Going Beyond the Theory/ Practice Divide in Early Childhood Education

Going Beyond the Theory/Practice Divide in Early Childhood Education focuses on the use of pedagogical documentation as a tool for learning and transformation. Based on innovative research, the author presents new approaches to learning in early childhood education, shifting attention to the force and impact that material objects and artefacts can have in learning. Drawing upon the theories of feminist Karen Barad and philosophers Gilles Deleuze and Félix Guattari, Hillevi Lenz Taguchi discusses examples of how pens, paper, clay and construction materials can be understood as active and performative agents, challenging binary divides such as theory/practice, discourse/matter and mind/body in teaching and learning. Numerous examples from practice are explored to introduce an intra-active pedagogy. 'Methodological' strategies for learning with children in preschools, and in teacher education, are brought to the fore. For example:

- the neighbourhood around the preschool and children's homes is explored, using drawing and construction-work on the floor;
- mathematics is investigated in teacher education, using the body, dance and music to investigate mathematical relationships and problems;
- taken-for-granted forms of academic writing are challenged by different forms of praxis- and experience-based writings that transgress the theory/ practice divide;
- children, students and teacher educators use pedagogical documentation to understand their own learning, and to critique dominant habits of thinking and doing.

Challenging the dominant understanding of 'inclusion' in educational contexts, and making 'difference' actively visible and positive, this book is rooted in the experiences, practices and words of teachers, teacher educators and student teachers. It will appeal to all those involved in early childhood education and also to those interested in challenging educational thinking and practices.

Hillevi Lenz Taguchi is an Associate Professor in the Department of Education, Stockholm University, Sweden.

Contesting Early Childhood

Series editors: Gunilla Dahlberg and Peter Moss

This groundbreaking new series questions the current dominant discourses surrounding early childhood, and offers instead alternative narratives of an area that is now made up of a multitude of perspectives and debates.

The series examines the possibilities and risks arising from the accelerated development of early childhood services and policies, and illustrates how it has become increasingly steeped in regulation and control. Insightfully, this collection of books shows how early childhood services can in fact contribute to ethical and democratic practices. The authors explore new ideas taken from alternative working practices in both the Western and developing world, and from other academic disciplines such as developmental psychology. Current theories and best practice are placed in relation to the major processes of political, social, economic, cultural and technological change occurring in the world today.

Other titles in the series:

Art and Creativity in Reggio Emilia
Exploring the role and potential of ateliers in early childhood education (Forthcoming)
Vea Vecchi

Contesting Early Childhood . . . and Opening for Change (Forthcoming)
Gunilla Dahlberg and Peter Moss

Movement and Experimentation in Young Children's Learning
Deleuze and Guattari in early childhood education
Liselott Mariett Olsson

Doing Foucault in Early Childhood Studies
Applying post-structural ideas
Glenda MacNaughton

Ethics and Politics in Early Childhood Education
Gunilla Dahlberg and Peter Moss

Forming Ethical Identities in Early Childhood Play
Brian Edmiston

In Dialogue with Reggio Emilia
Listening, researching and learning
Carlina Rinaldi

Unequal Childhoods
Young children's lives in poor countries
Helen Penn

Going Beyond the Theory/Practice Divide in Early Childhood Education

Introducing an intra-active pedagogy

Hillevi Lenz Taguchi

Routledge
Taylor & Francis Group

LONDON AND NEW YORK

First published 2010
by Routledge
2 Park Square, Milton Park, Abingdon, Oxon OX14 4RN

Simultaneously published in the USA and Canada
by Routledge
270 Madison Avenue, New York, NY 10016

Routledge is an imprint of the Taylor & Francis Group, an informa business

© 2010 Hillevi Lenz Taguchi

Typeset in Baskerville
by Keystroke, Tettenhall, Wolverhampton
Printed and bound in Great Britain
by TJ International Ltd, Padstow, Cornwall

British Library Cataloguing in Publication Data
A catalogue record for this book is available
from the British Library

Library of Congress Cataloging-in-Publication Data
Lenz-Taguchi, Hillevi.
Going beyond the theory/practice divide in early childhood education :
introducing an intra-active pedagogy / Hillevi Lenz-Taguchi.
p. cm.
Includes bibliographical references.
1. Early childhood education–Philosophy. 2. Early childhood teachers–Training of.
I. Title.
LB1139.23.L46 2010
372.2101–dc22
2009005117

ISBN 10: 0–415–46444–7 (hbk)
ISBN 10: 0–415–46445–5 (pbk)
ISBN 10: 0–203–87295–9 (ebk)

ISBN 13: 978–0–415–46444–4 (hbk)
ISBN 13: 978–0–415–46445–1 (pbk)
ISBN 13: 978–0–203–87295–6 (ebk)

Contents

Introduction by the series editors

Gunilla Dahlberg and Peter Moss

One way of understanding the educational arena in a wider perspective today is that there are two strong contradictory movements at work; one of complexity and diversity increase, and one of complexity and diversity reduction . . . The more we seem to know about the complexity of learning, children's diverse strategies and multiple theories of knowledge, the more we seek to impose learning strategies and curriculum goals that reduce the complexities and diversities of learning and knowing.

(Lenz Taguchi, 2008: 1)

This is the seventh book in the series *Contesting Early Childhood*. The aim of the series is to contest dominant discourses, those paradigmatic perspectives and theories of learning that act as if they were self-evident and as if there are no alternatives; for example, child development and 'developmentally appropriate practice' and their assumptions of a true or 'essential' child. Such discourses contribute to the strategies of complexity reduction in early childhood education (but also elsewhere in education) that the author of this book has noted in the quotation with which we start this introduction.

But the series has another, equally important, aim: not only to contest but also to relativise these discourses by showing that there are alternatives, and that the dominant discourses far from being self-evident are always just one of many choices facing us. In short, to free us from what Roberto Unger calls 'a dictatorship of no alternatives' (Unger, 2005: 1). This aim has been pursued not just through adopting different paradigmatic perspectives and expounding new theories, or rather theories that are new to the world of early childhood education. We (and others) have also shown, in book after book and other numerous examples, how they can be put to work in everyday circumstances, by children and adults, to create new understandings and enrich practice. In this very concrete way, the series has shown that there are in fact alternatives and that, to take a key theme of the present book, theory and practice do not represent a divide – an either/or binary; rather, 'practice is in fact continuously and already doing and enacting educational theories'.

The Swedish context

Hillevi Lenz Taguchi, in this book, looks at this close relationship between theory and practice in two everyday settings situated in a particular context: early childhood centres (*förskola* or 'preschools') and the education of preschool teachers (*förskollärare*) in Sweden. Before looking in more detail at the substance of her arguments, it may be helpful to non-Swedish readers to say more about these settings and their national context. Sweden, today, has one of the most extensive and developed systems of early childhood education in the world – a recent league table of 'early childhood education and care in economically advanced countries' places it first out of twenty-five rich countries (UNICEF, 2008). This has been the result of years of sustained policy development built on strong democratic processes and social responsibility for young children and a willingness to back this with adequate tax-based resourcing. The author of this book, writing earlier with a colleague in a review of recent developments in Swedish policy, has summarised this achievement of the Swedish welfare state:

> What was once viewed as either a privilege of the wealthy for a few hours a day, or an institution for needy children and single mothers, has become, after 70 years of political vision and policy-making, an unquestionable right of children and families. Furthermore, parents now expect a holistic pedagogy that includes health care, nurturing and education for their preschoolers.
>
> (Lenz Taguchi and Munkhammar, 2003: 23)

Central to this endeavour has been the *förskola* or preschool, the early childhood centre that provides for Swedish children between 12 months (before then they are at home with parents taking well-paid parental leave) and the age of 6 years, when children move into school. All Swedish children are legally entitled to attend the preschool from 12 months of age, whether or not their parents are employed or studying. In 2006, 43 per cent of 1 year olds, 85 percent of 2 and 3 year olds and 91 percent of 4 and 5 year olds went to these centres (Skolverket, 2006). It is truly a universal arena for early childhood education, where the society takes responsibility for the upbringing of its youngest members – education in its broadest sense ('holistic pedagogy') and as a community project.

The staff in these preschools, who we will meet in this book, are a mixture of preschool teachers (*förskollärare*) and assistants (*barnskötare*), the workforce divided roughly 50/50 between these two groups. The latter have a three-year education at an upper secondary school level. The former have a three and a half-year university education, leading to a graduate teaching qualification with a specialisation in work with young children between 1 and 6 years of age.

Preschools, since 1996, are in the education system, under the aegis of the Ministry of Education. Their purpose is to provide to all children a 'pedagogical approach where care, nurturing and learning together form a coherent whole' (Ministry of Education and Science, 1998: 14). Children under and over 3 years of age share the same provision, the same workforce and the same preschool curriculum, and a single system of funding applies across the system. Unlike many countries, therefore, Swedish ECEC is fully integrated, both conceptually and structurally.

Hillevi Lenz Taguchi, who works in the Department of Education at the University of Stockholm, draws on work undertaken both in preschools and in the education of preschool teachers at this university. Her scope is learning and education of both children and adults, with the application of similar perspectives and practices to both. Indeed, she and her colleagues 'basically decided that teacher education should be engaged in and perform the same kinds of educational practices with student-teachers, as we as educators wanted and taught the students to do with children once they become professional teachers'.

What is striking to someone from outside Sweden (as one of us is), both in this book and the previous volume in this series by Liselott Mariett Olsson – *Movement and Experimentation in Young Children's Learning: Deleuze and Guattari in Early Childhood Education* – is the way that 'ordinary' preschools, preschool teachers and teacher educators in Sweden come to be working with 'alternative' theories from theorists who have usually not written about early childhood education and who are unlikely to figure on the reading lists of 99 per cent of courses for early childhood workers, theorists such as the French philosophers Gilles Deleuze and Félix Guattari (in both books) and the feminist physicist Karen Barad (in this book). We do not wish to exaggerate by suggesting that this is the case throughout Swedish preschools and teacher education. But there does seem to be a potentiality in the Swedish system for working with new thinking and experimentation. If that potentiality and its realisation seems important, as we think it is, then we should reflect on how it may emerge and flourish. How can we create a context within which new thinking and experimentation are not only tolerated but positively encouraged and flourish?

Sweden suggests three possible components in such a context. First, *a strong decentralisation* of responsibility to both local authorities and individual preschools, epitomised by a preschool curriculum of only nineteen pages (in the English edition), a framework document which sets out broad values, tasks and goals, but leaves considerable space for local interpretation and implementation (Ministry of Education and Science, 1998). It steers without unduly prescribing, enabling preschools to combine working with this national document whilst exploring new approaches to learning and creating more local knowledges. Second, *a strong emphasis on democracy* which forms, the curriculum says, 'the foundation of the pre-school' (Ministry of Education and Science, 1998: 6). Democracy is a fundamental value in Swedish early childhood education, and this matters because democracy recognises, values and enacts pluralism, the idea that there are always alternatives, differing perspectives, other possibilities – and hence contestations to be had and choices to be made. Third, *a strong workforce* of well-educated preschool teachers, from among whom emerge substantial numbers who feel the need to be challenged, who are curious to know more about different theories and approaches to learning, and who are willing and able to work with them in their practice, especially in collaboration with gifted educators. Indeed, we might add to the third condition by noting a cadre of academics – both educating teachers and doing research – who have come to form a critical mass that desires to work with new discourses and to go deeply into their potential for learning and early childhood education. Hillevi Lenz Taguchi and Liselott Mariett Olsson are part of this cadre of experimenters.

The desire to experiment and create new thinking has been intensified from another source: the pedagogical work in Reggio Emilia, two of whose leading exponents (Carlina Rinaldi and Vea Vecchi) are also contributors to this series (Rinaldi, 2006; Vecchi, in preparation). No other country in Europe has been so closely connected to Reggio as Sweden, expressed through the wide-ranging work of the Reggio Institute in Stockholm, and the many networks of Swedish preschools connected with the Institute and working with inspiration from Reggio Emilia. Policy, too, has been explicitly influenced by Reggio Emilia's approach to early childhood education.

It has not been a simple matter of transmission, of Sweden buying the 'Reggio programme'. Rather there seems to have been much in common between the Italian city and the Nordic country: shared values, shared traditions, shared interests, shared ways of thinking about children and learning – 'the fact that the Reggio Emilia approach became so widely disseminated in Sweden could well be because in some respects it resembled that of the Swedish pre-school, but in a more audacious and sharper form' (Korpi, 2007: 66). This common ground – what might be termed a pedagogical meeting place – has enabled a productive and long-running exchange and dialogue, which has provoked experimentation. Neither Reggio Emilia nor those in Sweden working with inspiration from Reggio see early childhood education as a search for the one right answer, a time-limited project that will conclude with the application of a universal best practice or definition of good quality to the achievement of a set of predefined learning and developmental outcomes; both see early childhood education as a continuous process involving border crossings, the introduction of new perspectives and the creation of new understandings.

Central to this continuous process of dialogue and learning through experimentation is the tool of pedagogical documentation, originating in Reggio Emilia, but today in use throughout the world, and widespread in Sweden. It is not coincidence that pedagogical documentation plays such a central role in this book by Hillevi Lenz Taguchi as well as in the previous one in our series by Liselott Mariett Olsson. Nor that it features in other books in the series, by Carlina Rinaldi, Vea Vecchi and ourselves.

The idea is simple – making practice visible or material, thence subject to research, dialogue, reflection and interpretation (meaning-making). But its application, doing documentation, is anything but simple, as are its consequences. For it acknowledges and welcomes subjectivity, diversity of position and multiple perspectives: in short, it values plurality. As Hillevi Lenz Taguchi notes 'it produces different kinds of knowledge depending on the ontological and/or epistemological perspectives we bring with us in our usage of it'.

Documentation is not only a multi-purpose tool, of use in evaluation, researching, professional development and planning. Nor is it just a tool for bringing democratic politics into the preschool, opening up pedagogical work to the public gaze and to public argumentation, offering (as Loris Malaguzzi put it) 'the possibility to discuss and to dialogue everything with everyone' (Hoyuelos, 2004: 7). It also provides the means – vividly illustrated by Hillevi Lenz Taguchi in this book, and Liselott Mariett Olsson in the previous volume – to bring new ideas and perspectives into the preschool, to look at how new theories can offer new understandings and new directions for pedagogical work, and by so doing contributing to what Hillevi Lenz Taguchi describes in this book:

Giving up the search for and fantasy of finding the 'true' child and child development in your practices as preschool teacher, and instead engaging in a process of collaborative invention and creation together with the children of what a child might become.

Matters of substance

This book is rich in both its documentation of practice and its wide-ranging exploration of theories and concepts. It spans work in the preschool and in teacher education. Here we give just a hint of these riches, exploring two concepts and the theoretical context from which they are created, rather than mapping all the territory covered by the book.

An intra-active pedagogy

Both Liselott Mariett Olsson, in her book in our series, and Hillevi Lenz Taguchi in the present book have tried to find theoretical and philosophical perspectives that stimulate and support 'a process of collaborative invention and creation' among children and teachers. In this book, Hillevi Lenz Taguchi searches for concepts that can enable us to go beyond the theory/practice divide and open up for trans-disciplinary teaching and learning. By drawing mainly on the thinking of Karen Barad and of Gilles Deleuze and his co-writer Félix Guattari the book introduces what Hillevi Lenz Taguchi, with inspiration from Karen Barad's concept of 'intra-activity', calls an 'intra-active pedagogy'.

Hillevi Lenz Taguchi writes that an intra-active pedagogy shifts our attention from intra-personal and inter-personal relationships towards an intra-active relationship between all living organisms and the material environment such as things and artefacts, spaces and places that we occupy and use in our daily practices. She argues, like other material feminists, that not only humans have agency. Material objects and artefacts can be understood as being part of a performative production of power and change in an intertwined relationship of intra-activity with other matter or humans. How, for example, chairs and floors feel and sound matters in our intra-actions with them; from this perspective, sitting in a specific space can be understood as a material-discursive phenomenon that emerges in the interaction that takes place in-between a subject, who is inscribed in discursive meanings, the body, and the chairs and the surfaces. And it is in this intra-action that our sense of being emerges – a sense that can either be empowering or disciplining.

Developing this theme, Hillevi Lenz Taguchi asks an important question. What are the consequences if we start viewing pedagogical practices from a perspective in which learning and knowing occurs in the interconnections that take place in-between different forms of matter making themselves intelligible to each other? She seeks to answer this question through bringing in examples drawn from practices in both preschools and teacher education, interpreted with the benefit of a theoretical and philosophical journey on which she has been engaged.

The 'material turn' that Hillevi Lenz Taguchi proposes builds on the 'linguistic turn' in philosophy and social theory. The latter made explicit the importance of language as a constituting agent of our practices and realities. But the 'material turn' goes further by including the material as an active agent in the construction of discourse and reality. In contrast to 'old' materialism, which was connected to positivism or Marxism, the 'new' material turn, she says, is interested in the active role of the material world, material culture, material agency and artifactuality.

Like many other researchers and philosophers who have tried to open up towards a thinking that bridges the divide between the material and the immaterial, the human and the non-human, Karen Barad has taken inspiration from the Danish quantum physicist Nils Bohr. In the 1930s, Bohr challenged mainstream physics and the theories of Newton and Einstein, by arguing against their idea of an external world, independent of observers and the circumstances of their measurements. But before him others had challenged the conception of the material as a passive object. As far back as the eighteenth century the Italian philosopher Giovanni Battista Vico proposed what has been called a 'scienza nuova'. Vico was a critic of modern rationalism and he argued that humans can only know what humans have constructed and in this process of construction poetic imagination plays an important role (von Glasersfeld, 1991).

More recently, the chemist and Nobel Prize winner Ilya Prigogine and the historian of ideas Isabelle Stengers published their book *La Nouvelle Alliance*, in which they refer to the new alliance between the human being, nature and science (Prigogine and Stengers, 1984). A chapter in that book is actually called 'Active material', in which they talk about self-organising systems and dissipative structures – a system's exchange of material and energy with the outside world (Lagerroth, 1994). This move from an idea of a passive and mechanical world to what could be called a more dynamic and creative universe has also been the interest within second order cybernetics and it closely relates to the idea of autopoiesis, or self-production, which the two Chilean biologists Humberto Maturana (1991) and Franscisco Varela have studied (see further Steier, 1991).

Despite these antecedents, the idea of non-humans having agency – agency without a subject – remains controversial and provocative. It is perhaps best known today from Bruno Latour's and Michel Callon's interdisciplinary approach to social science – the Actor Network Theory (ANT) – in which they, like Barad, have integrated the material and the semiotic. However, Latour increasingly refers to 'actants' instead of actor and agency, and this change reflects how their thinking has developed over the years (Latour, 1999).

The implication is clear. We should focus neither on the material nor on the subject – but on the in-between. It is machinic, Deleuze would say, and by this he refers to the event of life itself as it enables and produces the connections between organisms, matter and human beings, life as an ongoing movement of living. These ideas are apparent in the pedagogical work Hillevi Lenz Taguchi documents in this book and what she calls 'entangled becomings' in relation to 'an ontology of immanence'.

An ethics of immanence

Hillevi Lenz Taguchi has, like Liselott Mariett Olsson in the former book in our series, tried to understand pedagogy and education in a different way through formulating new problems and new concepts as well as experimenting with these together with teachers in preschools and schools as well as with colleagues in teacher education. One could say that the teachers in the different events described in the book become activators of connections in-between themselves and the children as well as other phenomena. This is not a form of instrumentalism, as their practice eschews predictions and classifications, programmes and subjects; it pre-supposes another 'sense of machine' than instrumentalism.

The project work that Hillevi Lenz Taguchi describes in the book gives us suggestions of how to work with young children in relation to Deleuze's understanding of the productivity of thought. Thought is generated by problems, says Deleuze, and Hillevi Lenz Taguchi makes it possible for the reader to follow how very young children formulate and address different problems, and how they create connections through experimenting in many different languages; for example, conceptually, pictorially or spatially. In these processes children's thought manifests itself in the various forms taken by children's responses to the problems. To learn then means a form of experimenting in which no method pre-exists, only alliances and friendships. Working in this way requires trust: trust in another way of thinking, a more rhizomatic thinking instead of linear and aborescent thinking, and trust in increasing the power to live.

These ideas about thought have consequences for our ideas about quality of life; quality of life comes to mean a way of living that is capable of transforming itself in relation with the forces it meets, always increasing the power to live and welcoming new potentials, opening up for creativity and invention. However, as can be seen in the examples from the book, it presupposes that the teachers make themselves open for, and that they take care of, what the children are engrossed in, e.g. being open for the events that are already taking place; and that they have constructed conditions for experimenting by organising an environment that gives the children possibilities to address their problems through many different languages. Rather than programmes or commands, pre-planning and prescribed courses of action, teachers have to 'listen' to the situation and to learn to surf it. It is so easy for an adult to break children's movement and their awareness of the potentialities of the situation, and so difficult for a preschool to be a place where all involved act as becoming subjects in a relational field.

To work with experimentation, like children and teachers described in this book have done, can be seen as a form of ethics; as such, it connects to a theme of the first book in this series (Dahlberg and Moss, 2005), about the possibility of early childhood education being, first and foremost, a place for ethical practice. With reference to Deleuze and Colebrook, Hillevi Lenz Taguchi proposes an ethics of immanence and potentialities. In an ethics of immanence she says, the teacher cannot understand the student, the content or the methodology as a fixed entity, separated from everything else. Instead, an ethics of immanence in education

> is concerned with the inter-connections and intra-actions in-between human and non-human organisms, matter and things, the contents and subjectivities of students that emerge through the learning events. It is concerned with students and teachers in processes of mutual engagement and transformation. This means that we have to view ourselves in a constant and mutual state of responsibility for what happens in the multiple intra-actions emerging in the learning event, as we affect and are being affected by everything else. The flow of events thus becomes a collective responsibility on behalf of all organisms present, whether they are human or non-human. Responsibility is thus built into the immanent relationship between all matter and organisms.

This responsibility is not something we can choose to have, she states with reference to Deleuze. It comes with living and with our potentialities of affecting and becoming affected.

An ethics of immanence opens up for an ethics, as well as an aesthetics, that has trust in the potentials of the world we are living in now instead of a trust in another world (Rajchman, 2001: 139). This means a desire for experimentation instead of redemption and judgement through transcendental categories. This means giving up a search for the 'true' child, 'true' knowledge, and 'true' development, in favour of collaborative innovation and creation.

Welcoming complexity and diversity

We now return to the contradiction and question raised in Lenz Taguchi's quote at the beginning of this introduction. In a world of increasing complexity and diversity (or, perhaps we should say, of increased appreciation of complexity and diversity, since the world was ever thus), how do we recognise, value and work with, rather than work against and reduce, complexity and diversity? We recognise that this poses enormous challenges. But this book adds to our understanding of the possibilities.

It means turning away from learning as a technical process of representation, reproduction, categorisation and normalisation. It means working with new theories and perspectives, which require new ways of thinking and relating, which offer no certainties and predetermined outcomes, and which call for us to take responsibility – for our own meanings and for our relationship with difference: 'To think another whom I cannot grasp is an important shift and it challenges the whole scene of pedagogy. It poses other questions to us pedagogues. Questions such as how the encounter with Otherness, with difference, can take place as responsibly as possible' (Dahlberg, 2003: 270).

Local experiences such as those written about in this book and others in our series show what may be possible; they show how we can not only think differently to the dominant discourse, but also do differently, bridging the theory/practice divide. But a lot of further work needs to be done to understand better how to bring new perspectives and theories into the everyday work of early childhood education and how to support the educators who wish to work with them. Can we move from isolated instances of experimentation to extended networks, so that it might be quite normal to visit a preschool (or its equivalent in other countries) to find its community of children and adults working with unfamiliar theories, experimenting in practice to realise their potential?

Consideration needs, too, to be given to the implications of working with complexity and diversity for key areas of policy. What about, for example, curriculum and evaluation? Both have a worrying capacity to govern and normalise through reducing complexity and diversity. But neither, we think, can be avoided by being wished away. To try to do so risks replacing public and contestable processes with invisible and unaccountable ones. A democratic nation state that takes responsibility for its children's education must also take some positions on the values and goals of that education.

So we need to seek new relations between diversity and norms, not seek to do away with one or the other entirely. Some parts of the relation can be discerned: a broad framework curriculum, open to interpretation, leaving room for experimentation and taking diversity and complexity seriously; a key role for pedagogical documentation in many educational tasks, including evaluation; a very well-educated workforce, critical thinkers, aware of different paradigms and theoretical perspectives, able to listen and surf; highly skilled pedagogical coordinators (*pedagogistas*) to support them in their continuous professional development; active policy support for academics and teachers wanting to work with new theories – an 'experimenting welfare state'; and an active public debate about the meanings of learning, knowing and the (pre)school. The relationship will never be stable and finalised; there is no final point of permanent and perfect equilibrium. Our best hope is to openly work the tension between the two directions.

References

Dahlberg, G. (2003) 'Pedagogy as a loci of an ethics of an encounter', in M. Bloch, K. Holmlund, I. Moqvist and T. Popkewitz (eds) *Governing Children, Families and Education: Restructuring the Welfare State*. New York: Palgrave, pp. 3–35.

Dahlberg, G. and Moss, P. (2005) *Ethics and Politics in Early Childhood Education*. London: Routledge.

Hoyuelos, A. (2004) 'A pedagogy of transgression', *Children in Europe*, 6: 6–7.

Korpi, B.M. (2007) *The Politics of Preschool: Intentions and Decisions Underlying the Emergence and Growth of the Swedish Preschool*. Stockholm: Regeringskansliet (Swedish Ministry of Education and Research).

Lagerroth, E. (1994) *Världen och vetandet sjunger på nytt. Från en mekanisk världsbild till ett skapande universum. (The World and the Wisdom Enchant Anew. From a Mechanistic Worldview Towards a Creating Universe)*. Göteborg: Korpen.

Latour, B. (1999) 'On recalling ANT', in J. Law and J. Hassard (eds), *Actor Network Theory and After*. Oxford: Blackwell/The Sociological Review, pp. 15–25.

Lenz Taguchi, H. (2008) 'Doing justice in early childhood education? Justice to whom and to what?'. Paper presented at the *18th Annual EECERA Conference*, Stavanger, Norway, 3–6 September.

Lenz Taguchi, H. and Munkhammar, I. (2003) *Consolidating Governmental Early*

Childhood Education and Care Services under the Ministry of Education: A Swedish Case Study (UNESCO Early Childhood and Family Policy Series No. 6). Paris: UNESCO.

Maturana, H.R. (1991) 'Science and daily life: the ontology of scientific explanations', in F. Steier (ed.) *Research and Reflexivity*. London: Sage Publications, pp. 30–52.

Ministry of Education and Science (Sweden) (1998: English edn) *Curriculum for Pre-school (Lpfö 98)*. Stockholm: Regeringskansliet.

Prigogine, I. and Stengers, I. (1984) *Order out of Chaos*. New York: Bantam Books.

Rajchman, J. (2001) *The Deleuze Connections*. Cambridge, MA and London: MIT Press.

Rinaldi, C. (2006) *In Dialogue with Reggio Emilia: Listening, Researching and Learning*. London: Routledge.

Skolverket (2006: English edn) *Descriptive Data on Pre-school Activities, School-age Childcare, Schools and Adult Education in Sweden, 2006*. Stockholm: Skolverket.

Steier, F. (ed.) (1991) *Research and Reflexivity*. London: Sage Publications.

Unger, R. (2005) *What Should the Left Propose?* London: Verso.

UNICEF (2008) *The Child Care Transition* (Innocenti Research Centre Report Card 8). Florence: UNICEF Innocenti Research Centre.

Vecchi, V. (in preparation) *Art and Creativity in Reggio Emilia: Exploring the Role and Potential of Ateliers in Early Childhood Education*. London: Routledge.

von Glasersfeld, E. (1991) 'Knowing without metaphysics: aspects of the radical constructivist position', in F. Steier (ed.) *Research and Reflexivity*. London: Sage Publications, pp. 12–29.

Acknowledgements

This book is to great extent a collaborative learning endeavour that I have had together with my colleagues Anna Palmer, Karin Hultman and Kajsa Ohrlander during the last years. Central to the process of writing this book have also been Klara Dolk and Hedda Schönbäck as important members of our research group. I also want to thank Gabriel Kuhn for his philosophically initiated editorial advice. I am immensely grateful to Gunilla Dahlberg and Peter Moss for giving me the opportunity to write this book. Gunilla Dahlberg introduced me to the Reggio Emilian practices and to the projects and networks of teachers and practitioners in Sweden working with inspiration from Reggio Emilia in 1993. Everything I have done connects to these practices in one way or another. Throughout my career I have also found very strong inspiration in the writings, collective biography work and friendship with Bronwyn Davies. Lastly I want to thank Anders Stenberg for intertwining his life with mine in all possible ways.

I am grateful to Malin Kjellander for permission to use her photographs in Chapter 3. All other photographs are taken from the pedagogical documentation and research data from either the project 'Gender perspectives in practice-oriented research in university education' (2003–6), funded by the Swedish National Research Council, or my doctoral project 'Emancipation and resistance: pedagogical documentation and co-operative learning-processes in preschool' (1997–2000), both at the Stockholm Institute of Education, Sweden.

The following material is used with permission:

Data in Chapter 5 are taken from 'Getting personal: how early childhood teacher education troubles students' and teacher educators' identities regarding subjectivity and feminism', *Contemporary Issues in Early Childhood* (2005), 6(3) (Symposium Journals, a division of wwwords Ltd).

A section of the Introduction and Chapter 6 are rewritten versions of 'Writing practices in Swedish teacher education and the inclusion/ exclusion of subjectivities', *Critical Studies in Education* 50(2) (2009): 145–58. The example in Chapter 7 is a rewritten version of a section of 'An "ethics of resistance" challenges taken-for-granted ideas in Swedish early childhood education', *International Journal of Educational Research* (2008), 47(5) (Elsevier), which was previously published as a chapter in J. Johanna Jonasdottir and J. Wagner (eds) *Nordic Childhood and Early Education: Philosophy, Research, Policy and Practice in Denmark, Finland Iceland, Norway and Sweden* (Information Age Publishing).

Introduction

I remember entering the vice-chancellor's conference room at Stockholm University and being overwhelmed by the impact of this room. Stockholm University is a comparably young university partly built in the late 1960s at the height of the democratic and feminist movements, with modest and minimalist 1960s furnishing, airy, light, high-ceiling corridors and exquisite abstract art. But the furniture of this room was old and similar to what I had seen in movies from colleges at Oxford or Cambridge. With its large heavy-framed paintings of men in robes with distinctions and honours in straight rows on the wooden panelled walls, it constituted a distinct contrast to the university as I knew it up until that day. Upon encountering the stuffy air lingering in this room, I was almost forced to a halt. It felt hard to breathe in here and smelled like an old museum that had never been aired. The wooden chair, with its backrest taller than the top of my head, creaked quietly as I sat down on it at the large oval shiny table. The wide leather seat was quickly heated from the warmth of my jeans-clothed buttocks. The chair embraced me as I leaned back and put my arms on the generous armrests, giving me a feeling of authoritarian comfort, excitement and inferiority, all at the same time. The low voices of the assembled professors were almost drowned by the intensive creaking of their chairs as they turned and twisted in their seats during polite exchanges and greetings. As the chairman rose from his chair at the end of the table, the human voices quickly silenced. Only a few mocking creaks from chairs penetrated the mat of silence that had spread out into the room. He gave a welcoming speech and outlined the agenda for the meeting. Being embodied by and simultaneously embodying this entirely new room, inhabited by people I did not yet know, in a meeting which was new to me, I was thrown back into my childhood and the first day at preschool in the year of 1968.

On my first day of preschool the teacher took all of us into the large and light playroom. She told us to sit down on an assigned dot glued to the floor. The dots formed a large circle and by the main wall there was a soft red pillow where the teacher seated herself crossing her legs in front of her, telling us to do the same. I could feel the icy chilliness from the cool linoleum floor through my tights. My dot was in-between two boys that I had never met before. They talked lively to each other and sat somewhat too close to me, so that our crossed legs would touch. I therefore stretched out my legs instead, which caused the boys to immediately fill out the vacant space with their legs, so I could feel them against the side of my thighs. I felt sandwiched in-between them, almost not being able to breathe. 'You're not sitting on your dot', I told the boy to my right. 'Can you move onto your dot, please?' The boy mocked me as the teacher told me to be quiet. I felt as if the dot on the floor was burning under my buttocks, screaming out to me 'Sit still!' 'Don't move!' 'Be quiet!' I couldn't understand why the dots under those boys didn't do their job, not keeping them in place at all. The boy on my left suddenly swirled around and his feet hit my arm and the side of my stomach. I straightened and nailed my body even more firmly to the dot without saying anything. I was doing it right, but I was not in a position to do the reprimanding. The teacher simply laughed lightly at what had happened. Then she said something about how difficult it was to learn how to sit still – especially for boys this age – but, she explained, that this was exactly what preschool was all about: learning how to sit still on your dot.

In the warm and somehow comfortably authoritarian atmosphere of the vice-chancellor's room, we discussed the consequences of merging the Stockholm Institute of Education, where I worked, with the University of Stockholm. I enthusiastically urged the professors to understand the importance of maintaining the inter-disciplinary teaching practices that we had developed during the last eight years in teacher education. I described teaching which was performed not sitting still on chairs in hours of lectures or seminars but in a trans-disciplinary fashion with collaborative and inclusive strategies. I claimed that such teaching, in for instance mathematics, achieves deep understanding of mathematical thinking by analysing music, choreographed bodily movements or the architecture of the room or a building. I explained about how students, just like small children, learn from their bodies and from interacting with different materials. Mathematics can be felt through the body – walking, skipping, dancing – and through the different kinds of music that correspond to mathematical formulas in their rhythms and compositions. I described the documentations we did throughout these investigations, and how we collaboratively analysed them, not just mathematically but also using a wide array of social science theories. Sorry to say, I didn't have sufficient language then to be able to tell them how we can think about and practise teaching and learning in these new and other ways. Ways which make us more aware of the importance of the body, and the inter-connectedness between bodies, matter, space, theory, rational thinking and the bodily senses; and practising teaching and learning in ways that go beyond the theory/practice binary divide, as well as a range of other binary divides, such as mind/body, discourse/matter and science/art. I left the meeting with a strong insight and an empowering feeling of having been challenged to develop a richer and more theoretically efficient and productive language, to be able to express my experiences from the last fifteen years of reconceptualising practices in both preschool practices and in higher education. Developing such a language is necessary – not just to convince the academy of the advantages of trans-disciplinary teaching and learning – but for us to be able to keep on challenging ourselves in our own work as well. Our practices need to be theorised in new ways, as new theory help us to challenge our practices into different ways of teaching and learning.

What is this book about?

This book is about searching for a language that my colleagues and I, as well as many other teachers, pedagogues and researchers in education around the world, need to be able to work in ways that enable us to go beyond the theory/practice binary divide. The book will address the intertwined discursive and material reality of pedagogical practices or events, such as the ones the stories above are trying to tell. It addresses the problem of an ontological divide between theory and practice, between academic knowledge and our sensing bodies, matter, rooms and material environments – spaces and places. It will mainly draw on the thinking of the feminist physicist Karen Barad and the French philosopher Gilles Deleuze and his co-writer Félix Guattari. My writing is situated in a theoretical context that I will outline in more detail below, often referred to as the 'material turn' in philosophy, feminist theory and the social sciences. However, my writing of this book is just as much situated in the pedagogical context of the practices in Sweden that have taken their inspiration from the municipal preschools in the Italian city of Reggio Emilia (active since 1960), but also from the critical and feminist pedagogies emerging in Western universities in the 1980s. The way I see it, the consequences for education are vast if we take the 'material turn' seriously. (I will explain this turn in more detail later.) In writing this book I also want to trouble and challenge what is going on in the educational arena today, where pedagogical practices are being increasingly mainstreamed and normalised in relation to universal standards. These tendencies reduce the complexities of teaching and learning in an increasingly complex and diverse world. I argue that we need a language that encompasses more of these complexities, and which can enable us to make use of them and thereby go beyond the prevailing binary divides that still haunt educational practices and theories.

In this book I want to introduce my thinking about what I have called an intra-active pedagogy, based on Barad's concept of intra-activity and what she refers to as an onto-epistemology (Barad, 1998, 1999, 2007, 2008). The latter term relates to the interdependent and intertwined relationship between theories of being (ontology) and theories of knowing (epistemology). Barad's thinking challenges dominant divisions between humans as active and intentional on the one hand, and matters as passive backgrounds on the other. I will explain what this means by briefly introducing here the core thinking that will run through this book and which will be developed further in the unfolding of the different chapters to come. Thinking in line with Barad, both the dot on the cool linoleum preschool floor and the chairs in the vice-chancellor's room can be understood as performative agents. This means that material objects and artefacts can be understood as being part of a performative production of power and change in an intertwined relationship of intra-activity with other matter or humans. How chairs, dots and floors feel and sound matters in our intra-actions with them. They have force and power to transform our thinking and being in a particular space or in the world at large. Intra-activity is different from inter-activity, which refers to inter-personal relationships between at least two persons. Intra-activity here relates to physicist terminology and to relationships between any organism and matter (human or non-human). Hence, what Barad and other material feminists (Alaimo and Hekman, 2008) are suggesting is that it is not only humans that have agency – the possibility of intervening and acting upon others and the world. Rather, all matter can be understood as having agency in a relationship in which they mutually will change and alter in their on-going intra-actions. Consider for instance the simple example of how hot tea or coffee intra-acts with our bodies to heat them from within and perhaps somewhat relaxing them when they tense. Or the more complicated interconnections between that which we conceptualise as our body and mind, when somatic illnesses can emerge from emotional events that will profoundly affect the body in different ways. Or, consider how birds and crickets sing and sound more loudly and develop better 'sound-instruments' as an evolutionary process living in the noise of the big cities.

Intra-actions are simultaneously material and discursive in an intertwined relation. 'Matter and meaning are not separate elements', writes Barad (2007: 3). This means that it matters what notions and beliefs are at work in our intra-activities with the material world. It also means that notions and beliefs can change as a result of the force of intra-activity with material objects and artefacts. Hence, Barad consequently refers to the material-discursive to make this clear, and writes that knowing can be understood as a result of a process where 'the material and the discursive are mutually implicated in the dynamics of intra-activity' (Barad, 2007: 152). She explains:

> The relationship between the material and the discursive is one of mutual entailment. Neither discursive practices nor material phenomena are ontologically or epistemologically prior. Neither can be explained in terms of the other. Neither is reducible to the other. Neither has privileged status in determining the other. Neither is articulated or articulable in the absence of the other; matter and meaning are mutually articulated.
>
> (Barad, 2007: 152)

In line with this thinking, the chair and the dot – both material objects – can be understood to actively work on my body and make it sit in specific ways, depending on the meaning I make in a specific space as girl or boy, or as a female or male, young or old, ethnic minority or ethnic majority, etc. Sitting in a specific space can thus be understood as a material-discursive phenomenon that emerges in the intra-action that takes place in-between a subject, who is inscribed in discursive meanings, the body, the dot on the cool floor or the wide high back-rested old creaking chair. In this way, chairs and dots can be understood to keep us in place and force or enable us to sit in specific ways, depending on whether we are at a lesson, assembly, seminar, lecture or staff meeting. In this sitting, our sense of being emerges in the material-discursive intra-actions taking place – being empowered, or being subjected to disciplining, etc. Moreover, sitting on a specific chair in a specific space with specific other human and non-human organisms and matter will regulate how and what we might say or do, or not say or do. All spaces, and certainly pedagogical spaces, call upon us and demand specific ways of sitting or moving, talking or socialising with different affective force and intensities, depending on the material-discursive interconnections and intra-actions at work in this space (Hultman, 2009). Now, as a contrast to the many different practices of sitting (listening, reading or writing) in our pedagogical spaces on all levels of education, consider what might happen in the pedagogical space when the maths teacher asks the children to dance their favourite break dance and then figure out the maths of the music on large papers on the floor (Palmer, 2009b). Or, when student-teachers are asked to make or compose music from the architecture of the room and figure out its maths, as in the example shown in Chapter 5 of this book (see also Palmer, 2009a). Imagine all the many new and other possibilities of multiple and complex intra-activities that will emerge in-between all these performative agents at work; the music and children's and students' bodies, and their movements translated into geometrical symbols, as well as the numbers and calculus of the beats and melodies.

Learning and knowing takes place in the interconnections in-between different matter making themselves intelligible to each other, writes Barad (2007: 140). If she is right, what consequences does this have for pedagogical practices of all kinds? Intra-actions take place in-between children, students, teachers, chairs, books, pens and papers when they read, write and talk while sitting in rows or circles etc. Multiple and complex sets of intra-actions also take place when we transform our teaching practices into trans-disciplinary practices in the spaces of open classrooms and using, for instance, music and dance to think mathematically. If learning can be understood in terms of different matter – human and non-human – making themselves intelligible to each other, the inter- and trans-disciplinary classroom and its practices that set out to go beyond the theory/practice binary divide will offer multiple possibilities of understanding and knowing. In what follows I will make a brief outline of how I understand the context of contemporary education and especially early childhood education, and then move on to situate an intra-active pedagogy in relation to the pedagogical practices from which it has emerged, as well as the theoretical context of the 'material turn' and a philosophy of immanence, inspired by Deleuze and Guattari.

The contemporary context of education: two contradictory movements

One way of understanding the educational arena today is that there are two strong contradictory movements at work: one of complexity and diversity increase, and one of complexity and diversity reduction. On the one hand, increased complexity, multiplicity and diversity push for increased inclusion of children and families with diverse ethnic, racial, religious, cultural, social and economic backgrounds into early childhood education (ECE). Provisions increase around the world, not least as a result of women wishing to participate in the labour force. More and more governments become aware of the economic benefits of women participating in the labour market, as well as the benefits of ECE provisions for national finances and fighting illiteracy and crime. Moreover, in terms of theoretical perspectives on children's learning and development, there exists a multitude of different theories. These are based on different epistemological paradigms and sciences that both support and, at times, severely contradict each other in terms of their results and consequences for pedagogical practices in early childhood provisions.

On the other hand, these circumstances of increased complexity seem to enforce strategies of complexity reduction on the political and administrative arena when it comes to the realisation, accomplishment and evaluation of educational and early childhood education practices around the world. In a globalised perspective there seems to be an international mainstreaming of ECE practices towards developmentally appropriate practices – DAP (Bredekamp and Coople, 1993; Bredekamp et al., 2000; Gestwicki, 2006). Formulated within the discipline of developmental psychology, ideas about universal, age-related stages have produced widely held truths about children's development and learning. These truths have been translated into accepted practices designed to educate and normalise children into healthy, enlightened and free citizens (Burman, 2007; Rose, 1999).

Practices of observation and documentation have been used in the Swedish context very extensively for the last 100 years based on developmental psychology in order to determine deficiencies in children's development and learning and to identify the need for early intervention with the goal of normalising children and their families (Lenz Taguchi, 1996, 2000). In the late 1990s developmental psychology had a revival in early childhood education after the critique of the 1970s and 1980s. Now developmental plans of various kinds are issued to monitor children's cognitive, psychological and social development as well as their physical motor abilities throughout the preschool years and into primary schooling (Elfström, 2004). Noting how deeply developmental stage theory has taken root, MacNaughton (2005: 1) writes that it has 'settled so firmly into the fabric of early childhood studies that its familiarity makes it just seem "right", "best" and "ethical"'.

During the last twenty years of increasing diversity and complexity in many areas of Swedish society, contemporary developmental theories and practices have been used continuously as inspiration for incessantly new ways of normalising children's development. Developmental theories have been supplemented with constructivist learning theories thriving upon ideas about 'learning how to learn', concept mapping and meta-cognitive practices (Doveborg and Pramling, 1999; Doveborg and Pramling Samuelsson, 2000; Marton and Booth, 1997; Novak and Gowin, 1984; Pramling, 1990). In these practices, observation and documentation have found another usage in mapping out the cognitive development of the individual child in relation to a specific learning content to be learnt. The idea of these constructivist and meta-cognitive learning practices, which today have taken on the label of 'learning studies' in Sweden as an adaptation of the Japanese 'lesson studies', is that the documentation is used by the teacher to identify where in the cognitive development the child is situated and how a specific child learns. Thereby the teachers can challenge the child to pick up the specific content on a higher level of cognition and knowing (Holmqvist, 2006; Marton and Tsui, 2004; Pramling Samuelsson and Pramling, 2008). The aim is to have the child learn exactly what it is we as teachers and adults want them to learn.

The overall benevolent aims of both developmentally appropriate and constructivist learning practices have been to reduce differences and complexities among children, to bring them to a mastery of basic skills and to allow them to assimilate well into the school system. Many policy-makers and practitioners view these practices as a way to foster the tradition of ensuring the good childhood and a solid base for lifelong learning, by treating and evaluating everyone the same way through universal, comparable, and centralised standards (Dahlberg *et al.*, 2007; Dahlberg and Moss, 2005). It appears to be against our better judge-ment, but the more we seem to know about the complexity of learning, children's diverse strategies and multiple theories of knowledge, the more we seek to impose learning strategies and curriculum goals that reduce the complexities and diversities of learning and knowing. The more complex things become, the more we seem to desire processes of reduc-tion and thus control, but such reduction strategies might simultaneously shut out the inclusion and justice we want to achieve (Biesta, 2008; Osberg and Biesta, 2009).

The context of pedagogical practices from which an intra-active pedagogy has emerged

One of the aims with this book is to challenge what I consider the reductionist thinking outlined above, and to suggest a pedagogical practice which is based on another philosophy of becoming and learning that is different to those that dominate the field of education at large and especially early childhood education. This is a pedagogy that works with and makes use of – rather than working against – differences, diversities and increased complexities of learning and knowing. It is a pedagogy that is inclusive of children's and students' thinking and different strategies and ways of doing, as well as their subject positionings on the margins of social class, ethnicity, race, gender and sexuality.

In the field of early childhood education, an intra-active pedagogy builds on practices in early childhood education that are already in place in Sweden since the early 1990s with inspiration from the preschool practices of the city of Reggio Emilia in northern Italy (Dahlberg *et al.*, 2007; Reggio Children, 2001, 2008; Rinaldi, 2006; Ceppi and Zini, 1998). The so-called Stockholm project became the first major project. It was led by Professor Gunilla Dahlberg and ran in collaboration with a municipality – Hammarby – south of Stockholm, the Reggio Emilia Institute in Stockholm and their national and local networks (Dahlberg *et al.*, 2007). All the experiences we have made during the last fifteen years basically emerged from this first project and its intensive work with developing the tool of pedagogical documentation as a tool for learning and change. The basic idea of all this work has been to engage in collaborative knowledge-production with children that challenge their and our own possibilities and potentialities beyond what we already think we know. In my own research I have investigated how different types of observational and documentational practices have been and are used also as tools for a professional development and change, in both preschools and teacher education (Lenz Taguchi, 1997, 2000, 2005, 2006, 2007, 2008d).

The pedagogical theories developed in Sweden with inspiration from the practices performed in Reggio Emilian preschools are theories which are affirmative of children and adults being in collaborative processes of creation, invention and becoming. This is in contrast to cognitive and constructivist learning theories where the practices inevitably focus on judging individual achievement in relation to pre-set goals and outcomes (Dahlberg and Bloch, 2006; Dahlberg and Moss, 2005; Lenz Taguchi, 2008b, 2008c, 2008d, 2009a, 2009b). In the former theories, the ideas and strategies of children and students are treated in ways that give them equal value and importance to those of adults, teachers and teacher-educators. Thus, children and students are seen as co-constructors of culture and knowledge in an interdependent relationship with adults, families and the rest of the world (Dahlberg and Lenz Taguchi, 1994).

The pedagogical practices in Reggio Emilia, which have been such an important source of inspiration for both theoretical and practical development in Sweden, are built on strong democratic values. There is a very strong affirmative belief in the collaborative processes of meaning-making with children and that it can actually benefit and alter society at large, by making us more open to new and different ways of understanding the world. The Reggio Emilian philosophical and pedagogical approach has been called a 'pedagogy of listening' that activates 'the hundred languages', referring to the usage of a multiplicity of aesthetic tools and strategies for inter-disciplinary learning, as well as to aesthetic means of observing and documenting children's learning processes (Edwards *et al.*, 1998; Rinaldi, 2006). The tool of pedagogical documentation is necessary both to the more intimate process of 'listening' and making visible and challenging children's learning-processes, and to the political aspect of making children's meaning-making visible to the world outside the preschools and schools. Moreover, it is the central tool for professional development with the teachers doing research on their own practice. All this work has given the preschools of Reggio Emilia an unquestionable international status and *Newsweek* magazine pronounced them the best schools in the world in 1991 (Bruner, 2004; Gardner, 1994; Edwards *et al.*, 1998; Helm and Katz, 2000; Katz 1998; New, 1990, 2000). This grass-roots movement can be viewed as a resistance to taken-for-granted and normalising views of development and knowledge production that imply the existence of a single best and most efficient theory of learning and development, or a universal tool to evaluate specific developmental or knowledge construct outcomes. In this book, pedagogical documentation will be somewhat of a main character, taking on the lead role. It is to be understood as a performative agent in itself and as such also a 'methodological' tool for learning and change in any pedagogical practice.

The intra-active pedagogy shifts our attention from only giving attention to the intra-personal (self-talk and inner speech – Bateson, 1979; Vocate, 1994) and inter-personal (between two or more human subjects – Hartley, 1999) to give explicit attention to the intra-active relationship between all living organisms and the material environment: things and artefacts, spaces and places that we occupy and use in our daily practices, as I have tried to illustrate in the introductory examples. Hence, this pedagogy is inclusive of the material as a strong performative agent in learning. The pedagogues in Reggio Emilia have long since expressed a deep awareness of the significant force of the material environment. They have called the environment 'the third pedagogue' with reference to its strong agency in the events of learning (Edwards *et al.*, 1998; Reggio Children, 2008; Rinaldi, 2006). They usually only have two teachers in a group of twenty-five children aged 3–5 years old, which is why the environment, the materials and the organisation of time, space and place are considered to be the 'third pedagogue'.

When my colleagues and I were given the opportunity to design an alternative Early Childhood Teacher Education class in 1999 at the Stockholm Institute of Education, we basically decided that teacher education should be engaged in and perform the same kinds of educational practices with student-teachers, as we as educators wanted and taught the students to do with children once they become professional teachers. In 2001 we were able to construct a new one-year long course in the early childhood teacher education programme for students interested in Reggio Emilia-inspired work. This course is still running and has been researched by myself and my colleagues Ulla Lind and Anna Palmer (Lenz Taguchi, 2005, 2007, 2009b; Lind, 2003; Palmer, 2009a, 2009b). It was no easy task to transform higher education practices into practices in preschools. We built our work on 'high theory', including Foucauldian power-productions, Derridean deconstructionist analysis, feminist post-structural subjectivity theories and philosophies, Piercian semiotics, etc. Another extremely important source of inspiration for our work was the experience and research from critical and feminist pedagogy that had developed since the late 1980s. The aim of such work has been to create interdisciplinary knowledge, raising questions about the relationships between the margins and centres of power in educational contexts and with a specific interest in race, gender, class and ethnicity (Apple, 1982; Aronowitz and Giroux, 1991; Ellsworth, 1997; Freire, 2001; hooks, 1981, 1994; Lorde, 1984; MacLaren, 1994; Malka Fisher, 2001; Mayberry and Rose, 1999; Richardson, 1997; Walkerdine, 1988, 1998). We especially turned to the important self-critique of foremost feminist post-structural educators and researchers (Davies, 2000; Jones, 1997; Lather, 1991, 2007; Luke and Gore, 1992; St. Pierre and Pillow, 2000; Yates, 1993). In this inter- and/or trans-disciplinary work, both concerning teaching and learning of contents and academic writing practices, we seriously challenged the taken-for-granted practices in higher education, as you will be able to see in more detail in Chapters 5 and 6.

Building on what is already in motion: the 'material turn' and an ontology of immanence

We cannot privilege reality over construction, and we cannot privilege construction over reality either, writes Susan Hekman (2008). She continues to say that what we need is a conception that does not presuppose a gap between language and reality that are opposites that must be bridged; rather, we need to go beyond the binary divide of the real vs social construction or discourse, just as we need to go beyond the binary divide of theory/practice. The recent 'material turn' in the social, humanist and techno sciences has influenced my thinking a lot in writing this book. It can have very important effects on research and practices in the field of education at large as well as in early childhood education. In the social and educational sciences, the 'material turn' can be understood as building on what has been called the 'linguistic turn': an expression first used by the American philosopher Richard Rorty (1967). The 'linguistic turn' in philosophy and social theory makes explicit language as a constituting agent through humanly constructed discourse. What we understand as reality is conditioned by collectively constructed (discursive) meaning in language. Language thus constitutes our practices and realities. The 'material turn' builds on the linguistic but goes further to include the material as an active agent in the construction of discourse and reality. Physical matters become dynamic materials or trans-materials with a capacity of changing to its form in various ways, as well as intra-acting with other matter and organisms in processes of transformation. Hence, unlike the 'old' materialism, which was either connected to positive science (positivism) or to Marxism in the social sciences, the 'new' material turn is about an increased interest in the active role of the material world, material culture, material agency and 'artifactuality' (Daston, 2007; Hansen, 2000; Hayles, 2002; Miller, 2008; Tilley *et al.*, 2006). It was in philosophy of science that these ways of theorising first appeared in writings by Bruno Latour (1999, 2005), Andrew Pickering (1995), Joseph Rouse (2002) and Karen Barad (1998, 1999, 2007, 2008). Barad, who is the theorist that I draw heavily upon for my own work, builds on the theories of the Danish physicist Niels Bohr, who with his quantum physics challenged mainstream physics and Albert Einstein in the 1930s. Today the 'material turn' appears in literature studies, philosophy, history, cultural studies, sociology and feminist studies, as well as design, architecture, biology and medicine. For an elaborate outline on the 'material turn' in feminist studies and feminist philosophy see Alaimo and Hekman (2008) in their introduction as well as in their respective chapters of their edited volume *Material Feminisms*.

In the field of childhood, the ideas of the 'material turn' has influenced sociologist Alan Prout (2005). He outlines how the field of childhood studies is still dominated by a prevailing divide between viewing children's development as a consequence of either nature or culture; that is, biology and genetics or upbringing, social relations and education. We tend to choose either side depending on the issue of discussion. In the field of education, we often make diffuse claims about children's development and learning as a result of both–and (biology and culture). However, our teaching and learning practices imply that we rely more on biology and less on culture and social construction. This is quite remarkable, I think, since a vast body of critical pedagogy and educational research convincingly has shown how the idea of childhood and children's development and learning can be understood as results of constructions in specific socio-historical contexts (Burman, 2007; Hultqvist, 1990; James *et al.*, 1998; Ohrlander, 1992; Prout and James, 1990; Walkerdine, 1988). Hence, in education there is a divide between, on the one hand, theories of development and learning, which derive from developmental psychology and cognitive theories. These are close to biological theories which think of learning basically in terms of an individual cognitive process. I will talk about them in terms of cognitive and constructivist learning theories in the upcoming chapters. On the other hand, there are educational theories and research that are mainly involved with understanding the mechanisms in education and pedagogical work, which rely heavily on theories of social construction or discursive analysis, such as social constructivism and post-structural theories. This body of educational research has emerged from philosophy, ethnology, anthropology, sociology and cultural theory. There are some quite significant differences between these theories that are all interested in the constituting force of language and discourse. In this book, however, I will often deal with them in terms of discursive and social constructivist theories grouped together, to be able to show how they all emphasise the discursive so much that the constitutive force of the material is not acknowledged. What is important to my argument of an intra-active pedagogy is that we tend to fall into the trap of either/or: of essentialising biology, cognitive and constructivist learning-theory or discursive social constructivist theories, which often also include parts of the post-structural theories. This relates to the either/or of the binary divides of reality/discourse and nature/culture. In relation to the new 'material turn', Prout writes that a one-sided emphasis on 'culture' and language in discourse analysis can actually be understood as just as reductive as a one-sided emphasis on biology and 'nature'; neither view is an adequate starting-point for a satisfying analysis of early childhood (Prout, 2005: 84). He urges us to explore the possibilities of going beyond the biology/culture opposition and divide by engaging in reconceptualised evolutionary perspectives on childhood and the sociology of the body, inspired from the early post-structuralist and material feminist philosophers and biologists.

In his analysis Prout refers to the early work of the biologist and philosopher Donna Haraway (1991, 1997, 2008). Like other feminist biologists that are central to the 'material turn', such as Anne Fausto-Sterling (2000) and psychologist Elizabeth A. Wilson (1998, 2004), as well as feminist philosophers such as Elizabeth Grosz (1995, 1999, 2001, 2005) and Moira Gatens (1996), Haraway does not want to make a distinction between sex and gender, since they interconnect and are interdependently constructed. In other words, there is no way we can draw a border between what is to be understood as our biological body and what aspects of the body that are socially constructed, since our bodies are a mixture of both. It has developed as a result of an intertwined relationship between what we still insist in separating out as nature and culture. In line with this thinking, most recent feminist post-structural theories have consistently worked against and tried to go beyond the power-production in asymmetrical binary divides such as the male/female divide, and also mind/body, rationality/affectivity, objectivity/subjectivity, etc. In these dominant binary divides, the first concept is culturally considered to relate to masculine traits and the second is generally connected to feminine traits. Understanding gender as performative and subjectivities as discursively inscribed, multiple and shifting has made possible a growing field of research that offers a totally new and relevant understanding of how we become female and male subjects in the world. However, and again, as Barad (2007) points out, the agency of the body itself has been lost in the rejection of the material, reality and nature. This happens as we have overemphasised the discursive performativity of the body in our investigations, and when trying to develop ways of theorising and understanding that move away from and do not take the biological as the natural, sole and only origin. Hence, Stacy Alaimo and Susan Hekman claim that although the linguistic and discursive turn has been enormously productive for feminism in allowing feminism to understand gender from a new perspective that is based on the interconnections between power, knowledge, subjectivity and language, it has often meant a rejection of one side of the binary to embrace the other – culture is embraced over nature, language over reality, and discourse over the material (2008: 1–3). This means that material feminisms understood by Alaimo and Hekman and their co-writers are critical not just about the early socialist and Marxist understanding of the material, but also of the concept of materialisation with its exclusive discursive claims in relation to the construction of human subjectivity. Thus, material feminisms are about revising just about all these different theories emerging after the 'linguistic turn' – post-structuralist, postmodernist, social constructivist and cultural studies feminism – 'in ways that can more productively account for the agency, semiotic force, and dynamics of bodies and natures' (Alaimo and Hekman, 2008: 6). Or, in other words, material feminisms outline theories and examples that show how the body, reality and socially constructed discourse are in an interdependent relationship and in a process of mutual ongoing transformation by going beyond the nature/culture and reality/discourse binary divides. Alaimo asks a series of questions in relation to such thinking: 'How is it possible to understand agency without a subject, actions without actors? How can we rethink matter as *activity* rather than passive substance?' (Alaimo and Hekman, 2008: 245, my emphasis).

To be able to answer these questions and put them in relation to an intra-active pedagogy, my thinking in this book relies on an ontology of immanence. An ontology of immanence means that we also need to go beyond the human/non-human divide, as we understand our existence as a co-existence with the rest of the world. There is no hierarchical relationship between different organisms (human and non-human) and the material world around us, when we think in terms of immanence. We are all in a state and relationship of inter-dependence and inter-connection with each other as human or non-human performative agents. 'Existence is not an individual affair', writes Barad, both human individuals and non-human organisms and matter emerge through and as a part of entangled intra-relations (2007: ix). Everything around us affects everything else, which makes everything change and be in a continuous process of becoming – becoming different in itself – rather than being different in relation to another (Deleuze, 1994). In these processes there is a central element of unpredictability, creative and inventive change in the interconnections between different matter and organisms with different potentialities. All matter and organisms have agency and affect each other in a continuous flow of force and intensities that work in both predictable and sometimes in totally unpredictable ways (Grosz, 2005, 2008). What happens here and now in the actual present is a result, just as much of the repeated habitual self-organising behaviours of all organisms and matter, as it is of chances, mistakes or an act of creativity and invention that occurs in the intra-activities between all things and organisms at work. The limits of change, and the potentialities of all organisms and matter to develop and change, are unknown to us in an ontology of immanence. It is because we don't know what might be possible for a child or student to learn, to know or become, that this unknown potentiality and change becomes the most important subject for investigation in pedagogical theory and practice.

The influence from the French philosopher Gilles Deleuze and his work with psychoanalysist Félix Guattari has grown in the humanities, social sciences, architecture and theory of science since the turn of the last century. Here are some examples that have been productive for me: Bonta and Protevi (2004), Braidotti (1994, 2002, 2006), Buchanan and Colebrook (2000), Buchanan and Lambert (2005), Colebrook (2002, 2006), Grosz (1995, 1999, 2001, 2005), Hickey-Moody and Malins (2007), Patton and Protevi (2003), Sand (2008) and Williams (2008). Deleuze's immanence seems to go beyond the gap between science and the social sciences and humanities and do something else that transgresses this divide. There has been some interesting commentary that establishes the importance of the developments in biology for Deleuze's philosophy (Marks, 2006a). Moreover, there are writings on Deleuzian influence on the philosophy of technology and the philosophy of science (Marks, 2006b). His philosophy is discussed alongside the latest biological and evolution theories (Protevi, 2008a, 2008b). These new theories have revised and expanded traditional evolutionary theories to make biology merge with aspects of the social sciences in ways that make us understand how biology and our genes will change throughout our lives, depending on social and cultural environmental influences and circumstances (Jablonka and Lamb, 2005; West-Eberhard, 2003).

When it comes to the field of education and philosophy of education, Deleuze's philosophy also has significant ethical and political implications. Gunilla Dahlberg and Marianne Bloch (2006) have connected the philosophy of Deleuze to the pedagogical practices of the Italian preschools in Reggio Emilia. Their work is partly in line with the educational philosopher Inna Semetsky's (2006, 2008) call for a more philosophical pedagogy that primarily deals with creating new concepts in order to make us simultaneously feel, know and conceive in such a process of creation. Semetsky has also edited a special issue of *Educational Philosophy and Theory* on Deleuze and education with Michael A. Peters (2004), as well as published an edited book on Deleuze and educational philosophy (Semetsky 2008). Both of these include a number of philosophers trying to think Deleuze's philosophy in relation to education on a philosophical level. In the field of education methodologies, some researchers have outlined methodologies for education research inspired by Deleuze and Guattari. Elisabeth Adams St. Pierre (2000, 2004, 2009), Eileen Honan (2004), Glenda MacNaughton (2005), Lisa Mazzei (2008; Mazzei and Jackson, 2009) and Eileen Honan and Marg Sellers (2008) have all in different ways dealt with putting to work some of Deleuze's and Guattari's concepts in terms of methodology for educational research. Moreover, Bronwyn Davies and Susanne Gannon do Deleuzian readings on data that get closer to the reality of pedagogical encounters in practices in a forthcoming book.

Only a few educational researchers have, to my knowledge, seriously dealt with connecting Deleuze's and Deleuze and Guattari's thinking to concrete pedagogical events of learning in preschools, schools and universities with an aim to support and challenge the development of pedagogical practices. Christa Albrecht-Crane and Jennifer Daryl Slack (2007) have suggested a pedagogy of affect, drawing upon Deleuze. Dahlberg and Theorell (2009) write on children's dialogue with nature with strong Deleuzian influence. But the most significant contribution so far along these lines is provided by Liselott Olsson (2009). In various examples, closely connected with Deleuze's and Guattari's writings, she shows how teachers can put in motion collaborative processes of movement and experimentation in preschool children's ongoing construction of subjectivity and learning. It is along this line of trying to put theory to work in relation to the materiality of pedagogical practices that I have engaged with material feminisms, Barad and Deleuzian philosophy in my latest writings on graduate course-work (Lenz Taguchi, 2008a) and undergraduate academic writing (2009b), as well as in relation to examples of concrete learning practices and the lived experiences of children and teachers in preschools, schools and higher education (Lenz Taguchi, 2008b, 2008c). With this book I hope to make a further contribution that has the potentiality to challenge and change practices in preschools, schools and higher education.

The structure of the book and organisation of chapter contents

The first chapter of this book deals with my understanding of what going beyond the theory/practice binary divide as well as the discourse/matter divide can mean. The chapter discusses two very different learning events. The first event concerns our collective struggle in the Stockholm project with understanding issues of power-production as a way to displace our hierarchical thinking. We worked towards a 'flattening out' of the taken-for-granted hierarchical relationships, as well as with complicating our understanding of power-productions in-between subjects, subjects and objects, thinking and doing, theory and practice. The chapter then goes on to discuss an example of young children playing with sticks. I want to show how we have worked towards an understanding of learning-processes as flows and forces of interdependent intra-actions that involve the child's discursive conceptualisations, things, materials and the environment.

How can we think of learning if we are not outside observers of the world but, as Barad suggests, if we are rather part of the world in its ongoing intra-activity? Chapter 2 outlines some of the theories and concepts that I have used to understand learning in an intra-active pedagogy. I offer an example with student-teachers constructing clay figures to show how to understand learning in different ways, from different ontologies and epistemologies, that is, different ways of understanding our being and becoming in the world as well as our knowledge-production and learning.

The central tool for learning-practices in an intra-active pedagogy is pedagogical documentation. Pedagogical documentation is the topic of Chapter 3. How do we construct meaning with our tools of observation and documentation? What kind of knowledge is produced by the instruments or 'apparatuses' we use in our learning activities with children and students? What we call pedagogical documentation will be described as an apparatus of knowing that produces different kinds of knowledge depending on the ontological and/or epistemological perspectives we bring with us in our usage of it. I will use three different examples of observing and documenting children's learning and development in this chapter.

Chapter 4 deals with and exemplifies practising investigative learning processes with children, using the tool of pedagogical documentation. Pedagogical documentation is used 'methodologically' by putting in motion a 'circular' and a 'horizontal' movement. To illustrate these movements I use an example of learning experiences with 4 and 5 year olds investigating their neighbourhood on their way home from their preschool.

In the following two chapters the institutional context is teacher education. In Chapter 5 I will focus on the interdisciplinary, investigative and transgressive learning processes in mathematics during a ten-week course. I will give examples from different aspects of these reconceptualising teaching practices, taking into account that learning and construction of subjectivity cannot be separated in an ontology of immanence.

What is considered academic writing? How do you perform academic writing from an onto-epistemology? Chapter 6 is about writing practices that try to go beyond the theory/practice divide in academic writing by writing a collaboratively supervised multi-genre text. I have called this a hybrid-writing process. This writing process takes the student-teachers through the complexities of learning when trying to merge and go beyond the theory/practice divide in the writing, and simultaneously write in accordance with academic requirements.

In Chapter 7 I turn to the question of the ethical and political and ask: What are the ethical and political consequences of different worldviews and ways of understanding knowledge and learning in educational practices? An example of map drawing with 5 year olds is discussed to show the ethical and pedagogical consequences of different developmental and learning-theories that are at work in the educational arena today. I then make a re-reading of the example in line with my thinking on an intra-active pedagogy. The chapter ends with summing up my understanding of what I call an ethics of immanence and potentiality with reference to Deleuze and Claire Colebrook (2002).

The chapters in this book follow each other in a way that makes understanding easier if you have already read the previous chapter or chapters, where a concept has already been introduced and dealt with. As the chapters progress I will also refer back to previous chapters and sequences that might be helpful to return to if there is a need to refresh the reader's understanding of a concept or line of thinking. Since many readers might find the references to and writings by Deleuze and Deleuze and Guattari difficult, I want to direct the reader to three books that I have found useful when in need of a closer definition of various Deleuzian concepts that will appear in this book. The first is Mark Bonta's and John Protevi's book *Deleuze and Geophilosophy: A Guide and Glossary* (2004). The second is an edited volume by Charles J. Stivale (2005) *Gilles Deleuze: Key Concepts*, which consists of essays dealing with key concepts. The third is Claire Colebrook's book *Gilles Deleuze* (2002), which I have used extensively throughout the writing of this book, and which is a very well-written guide to understanding Deleuze's philosophy.

Chapter 1

Going beyond the theory/ practice and discourse/ matter divides

> Theory is ongoing, contingent and experimental, as well as dependent on an interaction with an environment and materials that it does not control . . . [N]o practice is free of theoretical dependencies.
>
> (Williams, 2007: 1)

Binary divides structure our thinking in simplifying and reductive ways – good/bad, mind/body, theory/practice – where one quality excludes the other and makes mixtures as well as states of both–and and in-between impossible. Going beyond the theory/practice divide in educational practices can be a complicated process, but for some reason it seems that the rewards are so great that there is no turning back to pedagogy-as-usual once you have started to engage in displacing your understandings and thinking differently (Lather, 1991; Lenz Taguchi, 2000). A preschool teacher once told me that being involved in processes questioning taken-for-granted thinking and habits of doing pedagogical practices at first felt frightening and difficult. Soon, however, it turned into the most exciting feeling she had had during her whole career. However, it felt somewhat like walking through a quagmire, not knowing when she would fall into traps of taken-for-granted habits or encounter unknown situations and not immediately knowing what to rely on and do next.

This chapter discusses two very different examples from Reggio Emilia-inspired practices in Sweden. The first example concerns our struggle with understanding issues of power-production in collaborative work among teachers, civil servants and researchers in the Stockholm project which started in 1993. We met once a month for one whole day to develop ways to use pedagogical documentation to organise and plan pedagogical activities that would challenge children's strategies and construction of knowledge. Pedagogical documentation became our most important tool for professional development. We also discussed and critically analysed the dominant views on children, learning and the activities of the preschool itself. In each meeting a teacher presented documentations from her or his practice focusing on the learning processes of children. The purpose was to collaboratively reflect upon and learn something about how children think and learn, as well as reflect upon the pedagogical preconditions for such learning (Dahlberg *et al.*, 2007; Lenz Taguchi, 1997, 2000, 2006). With the second example, I set out to introduce an intra-active pedagogy by describing a learning event with small children. It shows how we worked ourselves towards an understanding of learning processes which involves flows and forces of intra-actions in-between the child's discursive conceptualisations, things, materials and the environment.

The problems of the theory/practice divide

The dominant notion in the field of education is that there is a gap between what is understood as theory and practice. Theory and practice can also be said to constitute a binary opposition in the way we often think. For some this binary assumes the image of a visionary, rational, logical, clean and flawless theory, on the one hand; and on the other, a 'messy', 'dirty', disorderly practice, in need of being organised, cleaned up and saturated by the rationales and visions of theory. Proponents of the latter view would argue that the best and most appropriate theories should be applied to make practice better. If this is dominant thinking among many researchers and teacher educators, another line of thinking is sometimes just as dominant among practitioners. According to this line, practice constitutes a kind of truth in itself, based on unformulated, unwritten experiences and tacit knowledge, owned and embodied by the practitioners themselves. Proponents of this view would say that no theories can formulate and represent the truth of tacit knowledge in practice; therefore, what we need is to bring out that tacit truth from practice itself (Polanyi, 1997). What both of these notions fail to acknowledge is that practice is already and simultaneously theoretical and material, and that theory is totally dependent on experiences and fantasies of lived material practices.

The problem, then, is not that practice is not doing what we think it theoretically should be doing, or that theory is not representing practice in proper ways. Rather, practice is in fact continuously and *already* doing and practising educational theories, whether we are aware of it or not. We are already speaking and performing theories and ideas into existence of practice, along lines of thinking that are sometimes also contradictory or counter-productive. Practice can be understood as a dense material-discursive mixture of events that are folded upon each other. Educational theories are already materialised as developmentally appropriate, constructivist, response-ready, child-centred practices, etc. Materialisation is thus to be understood as an active ongoing process where specific notions and ideas are not only performed but have become an embodied routine and habit in our daily practice, rendering them into a state of 'naturalness' and taken-for-grantedness. In these materialising processes matter and meaning are intertwined to a state where we cannot distinguish what notions shaped our bodies and motions, or how the material preconditions of our bodies, architecture or organisation of practices shaped our notions and beliefs. Material bodies, matter and artefacts are constitutive of discourse, just as much as discourse is constitutive of how we decide to do and organise things in the material world and act as embodied subjects. Moreover, social positionings of gender, class, sexuality, ethnicity, race, age and disability are materialised as we talk and actively materialise ourselves into existence as, for instance, white, working-class female teachers (Butler, 1990, 1993, 2004). Children and students can be understood to be materialised and materialising themselves into existence as girls/women or boys/men, white, coloured, ethnic, religious, atheist, socially well or less well positioned, more or less intelligent, clever, emotional, practical, sensitive, etc. We *do* our gender, class, ethnicity, etc. as a continuously ongoing process of being constituted and constituting ourselves by a social world of discursive ideas and notions that we do not fully choose ourselves. Hence sociality – social norms, notions and discourses – has no single identifiable author or origin but is a collaborative construction (Butler 2004: 1–3). We do and materialise our own and the students' discursively inscribed subjectivities as teachers and learners as we handle books, learning material, furniture and school architecture in our daily practices. Hence, these materials and artefacts are to be understood as materialised ideas of knowledge and learning too, as well as active performative agents in a simultaneously ongoing process of change in societal notions and discourses.

After having presented these considerations to the teachers in the Stockholm project network, we suggested to the teachers that we should not be meeting to implement new methods with which to replace the old ones. What we wanted to do was to imagine opening up the toolboxes we carry, which are already filled with theoretical and methodological tools, to be able to look inside of them, temporarily un-pack them, investigate the tools inside, de-code them, re-code them and invent new ones. Professional development became a continuous process of un-packing and re-packing, un-coding and re-coding, un-folding and re-folding, and perhaps most importantly *re-inventing* what was in the toolbox to allow for something new to emerge. However, the new tools and experiences we made in our practices also needed to be de-coded, re-coded and re-considered in a continuous process. It is by looking into the toolbox and experimenting with the tools that the inseparability and inter-dependence of theory and practice becomes obvious to us.

Moreover, there is another central aspect of the theory/practice binary divide, a relation of power, where academic knowledge (being pre-dominantly theoretical and masculine) is valued higher than (feminine) preschool practices. Failure to lift the status of practice and the material to that of the theoretical is, I believe, a result of holding on to gendered notions: practice is implicitly understood as connected to and therefore contaminated by the less valued aspects of learning connected to the bodily or unformulated tacit and thus also most often the feminine. The conceptual divides that our Western thinking relies upon from Plato to Descartes to the twentieth century has been given explicit and implicit gendered values. The first concept in these divides has a privileged position with higher value and is considered to refer to masculine traits, whereas the concept on the other and opposite side of the divide is given a lesser value and is usually considered to refer to feminine traits: culture/nature; spirit/earth; mind/body; rational/emotional; thinking/feeling; discourse/ reality; language/material; linear/cyclic; active/passive; order/chaos; seeing/listening; stability/change; goal-orientation/process-orientation; fact/fiction (Davies, 2000; Lloyd, 2002).

This gendering of our binary everyday thinking, which entails valuing one side over the other, inhibits constructive change and makes us hold on to an *either–or* way of thinking. Educational discussions often polarise between teaching methods and practices that are *either* theoretical and text-based and easy to evaluate and measure, *or* investigative embodied hands-on experience-based teaching and learning, often using aesthetic means of expression as a way to learn differently. The latter are often considered difficult both to perform and to evaluate in a scientifically sound way. But, what would happen if we were to go beyond the either–or and instead focus on the inter-dependence between theory and practice? This could mean understanding theory and practice as decomposed or dissolved into what can be understood as inter-dependent powerful flows of mutual constitutive forces in constant intra-action with each other. These forces are impossible to separate from each other, nor can their boundaries be clearly defined (Barad, 2007). This thinking does not, however, imply that we give up practices of theoretical thinking or engaging in practising pedagogy. We just understand them as interdependent and inter-connected and thus equally valued and necessary. I will clarify all this in more detail below with the help of an example concerning understanding power in educational practices.

From 'either–or', 'both–and' or 'neither–nor' to entangled becomings

The first example of how the theory/practice divide can be challenged and dissolved is based on the learning processes we collaboratively undertook in the Stockholm project, as we tried to understand the mechanisms, forces and powers involved in what constitutes pedagogical practices. I will outline a journey of increased complexity, which made us reconceptualise our understanding of power-production in our practices and how power can be understood in relation to where it is produced. This journey is not linear or progressive, but rather circular and expansive. This means that in every new move or displacement of our understanding the previous move is included and still operating: we add another aspect or complication that makes us understand things in necessarily more complex ways. This process moves from an understanding of power as produced from above or outside of ourselves in terms of societal structures, which are acting on staff and material conditions as passive entities, to an understanding of everything as a discursive power-production that we all take part in and are collective producers of, whether we know it or not. The movement then expands into a third understanding, where discourse is no longer constitutive on its own as in the second understanding. Rather, discourses are understood to be intertwined and intra-acting with the agency of all other bodies, materials and artefacts in the world, with no clear-cut boundaries between them, as already suggested above.

'Outer structural and passive material preconditions determine qualities of early childhood'

When we met up in 1993 in the first network of the Stockholm project to discuss pieces of documentation, teachers were eager to question taken-for-granted routines and practices in their own practices and those employed in Sweden generally. They wanted to understand the mechanisms, forces and powers that produced these practices. We asked ourselves, what made us plan, organise, do and say things the way we

did. Most practitioners first mention over-arching structural circumstances, decided on by politicians and civil servants. These decisions
often involve inadequate space, staff, materials, time and money. Such
a view coincides and is supported by developmentally appropriate
practices (Bredekamp *et al.*, 2000) and evaluations, such as the ECERS
(Early Childhood Environmental Rating Scale), which have all become
more and more common in Sweden and around the world. These practices and evaluations build on ideas about what structurally constitutes
best practice, and best practices are defined in terms of standardised
criteria related to developmental learning theories. For instance, the
number of enrolled children structure the ideas of what it is possible to
do, according to what is believed to be the best possible group size for
different activities. Scientific knowledge about learning and children's
normal development informs politicians and civil servants directly or
indirectly about how best to organise learning activities and what
teaching-materials to buy. Politicians and civil servants, in their turn,
make decisions and construct evaluations according to this scientific
knowledge and in relation to the financial means available. What the
practitioners express in such cases is that any real power is basically not
in their own grasp, it is not something they can have. Rather it is imposed
on them from the 'outside' by societal structures built on systems of
organising society and knowledge production and seemingly upheld by
scientists, politicians and civil servants. Power is thus produced and
belongs to someone else in this way of thinking. Practice becomes an
arena of passive material entities that are regulated by active structures
and specific identifiable powerful subjects, who are a part of these over-
arching, power-producing and basically unchangeable structures.

'We are all collective producers of discursive power-production'

What if we were to reverse the above understanding of power owned
by the few in privileged positions within more or less fixed societal
structures, and claim that power is produced through collectively constructed discursive notions and meaning-making? The quality of practices
would then depend on the meaning-making and embodied practices we
are all (re)producing in our daily habits, routines and actions. Pedagogical
practices thus become *discursive practices* produced by collectively negotiated
meanings we ascribe to the world around us and ourselves. Hence,
power is produced and performed by all of us – collectively – in every little
thing we do.

The French theorist Michel Foucault has made us aware of this way of understanding power-production, by showing us how power embraces everything and comes from everywhere (1990: 93). He writes about power-production as something that operates through our own thinking and our own mentality. It operates through our self-government and self-regulation in accordance with dominating and socially constructed ideas, notions and discourses we have picked up and use as 'freely' choosing individual subjects. Foucault writes:

> There are two meanings of the word *subject:* subject to someone else by control and dependence, and tied to his own identity by a conscience or self-knowledge. Both meanings suggest a form of power which subjugates and makes subject to.
>
> (1982: 212, original emphasis)

Valerie Walkerdine was one of the first educational researchers to show how ideas and truths about children and learning are produced and maintained in classrooms by the teachers themselves. Ideas about children, produced in developmental psychology and mixed with ideas of learning, constitute practices that teachers materialise in classrooms. Walkerdine writes:

> The practices themselves, in their regulation, produce what it *means* to be a child: what behaviours, words, etc. are used and those are regulated by means of an apparatus of classification, and a grading of responses. 'The child' becomes a creation and yet at the same time provides room for a reading of pathology.
>
> (1988: 203–4, original emphasis)

When the team of researchers in the Stockholm project network suggested to the teachers to think about power-production in these terms and suggested that pedagogical practice emerges through our collective under-standings of what it is and should be, this at first felt quite uncomfortable to most teachers. How can practice be what we collectively *understand* it to be? When we explored the power of discursively naming, defining, writing and talking practice into existence by giving numerous examples, this way of thinking began to make more and more sense. Very soon it became quite easy to pick out any situation in daily practices and tell each other about how it is in fact discursively written, spoken and materialised as embodied pedagogical practice with specific goals and meanings by practitioners and children together. As an example, in the context of Nordic early childhood, even the situation of a very young child needing to go to the toilet is considered a pedagogical learning situation with normalising power-production. The visit to the toilet is not exclusively about learning hygiene, as you might first think, but about undressing, dressing and caring for your clothes all by yourself, and being responsible for flushing, turning out the light and closing the door. It thus becomes a learning situation that involves bodily coordination and motor skills, environmental, personal and social responsibility, where each thing is equally emphasised and thus pedagogised. There is an extensive body of research addressing these normalising practices in the context of education (Canella, 1997; Fendler, 2001; Hultqvist 1998, 2001; Lenz Taguchi, 1996, 2000; Popkewitz, 1998; Popkewitz and Brennan, 1998; Rose, 1999; Yelland, 2005).

Understanding power and pedagogical practice in terms of collectively constructed discursive meaning sometimes seems to stir up strong emotions. 'Everything that I have done up until now has been an unconscious power-production that might have had oppressive consequences for some children' is a common expression of this reaction. It can be overwhelming to realise that responsibility can be understood as shifting from being projected on to intentional subjects in power (such as politicians and civil servants in societal structures), to having become an intrinsic part of an undefined collective discursive power-production in which we are all inscribed and which we are all re-producing. In this way of thinking, individual agency must be understood as part of our collectively constructed meaning-making in our language and culture. That is, my possibility to make free choices and act upon my own thinking – my agency – is limited to picking up, using and repeating, but also to some extent transforming the discursive notions that we collectively produce and for which there is no single originator or author (Butler, 2004: 1). Some writers conclude from this that there is no individual agency or freedom at all (Popkewitz, 1998; Rose, 1999). The individual subject cannot 'free' herself from the language and culture she is inscribed in and through her daily life continues to reinscribe herself in. Following this perspective, the only agency we can have is through our usage and possible displacement of the discursive conditions to which we are already collectively subjected in terms of dominant notions that we repeat in our habitual living and practising. Agency is enacted through changes and displacements in these iterations as a resistance from *within* the collective discursive production of ourselves and others. Butler writes:

> Subjection consists precisely in this fundamental dependency on discourses we never chose but that, paradoxically, initiates and

sustains our agency. 'Subjection' signifies the process of becoming subordinated by power as well as the process of becoming a subject.

(1997: 2)

Most of us would say that it is scientists, politicians, media and artists that should be held responsible for the explicit construction of discourse and dominant notions and the naming of concepts and cultural expressions. But these discourses and notions cannot produce power unless the rest of us are using and repeating them.

After some time the emancipatory effects of the shift to a discursive understanding of power-production became evident among the participating teachers in the network of the Stockholm project. If practice is produced and emerges through all of us collectively thinking, talking and doing it into existence, we might also be able to collectively re-think, re-talk and re-do practice differently (Davies, 2000). Teachers who felt the collective emancipative effect of thinking of power-production in terms of discourses and discursive practices started to question more actively the way they have understood what a child is or should be, and tried to collectively think about what a child might or can be differently. This process of change in the Stockholm project has been described in several studies, and is not much unlike the experiences made in Australia by Glenda MacNaughton and her practitioner research project, based on Foucauldian, Derridean and Deleuzian theories to displace and learn about your own practices (Åberg and Lenz Taguchi, 2005; Dahlberg and Moss, 2005; Lenz Taguchi, 2000; MacNaughton, 2005).

A need to challenge and to go beyond the 'either–or' of the discourse/material divide

In the perspective of an intra-active pedagogy that I want to introduce to you later on in this chapter, both of the above described ways of understanding power-production end up separating out *the material* as passive or fixed, whether it is from the point of view of the structural or the discursive. We might collectively change the discourses and start to think about children as active investigators of the world, with consequences in how we organise practices to become more inviting to perform investigative learning; but the materials as such – the clay, sand or construction material – are still considered as passive and with no agency to affect the child. When we think about power being produced by discourses, it is important to see that this implies that only discourses can have what we would call agency – the active force to change and alter reality – rather than the material world of matter and artefacts around us (Barad, 2007; Hekman, 2008). Is it possible to think in another way that does not separate matter as 'dead' or passive in relation to the discursive? Is it possible to think of the material in early childhood practices as having agency of its own? Can we think of the material as being active in producing our meaning-making of the child and learning and of ourselves as teachers? Would it be possible to think of the material as being active in producing our discursive meaning-making? These were questions that we started to formulate and searched for ways to answer. If we answer the above questions in the affirmative, then power in pedagogical practices is produced and simultaneously materialised, not only by our discursive practices, but also by the materials actively and discursively materialising practice into existence through their agentic engagement in an intra-active production of our discursive understandings. Barad (2007) writes about the material as *performative agents*, a concept that has already been mentioned in the introduction. All kinds of organisms and matter are understood as performative agents. Everything is taking part in a dynamic process of intra-activity and materialisation as an ongoing flow of agency, through which a part of the world makes itself intelligible to another part of the world (Barad, 2007: 140). Even dots on the floor that children are supposed to sit on in a circle at assembly actively act upon the bodies of children. These dots actively make themselves intelligible to the child by keeping the child in place on the floor and signalling when a child is out of place by becoming visible to us (Hultman, 2009). Provided it is acknowledged to be the source of any kind of action, a performative agent can be both non-human and human (inorganic and organic).

When we think in terms of the material being just as agentic as humans, we are not locked into an *either–or* thinking, nor into a thinking of *both–and*. Rather, such thinking goes beyond the divide of the discursive and the material altogether. This is because the focus is on the in-between of intra-activities, as well as on the interdependent and intertwined nature of the relationship between discourses, things, matter and organisms. Now we can think of discourse and the material in new ways: in terms of the discursive being immanent to the material and the material being immanent to the discursive. This means that they depend upon each other and are mutually constitutive. It thus becomes impossible to say where the power-production on behalf of the material and the discursive meaning-making respectively starts or ends. In the perspective of intra-activity, there can be no clear divide between discourses, things, matter and organisms, since they are always in a relationship of intra-action and inter-connection and affecting each other mutually. This is why Barad writes about the *material-discursive*, which refers to the inter-connectedness and inseparability between discourse and matter. The material affects our discursive understandings just as much as our discursive understandings affect the material reality around us. As has been cited from Barad already in the introduction of this book, 'the material and the discursive are mutually implicated in the dynamics of intra-activity' (2007: 152). I will cite Barad further as she provides the very central explanation:

> The relationship between the material and the discursive is one of mutual entailment. Neither discursive practices nor material phenomena are ontologically or epistemologically prior. Neither can be explained in terms of the other. Neither is reducible to the other. Neither has privileged status in determining the other. Neither is articulated or articulable in the absence of the other; matter and meaning are mutually articulated.
>
> (2007: 152)

I will elaborate on this further below in relation to an example with young children, and in so doing also introduce some of the central concepts that we need in order to be able to understand what I call an intra-active pedagogy.

An example of transformation, transgression and learning as intra-active processes

One of our undergraduate students in early childhood education, Kristine Rende, showed a sequence of documentation from a small project she had done with children aged 2–3 years, during her vocational training in the second semester of teacher education. One of the aims of this vocational training was to learn how to use pedagogical documentation as a tool for learning and reflection on behalf of both the children and the staff, that is, making the learning visible to challenge the children further as well as critically challenging teachers' preconceptions about learning, taken-for-granted ways of thinking and organising practice. The students had been told to pick something that was 'going on' among the children – a question or issue that kept on reappearing in their play or everyday life at the preschool – document it and use the documentation to inform further play and learning.

For her presentation later at the Institute of Education, this student had made a short PowerPoint presentation. She immediately startled us as she started to describe how she had come to document 1- and 2-year-old boys using wooden sticks picked up from the ground as guns or pistols when playing outside in the afternoons. They were shooting and shouting, and hunting each other around the yard. So, when the student said that 'this is a project on ethics and gender', I could feel my heart beating faster and harder with a mixture of doubt and anticipation.

She told us how she had observed the boys and seen embarrassed staff members trying to calmly restrain the little bodies of the boys without succeeding in getting them to take an interest in something else than this aggressive play, which often ended up in tears. On other occasions staff became angry, forcing the boys inside and assembling them to talk about the norms and values of the preschool, stating that playing violent games was not allowed. This, however, did not seem to prevent the boys from picking up this game again. Rather it almost seemed as if it became even more desirable. The adults started to plan an extra parental meeting to discuss values and norms, and ask parents to please throw away toy guns and swords and forbid war games at home.

One day this student heard one boy shout out loudly 'My gun is alive and it wants to kill you!' pointing his stick, taken from an old pine tree, at his friend. The student called to this boy and, using what she described as an equally forceful but also very curious and interested voice, she asked him: 'If your gun is alive, it must have a name. What's the name of your gun?' The boy seemed startled and stood there quiet. 'Does it live with you?' she continued 'Or does it live here in the preschool yard?' The boy gave her a long silent look and then answered: 'His name is Erik and he lives with his mum under that tree', pointing at the tree under which he had found his stick. Then he ran off again. The student documented the short conversation in her process diary, which was a part of the pedagogical documentation she collected during her vocational training.

The next morning she asked the group of boys playing with sticks if she could talk to them for a minute. They agreed and she assembled them sitting down on the floor. She said that the previous day she had had a small talk with X that she had found so interesting that she wrote it down. She then asked X if it was all right for her to read out the short conversation they had had to the whole group, which he agreed to. The boys immediately started to talk out loud in unison, eagerly claiming their stick too had names and lived at home, or under the bench in the hall, etc. The student said: 'OK, let's listen to each of you one at a time', and as they each told their stories, they became increasingly full of imagination and humour, assigning the stick a certain look, specific traits

Figure 1.1 Painting sticks.

Figure 1.2 A finished stick.

and social contexts of families and friends. 'Go get your sticks and we can paint and decorate them so we can see which one is which', the student suggested.

Without getting into further details about the processes of this small project, I think you can imagine from these images how the boys' interest shifted from using the stick as a gun or pistol to making it into a friend – a doll – to play with, to make a family for, and to decorate in ways that made shooting with it impossible. Moreover, this shift of interest also invited girls to take part in the process. They too wanted to make dolls out of sticks. The play and aesthetic work with the sticks expanded to include more or less the whole group. Moreover, for some of the children the interest in sticks as being part of a tree evolved in the participatory discussions about the stick dolls and their lives. The children wondered about how the stick had been a part of the tree, which is a part of nature, dependent on rain, sun, soil, etc. Discussions about the life and death of sticks, after falling off trees, became interesting to some of the children. The sticks had been adopted into the community of the preschool as dolls instead of being a part of the tree or used as a weapon.

Figure 1.3 Investigating sticks.

I am telling this story to frame some of the aspects of an intra-active pedagogy that this book is all about. How can I, for instance, say that the theory/practice and the discourse/material divides were transgressed in this example? Were any other binary divides transgressed as well? Where were the inventive turning points in this process? How did matter – the material – come to matter in this example, both for children's learning and in the construction of children's subjectivities as learners?

In relation to this student's project it is easy to see the importance of taking into account and being inclusive of the children's world and their play, and negotiate with them from within their own language and life experiences. This is the basis for a listening pedagogy developed so successfully in Reggio Emilia, which has inspired Swedish preschools and schools (Åberg and Lenz Taguchi, 2005; Elfström *et al.*, 2008; Furness, 2008; Rinaldi, 2006). By being inclusive and actively making use of the children's ways of understanding their play and the way they spent their time in the preschool yard, maybe another way of theorising and doing practice would be the result? Maybe we would understand that the boys were simply bored and not seriously challenged to play in any other way than simply picking up sticks and running around? Maybe we would find that they imitated a television show that they frequently looked at, that we perhaps should know more about, and make use of, to challenge and expand their play? Or maybe these boys had just got the strong message in our culture about what a boy should be doing to perform masculinity in expected ways? Being inclusive of this knowledge, how are we to use it to challenge new ways of playing, thinking and doing that might expand their playfulness and/or deepen their learning of any aspect we chose to pick out as important or interesting?

There are many possible ways to go here, but either way, what is important in an intra-active approach is for us as teachers to try to make visible and do justice to what the learning child brings into the play or learning situation, without imposing our own moral values and aims of learning on them. Rather, we want to be in a listening dialogue, where we negotiate our different understandings, and learn about the diversities and differences in meaning-making and strategies of doing things. It is what the children already do and bring with them that we can make use of and further investigate or challenge to produce a deeper learning (Åberg and Lenz Taguchi, 2005; Dahlberg and Moss, 2005; Elfström *et al*., 2008; Furness, 2008; Lenz Taguchi, 2000, 2006; 2008b; Olsson, 2009; Reggio Children, 2001; Rinaldi, 2006). In this example the student decided to challenge the boys' play by offering them to intra-act with the sticks in a different way. In the dominance of our taken-for-granted worldview, the understanding that seems to lie most easily at hand is to think that the children 'humanise' their sticks by giving them names and human traits expressed in their usage of various aesthetic materials to transform the sticks from guns to dolls. Reading it this way the agency is still with the child who uses the passive materials to transform the stick. If we change our gaze to the perspective of the materials, it becomes possible to see how the material realities can be understood to have agency in relation to what happens in the material-discursive intra-active processes taking place between the materials, the children and the student. It becomes possible to see the agentic forces of the shiny papers evoking desires in the child to transform the stick in a way s/he first did not think was possible. It becomes possible to listen to the agentic rustle or swish of the thin coloured papers as they swirl around in the air from the top of the stick. This rustle connects to the discursive thinking of the child and the stick transforms again and again in the play taking place with other sticks and children.

The discursive meaning of the sticks agentially shifts in the different aspects of the play, depending on what the children are doing with the sticks. They come to know them differently as they play with them in different fashions and keep on adding materials to them. In a simple understanding, the stick shifts from being a weapon to a friend or doll to care for and interact with in the process of using and connecting to materials, such as paints, ribbons, shiny paper and glue. The materials thus *materialise* the looks and traits of the friend–stick–dolls, making them alive and 'humanised'. In the way Barad thinks about materialisation it is not just a matter of how discourse and meaning-making comes to matter, but how matter comes to matter in its agency (1998: 108). In a more complex way of understanding it, from the viewpoint of the material, the material *matters* and intra-acts with the boys in their play and their continuously displaced understandings of the sticks. The gaze shifts from the inter-action between the boys and the teacher in how they speak about the sticks and move them around, etc., to the wider and expanded gaze from the point of view of the swirl and rustle of the paper and its intra-action with the discursive understandings.

For the teachers, the focus shifts from being exclusively preoccupied with the individual children's cognitive knowledge constructions or the dialogue between the children, to the learning event taking place *in-between* the child and the material in the space and event of learning. How can pieces of shiny paper act upon a boy and his wooden stick with the help of a little glue in the atelier of the preschool? What will the transformation of the stick do to the boy's thinking and conceptualising of the stick as he now continues to play with it? Are new inter-connections made possible with other materials, ideas or children? We are of course as interested in the learning processes of the individual child in an intra-active pedagogy as in any other pedagogical approach to learning and play. However, to be able to know anything about what the individual child might have learnt or experienced, an intra-active pedagogy does not simply focus on and analyse the child and what the child says and does as separate from the environment and the materials it handles. We need to be just as attentive of the questions posed by the teachers that linger in the space of the learning event as we must be of the material possibilities in the room and the codes that regulate how children will use the materials and/or continue playing in this room. *It is the material-discursive forces and intensities that emerge in the intra-actions in-between the child and the materials in the room that together constitute the learning that can take place.* Hence, learning does not simply take place inside the child but is the phenomena that are produced in the intra-activity taking place in-between the child, its body, its discursive inscriptions, the discursive conditions in the space of learning, the materials available, the time–space relations in a specific room of situated organisms, where people are only one such material organism among others.

In this perspective all these organisms and matter in the event of learning must be understood as having agency of their own, being per-formative agents. They are intra-acting with each other differently, with different intensities and force, depending on the different potentialities of each organism or matter. Some matters cannot engage as easily or smoothly as others in change or transformation. For instance, the walls of the room cannot be moved, but the interior of the room can easily be altered in intra-action with furniture, things and materials. Water and clay can transform with great intensities and speed, but so can con-struction blocks when, for example, a construction of blocks is knocked down. The intensity and speed of the forces between materials vary depending on innumerable material-discursive conditions in the peda-gogical space. This also goes for the discursive production of words and meaning-making that the child is engaged in, in the intra-active processes. An older child with more available concepts might speed up the discursive-material intra-action when handling material and simulta-neously conceptualising what is going on. The phenomena that we call knowledge, experience or learning, are totally dependent on all these material-discursive conditions in intense intra-action with each other. The consequences of this thinking is that the teacher needs to make herself aware of how the room, space, time and things are organised and structured, and what kinds of intra-action between the different organisms might be possible.

Knowledge as phenomena can be viewed as material-discursive materialisations, that is, meanings negotiated in the material world within a material and discursively embodied being; for example, the child or the student-teacher. According to what Barad (1998) calls an *agential realism*, materialisation is understood in terms of the dynamics of intra-action (p. 106). And again, materialisation is not just a matter of how discourse and meaning-making comes to matter, but how matter comes to matter in its agency (p. 108). So, what is new in Barad's agential realism is to recognise matter as agentic in the process of an intra-active materialisation with other embodied beings, matter and discursive thinking (p. 109). Learning as an intra-action is thus a material-discursive process.

In relation to the example with the stick, intra-activity dissolves the divide between our discursive meaning-making (of a doll) and the material objects (of the stick, paint and papers), and between contents of learning (friendship, social relations and what a tree is and how it lives) and the learner's subjectivity (how the boys understand themselves as good or bad friends, or being curious about social life, or life of trees and wanting to learn more about these things). Understanding the processes of learning in this way means going beyond the theory/practice divide, but also the discourse/material and subject/object divides – the inseparability of the learner from what is learnt. Moreover, how the events of this example developed also entailed going beyond the masculine/feminine divide, as the boys transformed their play and started to investigate friendship and trees instead, in ways that should be labelled as neither feminine nor masculine. However, this displacement in content of their play made girls interested to participate and made the larger group of children take part in the different learning and play situations that emerged.

Moreover, we might think of what happened in this process in terms of a series of very specific events, where there were some very important turning points that would change the learning and becoming of the children. The first turning point emerged in the event when the student teacher asked the boy about the name of his stick. The second turning point took place as the children started to talk about the stick as part of the living tree in terms of life and death. In these specific events something entirely new was made possible. The questions posed and put out into the pedagogical space can, with inspiration from Deleuze, be understood in terms of evoking an inventive 'line of flight' (Deleuze and Guattari, 1987) into new becomings for the boys' understanding of their play with sticks, and the group of children's collective thinking on trees as living beings.

As you can see, it is very important how we as teachers choose to discursively understand – code, de-code or re-code – what the children do or say, or how we allow the children to code, de-code or re-code, what they do, that is, how we give and read meaning, and then re-construct such meaning-making in the intra-active processes taking place. This will determine what kinds of play and learning we will give the children the preconditions to enact, and thus what learning phenomena will emerge from this play. Or in other words, that which will eventually materialise as learning is dependent on what we say to children, how we encourage them or limit their possibilities to further investigation, how we organise the schedule for play or investigating processes, what materials we offer them, during what time span and in what environments, etc. (Åberg and Lenz Taguchi, 2005; Lenz Taguchi, 2000, 2004, 2006, 2008b). All this will be further developed in Chapter 4 with a detailed example.

Furthermore the words of the boys in their play and investigations took on a material reality in the form of documentation when they were written down and their play photographed. When the words were *made material* as written text, the documented words were given strong agency as the student decided to read them aloud to the boys from her process diary. This immediately made possible new intra-action taking place, that is, the documentation enabled new processes of meaning-making and investigative actions involving the offered materials. This student chose to use her photographed, taped and written documentation of the processes taking place as a way to enable adults and children to read, listen and look at what had been done and said, and collaboratively negotiate what to do, and challenge learning into new events of learning and questions to investigate. What was in the written notes and photographs constituted material limits to what could be understood, and intra-acted with the discourses available to the student-teacher. The meanings constructed in the discussion based on the documentation made the student-teacher direct her further investigations with the children to trees that the sticks once had been a part of, and the life of the living tree, needing to drink and breathe just like the children themselves.

Going beyond the theory/practice and discourse/matter divides means embracing an onto-epistemology

I have attempted to read the example above in terms of an intra-active pedagogy to try to illustrate that learning is not something an individual child achieves isolated from the material-discursive pedagogical space. Rather learning is produced in the intra-actions that emerge and where different organisms, matters and discourses intra-act with each other. We can identify phenomena of learning as we freeze the process to actualise the learning event in our documentation as written words or a photograph. This process is about becoming aware of how everything is connected and affects everything else in a state of *one-ness* and of being part of an interdependent whole – *univocity*, to use Colebrook's way of using the Deleuzian concept (Colebrook, 2002). As we will see below, Barad writes about this in terms of us being-*of*-the-world, rather than separate beings inside or above it. I will write more, in Chapter 7, on what the consequences are when we think about ourselves as in a total inter-connectedness with everything else, not the least in relation to issues of ethics. I want to end this chapter by introducing some of the basic theoretical underpinnings of going beyond the theory/practice and discourse/matter divides in this line of thinking. The concepts and thoughts below will also be further developed in relation to the example of student-teachers constructing clay figures in the next chapter.

Introducing an onto-epistemology

I want to emphasise how important it is to appreciate that we cannot separate the learner from what is learned in an intra-active pedagogy, when we plan, perform or evaluate our learning activities. We are in an interdependent relationship with the world that we come to know through intra-activity within the material-discursive embodied realities we live in and with, and that we are in a process of *'becoming-with'* (Haraway, 2008: 4). What teachers both in Reggio Emilia and Reggio Emilia-inspired preschools in Sweden have experienced is that there is no border between what the child *is* right now and what it continuously *becomes*. The child becomes, in a specific sense, what it learns, in a steadily ongoing flow of material-discursive events. Hence, what philosophers call ontology (theories of being) and epistemology (theories of knowledge and knowing) cannot be separated in the way they have been, if we are to understand the interdependent relationships between the subject, learning contents and the material reality in the way Karen Barad does. Hence, Barad (2007) talks about an *onto-epistemology*, defining it as 'the study of practices of knowing *in* being' (p. 185, my emphasis). She writes that it is impossible to isolate knowing from being since they are mutually implicated. She states:

> We don't obtain knowledge by standing outside the world; we know because we are *of* the world. We are part of the world and its differential becoming.
>
> (p. 185, my emphasis)

This means that practices of knowing cannot, as she writes,

> fully be claimed as human practices, not simply because we use non-human elements in our practices but because knowing is a matter of *part of the world making itself intelligible to another part.*
>
> (p. 185, my emphasis)

Learning events are, in this perspective, events of a materialised embodied reality. Learning is produced by our inevitable participation within these events and produces phenomena (knowledge) through complex intra-actions of multiple material-discursive (bodily, material and discursive) productions (Barad, 1998: 105). All these performative agents are busy learning to know each other – making each other intelligible to one another – and thus transform and change each other (in one way or another) in this process. Learning events are taking place just as much and simultaneously between your hands handling material things as they do in your thinking body/mind, handling concepts, notions and emotions. In such an understanding we go beyond the taken-for-granted ways of thinking of the binary divides of subject/object, theory/practice, intellect/body and discourse/matter, in order to make *matter* matter. Hence, we do justice to the material realities, spaces and places and the intra-active forces and intensities that are an inevitable part of learning (Barad, 1999, 2007, 2008; Alaimo and Hekman, 2008; Hekman, 2008).

The critical issues here are that there are no inherent and clear borders between matter and discourse, and no clear borders between being and knowing. This makes knowing just as much a matter of the body and the material as it is a matter of understanding and thinking through discourse/language, which of course has vast consequences for teaching and learning (Alaimo and Hekman, 2008; Barad, 1999, 2007). Thus, Barad's agential realism constitutes a post-humanist understanding of the 'human' where the ontological and epistemological cannot be separated but merge (Barad, 2007, 2008). She writes:

> [W]hat is at issue and at stake is a matter of the nature of reality, not merely as matter of human experience or human understandings of the world. Beyond the issue of how the body is positioned and situated in the world is the matter of how bodies are constituted along with the world, or rather as 'part' *of* the world (i.e., 'being-*of*-the-world,' not 'being-*in*-the-world').
>
> (2007: 160)

Individuals, just as non-humans and things, *emerge* through, and as a part of, their entangled intra-actions with everything else. Therefore we do not even pre-exist our interactions with the world. We are nothing until we connect to something else, even if it is simply the breathing of oxygen. Every organism is in connection with at least one other organism or matter to be able to live, as a condition of its existence. This is why we do not consider ourselves as an entity *in* the world, but rather as a consequence *of* the world. Everything that happens happens from within a mutual co-existence of a whole. Hence, what we are, or rather, continuously *become*, cannot be separated from our process of knowing (Barad, 2007). In the following chapter I will show the consequences of an ontology of immanence in relation to how we can understand learning.

Chapter 2

Learning and becoming in an onto-epistemology

We are not outside observers of the world. Neither are we simply located at particular places *in* the world; rather we are *part of* the world in its ongoing intra-activity.

(Barad, 2007: 184, my emphasis)

How can we think of the consequences for early childhood education, or in fact any educational context, if we were to take the quote from Karen Barad above seriously and start thinking of ourselves as learners as a part of everything around us, not just other humans? If we cannot clearly separate the learner from what is learned, and if ways of being in the world depend on our knowing of it, and our knowing depends on our being (and continuous becoming) in the world, how then do we go about teaching and learning?

In this chapter I want to outline how to understand learning and becoming from an onto-epistemological worldview. To accomplish this I will use an example of students in teacher education constructing clay figures. The basic idea that runs through this chapter is directly connected to the quote above: we are not put into the world in order to put ourselves above it, go beyond it or transcend it; rather, we are made from the same substances as the rest of the world, we are a part of it, and we are simply making ourselves intelligible to one another in a process of mutual and inter-dependent becoming. In other words, we cannot produce knowledge and learn about the world without being totally dependent on it. We are dependent on the world for our mere existence. What consequences does this have for pedagogical work? What do we do differently as teachers knowing this?

Understanding learning from different ontologies

Transcendence and immanence: in short, what's the difference?

I will start by describing some of the most dominant views on learning today that all refer to an ontology of transcendence. I want to show how these over-arching ontologies of transcendence and immanence in more general terms relate to the onto-epistemological view that the writing in this book seeks to encompass. In doing so I will rely on Todd May's (2005) accessible introduction to Gilles Deleuze where he makes this clear. In short, the dominant ontology of transcendence means that we as humans and the world around us are separated not just from each other but also from something above or beyond us that we consider universally true, unchangeable or infinite. Most people would either talk about this as universal and unchangeable laws or simply God. The world itself, in contrast, is understood as finite and changeable. Since God transcends the world, the world and God cannot be of the same substance. In the hierarchy of transcendent thinking, after God there is human subjectivity. The human subject transcends the material world, constituting it and giving it form and expression in our language, architecture, art, etc. In terms of epistemology then, the human subject is the seat of knowledge, but ontologically the subject follows in God's wake, since only God – or transcendent truth – can grant and guarantee the experiences of the subject (May, 2005: 27–8). The role of humans, May continues, becomes that of the observer and interpreter of the form of truth or God. May argues that our operation as knowledge-producers and learners in a transcendent view 'freezes living, makes it coagulate and lose its flow' (2005: 27). This happens, he says, when we submit to the judgement of a single truth, law or perspective that we allow to stand outside or above the complex mixtures of difference and transformations that constitute ongoing living life.

Immanence, on the contrary, is exactly about this complex mixture of differences in the world and universe, where all matter consists of the same substances, whether it is human or non-human matter. The hierarchical aspect of transcendence is thus 'flattened out' – nothing is considered to stand above or take a true or privileged position. There are no fixed or inherent borders between matter, organisms (human or non-human) and things. Instead, these are understood as in a constant flow of mutual intra-action and diffractions with each other. Diffraction is a concept from physics best illustrated with the rolling, pushing and transformation of waves in, for example, the sea, but in physics it deals with any kind of waves, such as sound-waves and light waves. Barad (2007) writes that, 'diffraction has to do with the way waves combine when they overlap and the apparent bending and spreading of waves that occurs when waves encounter an obstruction' (p. 74). She shows the example where barriers in the sea – such as huge stones – serve as an apparatus of diffraction where the waves are forced into bending and overlapping (pp. 74–5). It is this movement of overlapping where the waves change in themselves in intra-action with the obstacle of the stone and with each wave accumulating which signifies diffraction.

Diffraction as a force and movement is thus part of the productions, performances and phenomena created in processes of intra-actions in-between different matter; for instance, waves of water intra-acting with the stones, which together make up that which we call reality. This is a reality which is a non-hierarchical 'flattened-out' system of mutual inter-relationships between all matter and organisms (Barad, 2007). It can also be understood as a system of mutual and constantly ongoing communication, in which each wave affects the other, which affects the next, etc. by means of the agentic intensity and force of each matter or organism. Philosophers such as Spinoza, Nietzsche and Deleuze and Guattari, alongside leading contemporary physicists and biologists since at least the middle of the twentieth century, have found it necessary to abandon an ontology of transcendence, to be able to think more creatively and to better understand the world, evolution, life, living and knowing.

The learner and the world as separated

The learner and the world, or the subject observing and object of observation, are understood as separated from each other, in line with the dominant ontology of transcendence. In the perspectives on learning and teaching that emerge from this ontology, the world is either *represented* or being *presented* to the child or learner. Ever since modern schooling emerged in the seventeenth century, writes Osberg and Biesta (2007), it has been assumed that learning is about either one of two perspectives. The first perspective means that we try to *represent* the pre-existing world with the help of a language that is said to represent it. As a learner you reproduce these representing language constructs from books, lectures or other learning materials. These are thought of as entities of knowledge representing reality. In terms of teaching, what we get is basically instrumental or teacher-centred approaches. What is important in this perspective is that we accept knowledge constructs as true representations of the world 'out there' and apart from us. Only the world itself embodies the truths about itself. Humans are the 'discoverers' and 'disclosers', making the world transparent and knowable through our representations in language constructed into different discourses in science.

The second perspective on learning is about being *presented* to the pre-existing world in order to investigate it for yourself. In the history of educational theory this can mean very different things. It can, for example, relate to a representational paradigm as the first perspective does, with the difference being that learning is not to take place as instrumental transferences between the one who knows (the teacher) and the one who does not yet know (the learner), but rather as a result of active investigation on behalf of the learner. Such a perspective relies on the learner learning as a result of a natural and inborn curiosity, and only as much as s/he is mature enough to learn in accordance with her/his inherent abilities at different ages. Learning is thought of as a process that progresses from stages of low degrees of cognitive complexity and abstraction in language to increasingly higher stages. The learner will mature and develop her/his knowledge constructs in progressive stages and with increased age and maturity levels in these cognitive and constructivist learning-theories (Bredekamp *et al.*, 2000; Gestwicki, 2006; Marton and Booth, 1997; Marton and Tsui, 2004; Pramling Samuelsson and Pramling, 2008). These perspectives are probably familiar to the readers. They make the learner an object of learning in relation to her/his own levels of maturity and cognitive abilities in stage-like formations. When documentation is used it is to determine the positioning of the learner in relation to her/his development in learning a specific content or ability. What is learnt is also considered an object, most often being a well-defined language construct representing matters in a pre-existing world. Hence, these perspectives are built on an idea of reproduction of knowledge constructs and skills.

The second perspective, of being presented to the world to investigate it yourself, also has another meaning. This way of understanding learning is rarely taken up and practised in preschools and schools. It can be understood as based on a social constructivist and discursive understanding. In the field of early childhood education the preschools in Reggio Emilia can be understood to practise such learning processes. The child is understood as a competent constructor of its own language constructs about the world. Children take part in a collaborative construction of meaning and are thus constructors of both culture and knowledge in a community of learners (Dahlberg and Lenz Taguchi,

1994; Dahlberg *et al.*, 2007; Reggio Children, 2001; Rinaldi, 2006).
Although the learner is understood as an active agent in learning and in
constructing knowledge constructs, it is still only *human* languages and
expressions that possess valid agency in this perspective. Thus, the world
itself continues to be pre-existing, passive and separated from the learner.
It is human language and discourse that is constitutive of the learner and
how the subject understands and acts in the world.

In all the above ways of understanding learning, the learner is seen
as separated from the world itself. Learning is something that takes place
only within an individual learner's mind/intellect as an inner process or
in-between children, or children and adults in interaction processes.
Either learning is being represented in language, as in the representational paradigm, or it is understood as a constitutive discursive meaning-
making in language, as in the discursive and social constructivist
paradigm. The world itself remains 'dead' or passive and without agency.
Although the world and matter is understood as important to interact
with for learning to be constructed, it is, basically, a 'tool' and something
passive, 'out there' to construct knowledge about. Sometimes, however,
material tools are used to accomplish learning, but the tools in themselves
are considered passive and only the child handling them is active.

These ways of thinking inevitably refer to a dualistic worldview of
divides. The persuasive argument by many of the material feminists
(Alaimo and Hekman, 2008; Barad, 2007; Hekman, 2008) is that
constructivist, discursive and even post-structuralist views that specifically
emphasise the need to go beyond modernist binaries do not manage to
include in their equations the material world as an agentic producer of
meaning. They show in their writings that the material and the body are
merely discursive in these views of learning, and remain passive objects
upon which discourse is inscribed, rather than having agency on their
own. Only humans can learn about the world. The world itself is not in
a corresponding and interdependent process of learning or change.
Culture is constructed by humans as something different and apart from
the pre-existing natural nature 'out there'. The discursive meaning-
makings are active in inscribing, for example, the body as feminine,
whereas the material body passively awaits the discursive inscriptions.
Hence the binary divides remain in place and producing power instead of
being transgressed.

The learner and the world as entangled becomings

Next I will outline some of the most central aspects of thinking about the learner and the world as entangled becomings. Because this theory relies upon quantum physics as well as a reconceptualised evolutionary theory, it may seem unfamiliar at first, but hopefully things will make more sense to you as this thinking is put to work later in the example of the clay figures. Barad writes in the preface to her book *Meeting the Universe Halfway* (2007) that '[e]xistence is not an individual affair': our relation to the world is a relationship *as beings that are a part of the world*. Hence, there is 'no independent, self-contained existence' in the world (p. ix). Barad's onto-epistemology relies on quantum physics to challenge *both* a positivist and naturalist paradigm of representation, *and* a social constructivist paradigm that understands everything as discursive. Instead, she argues, the learner and the world cannot be separated, but are *of* the world in a co-dependency. As humans we must understand ourselves as material objects of the world, just as any other beings and matter.

In accordance with a reconceptualised evolutionary thinking, our potentialities are at the same time limited but also changeable in an evolutionary perspective (Jablonka and Lamb, 2005; West-Eberhard, 2003). Such evolutionary change of all organisms is ongoing and continuously taking place in the intra-actions in-between matter and organisms in the world. Our thinking and conceptualising minds are an intrinsic part of our bodies, which are in a flow of information between cells, fluids and synapses of thought. Biological and genetic research shows that development and evolution is a very complex process involving the genetic and structural potentialities of different organisms (such as the human body itself and the organs within it). These potentialities are actualised in unforeseen and unexpected ways depending on spatio-temporal intensities and forces that are determined by the environmental circumstances, but also by consciousness, affect and our socially constructed cultures. The biologists Jablonka and Lamb (2005) thus write about how we need to understand evolution in four dimensions: genetic, epigenetic, behavioural and symbolic/cultural. In other words, there are on the one hand limits to what our body can do depending on its construction, but on the other hand the body can and will inevitably change in ways that challenge these limitations depending on its intra-actions with both physical and cultural circumstances and preconditions.

In the following quote Deleuze (1988) describes how the philosopher Spinoza, in the seventeenth century, understood bodies of all kinds – an animal, a body of sounds, a mind or an idea, a social body or a collective body, and the human body (p. 127). His description is close to how many contemporary biological and physicist researchers would describe their understanding of the inter-connectedness of change in an ontology of immanence.

> In the first place, a body, however small it may be, is composed of an infinite number of particles; it is the relations of motion and rest, of speeds and slowness between particles, that define a body, the individuality of a body. Secondly, a body affects other bodies, or is affected by other bodies; it is this capacity for affecting and being affected that also defines a body in its individuality. . . . It [the body] is not defined by a form or by functions.
>
> (p. 123)

In the social sciences, feminist researchers have connected in different ways to aspects of this kind of thinking. The possibility of, for instance, literally 'thinking through the skin' is investigated in Sara Ahmed and Jackie Stacey's book (2001). The skin is not the border of our bodies but a territory or region of interference, a 'diffraction' of communicative 'waves' between matters, if we want to use Barad's way of talking about what happens in the in-between different matters (2007: 74–7). Physicists show that there are neither ontological nor visual edges nor boundaries between our bodies and the rest of the material world. Rather it is a mistaken psychological belief that bodily boundaries exist, writes Barad with reference to the Nobel-prize winning physicist Richard Feynman (Barad, 2007: 156). Bodies are, she concludes, not objects with properties or inherent boundaries; 'they are material-discursive phenomena' (p. 153). Human bodies are not, in such thinking, inherently different from non-human ones: 'what constitutes the human is not a fixed or pregiven notion, but neither is it a free-floating ideality', rather they [human bodies] are a result of an intra-action (p. 153).

Barad (2007) uses the thinking of the quantum physicist Niels Bohr as she theorises on the dissolved relationship between being and learning – onto-epistemology. Bohr challenged Newtonian classical physics and called into question several foundationalist assumptions that Western epistemology generally takes as essential to its project. The most important is the assumption of an inherent subject/object distinction and the representational status of language. He argued that it is impossible to separate out the object of observation from the agencies of observation – the subject. The 'cut' between the subject and object – what is observed – is enacted in the situatedness of a particular observation, using a particular apparatus of observation, rather than being inherent or fixed, as in the Newtonian tradition (p. 142). What Bohr challenged with his understanding of quantum mechanics was the notion in traditional physics of an independent real 'external' world, which is not dependent in any way on the observers. Hence, Bohr's theory interrupts the transcendent commitment to spatial separability and 'externality' put forward as a central precondition for knowing the world and a condition of objectivity by physicists such as Einstein (p. 173). Bohr did not share Einstein's metaphysical beliefs, which made it possible for him to think differently about borders, separability, and about difference itself. For Bohr, what appears to us as separated states in communication are in fact 'parts' of a phenomenom, which is a result of ontologically indeterminate intra-actions (pp. 174–5).

Hence, our meaning-making and the learning we do is dependent on the material world around us. The material world acts upon our thinking just as much as our thinking acts upon it (Barad, 2007). Our thinking can alter the stone, and correspondingly the stone can alter our thinking. Our thinking constructs ideas about what it is possible to do with stones from their qualities and shapes. We build something from the stone, or worship it like a God, or write on it to remember, or simply blast it to pieces to get to the metals embedded in it. Hence, discourse is just as much produced by way of the agentic qualities of the material world around us as it intra-acts with us, as it is produced by the limitations of our perceptive, intra-acting and conceptualising mind. As we are faced by global warming and environmental problems it is easy to accept the idea that the 'world kicks back at us' (Barad, 1998: 112) in unforeseen ways from within its own agentic logics that we sometimes know very little about. Our cultures and ways of living are shaped by nature, not as a fixed precondition, but as a living, changing performative agent, just like ourselves. Culture materialises from nature as nature is shaped and materialised by culture, that is, our ways of using it, living from it and altering it. There is no telling us apart, since what we are and our very existence are in total mutuality and interdependence.

One central consequence of an onto-epistemological perspective is that there can be no non-contextualised and universal 'best ways of learning' when applied to education. What we are engaged in, in pedagogical practices, can simply be understood as constituting habits – habits of teaching and learning that are tied to material-discursive conditions of things and matter, as well as ideas and notions of learning. Ideas and notions are of course also tied to socio-historical and political contexts. If we accept that pedagogical practices are a mixture of material-discursive phenomena actualised as habits of thinking and doing, what are the implications for practice? The consequences for educational practice of such thinking are for teachers to make themselves much more aware of, as well as find ways to make use of, the complexities, differences and diversities of the material-discursive contexts we inhabit. We need to critically analyse what taken-for-granted habits of thought and action the material-discursive intra-actions construct in our pedagogical spaces. These habits of thinking and doing in our teaching and learning-practices, which we arrange for children and students, are what we can observe, critique and change. Thus, we can engage in collecting an increasingly vaster body of experience from our documented practices. These collected experiences will make it easier for us to make use of and do justice to the differences and multiplicities among children, students, contents, matter and environments that are in intra-action with each other.

To sum up the above: what is new and unfamiliar to us is to start thinking of all aspects of learning – including the material – as being active and having *agency* in the construction of knowledge (Barad, 1999, 2007, 2008). This is what we can call the 'material turn' in the social sciences today. In a similar fashion, it took some time and felt quite unfamiliar at first, before we acknowledged the discursive as productive of practice and producing power – the 'discursive turn', which was discussed in Chapter 1. A few decades have passed since that 'discursive turn'. Now Barad and material feminism(s) (Alaimo and Hekman, 2008) state that it is time for the 'material turn' but without giving up on what we have learnt from the discursive one. However, we do need to ask ourselves the following legitimate question now that culture and discourse have been accepted as constituting forces:

> Why are language and culture granted their own agency and historicity, while matter is figured as passive and immutable? . . . Language matters. Discourse matters. Culture matters. There is an important sense in which the only thing that doesn't seem to matter anymore is matter.
>
> (Barad, 2007: 132)

In relation to learning and knowing, which is the key issue in educational practices? Barad urges us to go beyond all kinds of binary thinking, and especially going beyond the human/nonhuman, subject/object, discourse/reality, constructivist/realist binary divides, and rethink the concept of both 'agency' and 'realism' in this process. In conclusion, Barad clarifies what her agentic realist approach can do:

[It] provides an understanding of the role of human and nonhuman factors in the production of knowledge, thereby moving considerations of epistemic practices beyond the traditional realism versus social constructivism debates.

(1998: 89)

How knowing can be understood in an onto-epistemological approach: an example

In this section of the chapter, I will use an example to clarify the theoretical discussions above. This example will be read from three different perspectives: 'Being-*in*-the-world', where matter and organisms are still kept apart; 'Being-in-*discourse*', where everything is considered to be constituted by collectively constructed discourse; and 'Being-*of*-the-world', which is the onto-epistemology, theorised above, of an entangled state of interdependence. I will use some photographs and documentation from a learning experiment performed with some student-teachers within the reconceptualised teacher education, which I have mentioned already in the introduction of this book and which is described in more detail in Chapters 5 and 6. The learning event is about making a clay figure

Figure 2.1 Constructing a clay figure and turning it back into a lump of clay.

and later on transforming it back to a piece of clay, while observing and documenting the process very closely in writing and with photographs. The question posed to the students was: 'Can you make a clay figure that is about as big as your own hand – or larger – and is standing on one leg?' The photo-montage in Figure 2.1 on p. 51 illustrates this process.

'Being-in-the-world': a separate entity being in a relation to other entities

Let us begin by briefly recapitulating and applying a representational perspective, with its roots in the seventeenth century, that assumes that language is a transparent medium that transmits a true picture of reality to the knowing mind. The epistemology (theory of learning and knowing) of what has been called the modernist paradigm has been grounded in an idea of objective access to the real, with an ontology based on a taken-for-granted idea of clear boundaries between humans and non-humans, bodies and other matter, as has been shown earlier. Understood from this perspective the bodies and hands of the students making the clay figure and the pieces of clay are inherently separated from each other. The students observe how the clay transforms into a figure and back to a piece of clay. They take notes on, for instance, how the qualities of clay change from the warm temperature of human hands, from the oxygen in the air that makes it dry, and the water that softens and finally dissolves it. When they discuss their documentations they pose questions about the exact temperatures needed for a perfect softening of the clay and the time needed for the clay to dry and harden, depending on its thickness. They have scattered but no systematic and exact observations, but agree that they could have gained 'true knowledge' about the clay had they done so, as in a scientific experiment. With such a perspective humans become observers of the world and practices of knowing and being are separated from each other (Barad, 2007: 160).

'Being-in-discourse'

The above representational way of thinking is definitely and seriously challenged by a discursive thinking, which suggests that the real is a product of collaborative meaning-making discourses. Following the 'linguistic turn', the real is entirely constituted by us in our meaning-making expressed in language: what we call *discourse* (on the 'linguistic turn', see Introduction, p. 12). In this thinking discourse is not about linguistic representations, grammar or merely what is said, but those forms of meaning which constrain and enable what is possible to say and what counts as meaningful in a specific time, culture or context and group of people (Barad, 2007: 146; Butler, 1990; Foucault, 1990). When we now look at the group of clay figures and the observations at hand and critically analyse them from a discursive perspective, how are we to understand what has taken place in the construction of these figures? In the collaborative critical discussions the (female) students soon became aware that all the figures they had produced were 'clay men' or gender-neutral figures without feminine gender traits. They had moulded a head that was hairless, a body that was naked and breast-less, and legs and arms in different active postures: running, jogging, dancing, skating, etc. The students agreed that this was because of the Swedish cultural habit in our language of always referring to 'a man' when being asked to draw or make a human figure, irrespective of the material and even when baking gingerbread cookies. Why is the taken-for-granted figure always a male figure? And why is the 'neutral' word for 'it' in Swedish the same word as the word for man? This was easy to connect to basic feminist theory as these questions arose, and the asymmetry in power and value in the dominant male/female divide.

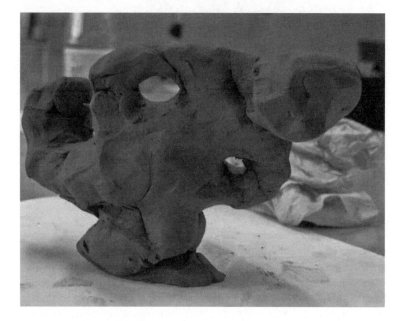

Figure 2.2 A clay figure skating.

Figure 2.3 A clay man from behind.

When the students discussed the scientific aspects of the qualities of clay, as well as the physics in terms of centre of gravity and balance, they agreed that their limited access to scientific discourse and its terminology constrained them to express themselves only in an 'everyday' discourse. Such a discourse, on the other hand, is strikingly domesticated. When discussing the clay they used what they understood as a more feminine language from familiar worlds of cooking, baking, dance and literature, rather than more difficult scientific words that more specifically define the qualities of the clay in the language of physics and mathematical geometry. So, what it is possible to say, they concluded, depends on your access to different discourses, and different discourses will enable you to know the clay figures in very specific and different ways.

If we think that our only way of knowing reality is discursive, there must, however, still be a reality 'out there' that remains separated from language, discourse or culture and that cannot, so to speak, 'speak for itself' (Alaimo and Hekman, 2008: 3). Although the material world of clay figures is constituted by discourse, that is, the clay figures take on a masculine appearance because of dominant discourse, the clay has no agency of its own and remains a passive material apart from us. What is embraced in the discursive paradigm is the idea of being and knowing as completely textual/discursive – *'being-in-discourse'*, in contrast to the former observer *in* a pre-existing world. There is a shift from one epistemological condition to another, from a reality-paradigm to a discursive-paradigm – it can be understood as a choice of *either–or*. However, I want to stress again that the discursive stance does indeed constitute an important effort to transgress binary divisions, by understanding everything as discursively constituted, instead of thinking the observing subject and the observed object as inherently separated. When we, however, choose to focus *only* on the discursive and avoid addressing what still must be understood as material, the threat of re-establishing the *discourse/reality* binary divide is definitely there. In our taken-for-granted ways of understanding what something 'is', its meaning-making depends on its excluded opposite – of what it is *not*. The binary is reinforced by what is absent or excluded. So, if the clay figures are merely discourse, then what they are *not* is *material and real*. Thus, the discursive paradigm – *'being-in-discourse'* – does not offer a way to address and theorise on how *matter* matters in relation to discourse and the binary cannot be dissolved or transgressed.

Even the important and far-reaching concept of *materialisation* in the writings of Judith Butler (1990, 1993, 2004) can, in this perspective, be understood as not having transgressed the binary divide to acknowledge the agency of the material in relation to discourse, writes Barad (2007: 63–4), who is in many aspects much indebted to Butler's theory. Discourses are, in Butlerian terms, inscribed on the 'surface' of bodies, and bodies are transformed and altered by discourse. This is done, writes Barad, by the agency of discourse only, *rather than in a mutual engagement with the material body itself*, where the body is granted agency on its own. Hence, she continues, Butler's theory reinscribes matter as a passive product of discursive practices rather than an active agent participating in materialisation (p. 151). In spite of the important ways that both Foucault and Butler have theorised on the body, what neither of them managed to show was how *the body itself actively matters* in the process of materialisation and subjectification (pp. 64–5). So, how do we make matter *matter* in how we come to know the world and ourselves, and in ways that go beyond and dissolve binary divides such as discourse/reality, culture/nature, language/material?

Thinking differently: an onto-epistemology and an ontology of immanence

If we want to challenge thinking either in terms of 'being-in-the-world' or 'being-in-discourse', we need to reject our instinct for trying to 'get out of' something altogether. There is nothing to get out of to observe from the outside, and there is no inside that we are forever stuck within. The inside is the outside, as has been materialised in the mathematical model for eternity in the Möbius strip, or in construction of the Klein bottle. The Möbius strip is a surface that has only one side and one edge. The Kein Bottle has no boundaries at all and is a non-orientable surface with no distinct 'inner' or 'outer' sides.

Or as Deleuze writes: 'We will say of pure immanence that it is A LIFE, and nothing else' (2001: 27, original capital letters). Deleuze describes immanence as a *life* and *a way of living*, where all substances are on a common 'plane of immanence' (2001: 26). His thinking relies heavily on his studies of the seventeenth-century philosopher Baruch Spinoza. In his book on Spinoza, Deleuze writes about what it means to be a part of the whole – there is only One. All bodies need to be understood in their living individuality, not as a form, but as a complex relation of particles that communicate, transform and become different from themselves at higher or lesser speed – infinitely (1988: 123). Deleuze continues:

> [O]ne Nature for all bodies, one Nature for all individuals, a Nature that is itself an individual varying in an infinite number of ways. What is involved is no longer the affirmation of a single substance, but rather the laying out of a *common plane of immanence* on which all bodies, all minds, and all individuals are situated. . . . Thus, to be in the middle of Spinoza is to be on this modal plane, or rather to install oneself on this plane – which implies a mode of living, a way of life.
>
> (1988: 122, original emphasis)

Immanence thus operates on what is generally described as a pre-human or un-human level, simply to emphasise that the world is not dependent only on human discursive thinking and a transcendent ontology (Colebrook, 2002; Grosz, 2005). Deleuze suggests, as has already been pointed out, that there is only one Nature or plane of univocal being, but with a pluralism and multiplicity of becomings – *Univocity* (Colebrook, 2002: 95).

To be able to think about this in a more concrete way and relating back to the students and the clay figures, we will look again at the dominating ontology of transcendence, which we take for granted in our daily lives and which is embedded in our language. This thinking, writes Deleuze and Guattari (1994), is based on *the habit of saying 'I'*: naming the self 'I', a self, apart from other selves and things. So, here am 'I', state the students making the clay figure, and here is a piece of clay that I am moulding into a 'clay man'. Everything in our thinking follows from this habit of saying 'I'. 'It is presumed', writes Deleuze, 'that everyone knows, independently of concepts, what is meant by self, thinking, and being' (1994: 129). Returning to the clay figures again: here 'am I' who is 'thinking about' and 'empirically observing' the clay figure from a position outside of and apart from it. It is dead matter made out of a pre-existing material, which is clay. 'The pure self of "I think" thus appears to be a beginning only because it has referred all its presuppositions back to the empirical self', writes Deleuze (1994: 129). What is not 'I' is different – *in place of the identical* – it is the negative, the contradictory or the opposite. Thus, the clay figure as material and clay is *not* a human and thinking self that can call itself an 'I'. Difference is a difference in relation to an identity – a difference *to* something – which is always the case in a transcendent thinking (Colebrook, 2002; Smith, 2003). To summarise this simply means that, by putting ourselves apart from and above the rest of the world as a human 'I', we cannot as easily understand our interdependence with other organisms and matter, which are given a lower status as matter in an ontology of transcendence.

In a pedagogical perspective this divide between 'I' and 'matter' makes us focus on what the subject of learning is capable of – what s/he understands, how developed and mature s/he is, and what s/he is able to conceptualise or perform. The force of what we call learning and knowing comes from within the learning subject in such thinking, rather than being a production of the intra-actions taking place in the processes of the material clay, the hands of the students and her discursive thinking body. From a perspective of immanence, we must instead focus on the whole of the learning event, including the environment and the agentic qualities of matter that intra-act with the learner. When thinking in this way, the clay is not separated from and different from the identity of the learner. Instead Deleuze proposes a difference without a negation, a difference that is a difference *in itself* and not as an opposite or negative to something (Deleuze, 1994). Thus, the clay figure – just as the learner – differentiates from itself or herself in every intra-active change taking place. It or she becomes anew in its or her transformative process, like the waves of diffraction. It is a clay man like this, *or* this, *or* this, *and* like this, *and* this. Difference *in* itself rather than different in comparison *to* something else.

Challenging and not accepting the taken-for-granted coherent 'I' constitutes an affirmation of the inter-connectedness between all organisms and matter. It is a *positivity* that moves beyond the transcendent binary thinking which is always constituted by a negation, as in thinking that something is because it is *not* something else (Deleuze, 1994). For pedagogy such a shift in our thinking can make us go away from making judgements of children in terms of deviations from the norm, and thus from the point of negativity. Instead we can practice to be affirmative of the iterative changes and differentiations in children in their intra-actions with other things in learning events. Moreover, it might make us change our hard reductive gaze on the individual child, to a softer and widened attentive gaze that includes that which takes place in the spaces in-between. The challenge for pedagogy then is not to do away with the 'I', but to start thinking about how this 'I' is constituted in a total inter-dependence with, not just other 'I's but all matters, artefacts and physical intensities and forces around it in the environment of a preschool situated in a socio-historical and geographical context.

Knowing in a state of 'being-of-the-world'

Knowing can be understood as a matter making itself understandable and intelligible to another matter, which are both part of the world, as has been already referred to in Chapter 1 (Barad, 2007: 185). Taking us back to our clay figure example, Barad might suggest to us that the hands of the students mould the clay while discursively thinking they are about to make a 'clay man'; while they are moulding what they discursively understand (in a gendered discourse) is a (hairless) head, (naked breast-less) body, legs and arms in different postures, such as running, dancing, skating. Discursively charged images of skating figures on cold winter mornings, or sweating joggers, etc. intra-act with clay that is softening from warm fingers and hands. So, discursively thinking hands mould the clay, *but the clay also moulds hands and the student's discursive thinking.* The clay with its

Figure 2.4 Student's hand moulding a clay man.

plasticity and three-dimensional agentic qualities *makes itself intelligible as clay* to the students, with its specific qualities and potentialities.

The clay works *with* and *against* the student's notions, conforming or resisting, as the 'clay men' are moulded and *moulding themselves* in their intra-acting with the hands, in a very intimate and borderless mutual relationship. The responsiveness and resistance of every lump of clay, with all its agentic qualities (infinite potentialities and temporal limitations) as this particular material piece of clay, materialises the notions of what a 'clay man' might become. But also what clay 'is' and might become, differently for each and every student. The students developed emotional affections towards their 'clay men', and gave them names and built a relationship through the process of discussing their observations of how they were constructed and turned back into a lump of clay. The affective relationships that were created had much in common with the children's relationships to the stick dolls in Chapter 1. Learning thus often involves emotions, affections, lust, desire and imagination that we do not usually acknowledge. By making ourselves aware of these aspects of learning we can also transgress the divides between mind/body and thinking/feeling (Colebrook, 2002; Deleuze, 1990; Grosz, 2005).

To summarise the above: what *becomes* a 'clay man' is the result of different matters making themselves intelligible to each other with all their potentialities and temporal limitations, in a specific series of events with specific preconditions. The clay is in a process of *becoming-with* and an *embodied thinking* in the discursively enacting hands of students. Simultaneously the students' discursively thinking hands are in a process of mutual becoming – *becoming-with* the clay (Haraway, 2008). Hence, Barad states that knowing and thinking can be understood as material practices of intra-acting (2007: 90). Such knowing is also about focusing on differences in themselves. This became clear to the students when they were asked to turn the figure back to clay again. They engaged in intra-active knowing with the clay as it altered, first into a soft and warm 'clay man', then turning dry and hard in intra-action with the atmospheric humidity of the air, and finally being transformed back to the state of a lump of clay. They observed the speed or slowness of drying – from head to foot apparently – in the intra-activity as the process of evaporation took place. Then, put into water, they experienced the intra-action between water and clay, the water slowly penetrating the clay and altering and transforming the substances until the 'clay men' were dissolved into a new state of becoming (see Figure 2.1).

As I will discuss in more detail in Chapter 4, an intra-active pedagogy can never be about planning exactly what kinds of learning processes will take place, or what kinds of learning will be achieved. There is no way to predict exact learning outcomes if you have an onto-epistemological understanding of learning and knowing, which is why teaching and learning needs to be thought about in other ways. Pedagogical documentation offers an invaluable tool in that it 'maps out' a fraction of a learning event and makes it materialise before us in the documentation. Using the documentation, you can read the learning event from its complexities and mixture of differentiations: from the perspective of the clay intra-acting with the water, or from the hands intra-acting with the clay, etc. You will be able to analyse what has taken place in the different intra-actions: how one matter or organism has made itself intelligible to another one. For instance, how your discursive thinking becomes intelligible to the clay, but also how the clay becomes intelligible to the moulding hands in the material-discursive intra-actions emerging in the process of moulding. From these analyses, you can, as a teacher, make new decisions on what intra-actions to make possible in the planning and organisation of the pedagogical environment, and questions to ask, etc. the next day.

Some of the pedagogical consequences of knowing as 'being-of-the-world'

If Karen Barad is right that being and knowing cannot be separated, and that we learn to know the world in intra-action with our being and the material reality around us, this must have consequences for how we teach, perform and evaluate learning processes in early childhood education. From the perspective of immanence and thinking in terms of an onto-epistemology, I ask myself if it is at all possible to teach without being in a state of a listening dialogue with children as well as with matter, artefacts and environments. How is it possible to teach without asking children or students about what they themselves think and bring into their play or the learning events we are involving them in? How can we teach without taking into account the complexities and diversities of children's and students' thinking and strategies of doing? How can we teach without taking into account how learning is enacted in intra-action with the materials we handle, the environments we inhabit and the organisation of time, places and spaces in our early childhood practices? This cannot simply be a question of observation of these intra-actions taking place, but must also have consequences for how we arrange, plan and pursue the learning endeavour in collaboration with the children and our colleagues.

Learning from an onto-epistemological perspective takes place *right in the middle of things*, in our very living and doing pedagogical practices. If we want to make ourselves aware of how and what we learn from within the events taking place, we need to open ourselves up to what happens right now and in the middle of the thickness of the actual present with all its multiplicities. When planning our work, which I want to emphasise as being of vast importance in order to be able to do this opening up, we need to take into account that such openings will occur at any time. We need to plan very thoroughly and imagine possibilities of challenging intra-actions that *might* take place. We plan also in order to be able to *diverge* from our plan. We need to be on our toes ready to insert a previously unimaginable question or comment into what is going on, or suggest a new way of doing or thinking, or offer a new material that was not already planned for. All this will be exemplified and discussed further in Chapter 4.

Different discourses will not just make you understand things differently, but will also make you *value* and *judge* things differently – in this case the clay figures. Hence, the question arose of why are we at all making this clay figure? What is it exactly that the teacher educator wants us to learn? And this is when the students discovered that the aim or goal of the learning endeavour determines what discourses to use when producing knowing in the intra-actions taking place. From this follows that we make judgements on what it is possible to learn, and then we make assessments of what kind and quality of learning has been achieved. The students thus realised that the aims we set up for our teaching, on the one hand, make possible a deepened learning into the chosen discourse(s), but, on the other hand, as a consequence of our choices of aims, we limit and exclude the possibilities of understanding what it is we are doing from the perspectives of a number of other discourses and possible intra-active events that could otherwise have taken place. For instance, we might exclude the possibility of knowing from the perspective of the agentic clay itself – the material – in intra-action with students. This is something that we so far have not had much of a language to talk and write about. I will discuss these important issues on learning goals and ethics in an intra-active pedagogy in the last chapter of this book. In the following chapter I will provide an in-depth understanding of how to understand the tool of pedagogical documentation so central to an intra-active pedagogy.

Chapter 3

The tool of pedagogical documentation

> Meaning is not a property of individual words or groups of words but *an ongoing performance* of the world in its differential dance of intelligibility and unintelligibility.
>
> (Barad, 2007: 149, my emphasis)

According to Barad in the above quote, meaning is an ongoing performance in a play or dance of different agentic bodies/matter, trying to make themselves intelligible to one another. What *kinds* of meanings we make matters. This means that our instruments, tools or apparatuses for meaning-making *matter*, not least in relation to how we think that children learn. Consequently we need to ask ourselves what kind of knowledge we produce with the tools or 'apparatuses' we use in our learning activities with children and students.

When we talk of pedagogical documentation in our everyday practices we sometimes refer to it as a tool of observation and constructing documentation from our practices. In this chapter I will outline a more precise definition of pedagogical documentation as a *material-discursive apparatus*. Relying on Barad's thinking, an apparatus used for observing something can be understood as taking part in a process of 'material (re)configurations or discursive practices' (2007: 184). This means that the apparatus of pedagogical documentation is *in itself* an active agent in generating discursive knowledge. It is part of the process of constructing meaning about children's learning, as it generates a material observation as a note, photograph, video-film, etc. If we become even more specific, the documentation we get (photographs, notes and objects made) is to be understood in terms of *matter/material*. Importantly, however, it is not a fixed matter with a fixed essence, but a substance in a process of intra-active performances and becoming – 'not a thing but a doing' (Barad, 2007: 183). However, pedagogical documentation is *not* about documenting the practice as a representation of what the practice *was* at the moment of documenting it. Rather, pedagogical documentation becomes what it actively *does and performs* in relation to the pedagogical practice where it is produced. I will develop and show what this means in much more detail in this chapter.

In the production of pedagogical documentation, what kind of documentation we produce and collect matters, such as photographs, video films, written observations, drawn sketches of what the children do or construct, or the very constructions themselves. *How* we use the apparatuses of observations matters, that is, which way we choose to turn the camera and what it is that we write, and what kind of meaning-making tools we use – all these choices matter. Pushing the button of a camera, focusing a video-camera, the decision of where to place the tape-recorder or our choice to write down what children do with their hands – all of these matter for what we are able to understand and learn. An observer and the apparatus for observing together construct what Barad in her context of physics would call a specific constructed '*cut*'. This cut is produced in the intra-action *in-between* an object and the agencies of observation (Barad, 2007: 115). This means, on the one hand, that there is no inherent distinction between the object and agencies of observation (the apparatus and the scientist or teacher), but, on the other hand, it means that the observation will in fact still produce a *temporary constructed distinction* – the constructed cut. This constructed 'cut' makes it possible for us to *at all* identify a material observation of practice that we can talk about and study as a piece of documentation. As a piece of documentation – or as a *performative agent* – the photograph, sketch or written words of an observation will also put things in motion by means of its own agentic force and materiality. Thus, new possibilities for intra-action with other matter and organisms will emerge.

In the first part of this chapter I will try to disentangle and give a theoretical introduction to how I understand pedagogical documentation as an apparatus of knowing. In the second part, I will put this theory to work in relation to a couple of examples. These new ways of thinking about observation and documentation practices might chafe at first, just like a pair of new shoes. However, the examples are intended to make these ways of thinking more comfortable in relation to your own thinking and practices.

Widening and expanding our perspectives of a pedagogy of listening

The practice of observing and documenting is understood in the pre-school practices in Reggio Emilia in terms of a 'listening made visible as traces of the learning event' in the written notes, photographs, videos, etc. (Rinaldi, 2006: 68). Although my understanding of pedagogical documentation in an intra-active pedagogy builds heavily on the Reggio Emilian pedagogy of listening, it supplements it when it comes to including the agency of the material in the production of knowledge. I would say, with inspiration from Barad (1999, 2007, 2008), that an intra-active pedagogy explicitly focuses on the phenomena produced in the inter-relations, inter-connections, interferences and waves of diffractions that emerge *in-between* the material, the discursive and human beings. In other words, in an intra-active pedagogy the emphasis is on an interdependent and mutual 'listening' and observing that expands the focus from merely dealing with the intra- and inter-personal relationships in and between children, children and adults and what is said and done, to be inclusive of the performative agency of the material in the intra-actions of learning events.

The agentic force and intensity of the material has only implicitly come to the surface in the writings from Reggio Emilia. The reason for this is not that the material is not important, as I have already pointed out in the introduction, but simply because we more or less lack a language and concepts to use in order to make visible or actualise the intra-active processes in-between organisms (human and non-human), objects, matter and things. In my understanding this is as a result of the taken-for-granted focus on the human subject and the intra- and inter-personal processes s/he is involved with in education. Pedagogy is understood to be about either internal cognitive process in the individual child, or emerging through an encounter with other human beings, and especially the teacher who knows what to learn. Thus, the equally important encounter with things, matter, artefacts, materials, furnished environments and architecture is not actively considered as being a part of the learning process.

In the context of this discussion, I want to point out that the forces and intensities of the material are nevertheless often present in the documentation of the projects from Reggio Emilia and the Reggio Emilia-inspired practices in Sweden. However, the material is basically presented as important but passive tools which outline a necessary precondition staged as a background to be used by active children and teachers. Objects and artefacts as living and agentic in themselves in an intra-active process of learning with the child only appear in the conversations and analyses done by the children themselves as we closely read the documentation. This mutual intra-activity is not explicitly identified and analysed by the teachers or researchers in the documentations and texts produced.

Rather, what is analysed by the teachers is what children do and say, which I think arises from a lack of language to theorise in this way. However, what the teachers in Reggio Emilia have done better than any educational practice is to document the most intimate processes of learning among children in a challenging environment that has indeed been consciously organised and planned by the adults. This documentation enables us to read and listen to how the children identify the agency of different organisms and objects around them in their learning-processes. As adults we often choose to understand this as a simple 'humanising' of the material, as with the sticks being 'humanised' and thus turned into a doll in the example in Chapter 1. However, I think it is possible to say that children's conceptual grammar while investigating the world around them seems to be an *intra-active and agentic realist grammar*. Hence, if we would listen better we would be able to 'hear' and observe other organisms, objects and things around us 'speak' and see them transform, as they intra-act with the children and their thinking in handling and intra-acting with them. For example, when children at a preschool outside Stockholm described what we as adults can identify as the complexity of photosynthesis, they did it in terms of the light having power, calling out to the plants, and forcing itself down into the roots, having different speed and intensity depending on resistance from other materials (documentation from Eken in Skarpnäck, outside Stockholm, presented by the atelierista Karin Furness). Thinking in terms of an intra-active pedagogy can make us better identify the 'voices' and 'language' of roots of plants, dirt, papers and pens, and observe their agency in processes of transformation and learning.

The 'machinic' quality of pedagogical documentation

Without having any specific identity in itself, pedagogical documentation can be understood as a movement or force that creates a space that makes our lived pedagogical practices *material*. It is the material films, images, observations, etc., that make up the documentation that together construct such a space where intra-active phenomena between children, concepts and materials can emerge and be actualised (i.e., made visible and readable to us). In other words, the documentation can be understood to create a temporary 'territory' or space where a constructed cut of the event is actualised and from which further intra-activity emerges. In this way pedagogical documentation can be understood in a Deleuzian and Guattarian way as working '*machinically*' (Colebrook, 2002: 57).

A *machine*, in their thinking, is not a mechanism or a metaphor for anything, but the event of life itself as it enables and produces the connections between organisms, matter and human beings that make life an ongoing movement of living. 'The machine' has no subjectivity of its own, writes Colebrook, and is nothing more than the connections it produces – 'it is what it does . . . it is a constant process of *de*terriorialisation, or *becoming other than itself*' (Colebrook, 2002: 56, my emphasis). Or, as Barad might have put it, the apparatus or practice of doing observations and documenting makes possible and is a producer of intra-actions. Moreover, the phenomena it produces in the intra-actions are more and other than the intra-acting bodies or matters themselves. In other words, pedagogical documentation puts in motion processes of learning and new becoming. Hence, the apparatus of pedagogical documentation is an apparatus that works machinically in the way I understand it in the context of education: it is an apparatus and machine, which should be understood as a movement or force in itself – a verb – and which can only be identified by what it produces. Thereby it should not be understood as a machine or apparatus in terms of a noun.

Let us repeat this again by taking the example of the camera and the photographs we take. Whereas the camera itself can be seen as a *mechanism* with specific functions, the photograph itself as a part of the documentation – just as the machine in Deleuze and Guattari's understanding – has no limitations of how it can inter-connect with other things (Colebrook, 2002: 56–7). It can produce endlessly new connections, interferences and thus new meanings in the intra-active events of which it is a part. Thus, the photograph should not be understood as a representation of the world and what is photographed. Rather, being a part of the pedagogical documentation, it constitutes a constructed cut of an event taking place in a pedagogical space. Pedagogical documentation can, however, offer constraints on or limitations to what is produced as knowledge, and even produce exclusions of ways of knowing, depending on what we are able to conceptualise and understand in terms of meaning-making. Since any event is both material *and* discursive at the same time, the limits of our discursive understandings, just as the limits of the material possibilities of the camera and the quality of the photographs that can be produced, will constitute a constraint or limitation on what is possible to produce in terms of a phenomenon of knowing from the event (cf Barad, 1998: 112).

In keeping with this way of thinking, I would describe pedagogical documentation as something that is *alive* and from which we can produce a multiplicity of differentiated knowledge from a specific event. Being aware of the complexity of this way of describing pedagogical documentation, which, after all, we first must conceive merely as written notes, photographs, video-films and the productions of children's investigative play, I would like to make the way of understanding I have outlined above more accessible in the examples that will follow in the second half of the chapter. Before getting there, I will continue this theoretical introduction with further discussion about who the teacher or researcher is as an observer, and what it means to see or observe in an intra-active pedagogical perspective. In this way it will be easier for the reader to see how this way of thinking seriously challenges the taken-for-granted ways of doing observations and documenting children's development that has been going on for more than 100 years now.

Who am 'I' as an 'observer'? A 'part' of the apparatus?

In Barad's (1999, 2007) understanding as a physicist and theorist of science, there can be no inherent and distinct border between the apparatus of observation (the observation protocol, camera and image produced) and the observer using it (the teacher or the child itself). Rather they depend totally on each other in the intra-active connections in-between them. In other words, it is impossible to separate the subject or knower from the object or known. This way it is also easy to see why Barad (1999) talks about the *material-discursive* as an intertwining of the conceptual (discursive meaning) and the physical dimensions of the material. Barad makes references to Niels Bohr, who argues that 'theoretical concepts are defined by the circumstances required for their measurement' (Barad, 1999: 3). This means that concepts emerge as a result of how they have been constructed through our lived experiences and concrete material observations of a specific phenomenon in the world (for instance using a microscope or camera). This material-discursive experience makes us name the concept and give it meaning in a specific way. Thereby all concepts are a result of 'phenomena made up of specific intra-actions of humans and non-humans', and thus the intertwining of the material and the discursive (Barad, 1998: 116). The observer and the observed are 'the physical and conceptual apparatuses [that] form a *non-dualistic whole*', with no inherent or given subject/object distinction, writes Barad (1998: 95, my emphasis). Written notes and photographs as materialised and actualised events and the discursive connections of meaning that we make are intertwined in the production of knowing by means of the pedagogical documentation. There are no observations that can be objective or 'free' from the material-discursive interconnections made in the intertwined process by the observer and the observational apparatus together.

As a consequence of the above, we are, as educational practitioners, entangled with our observations and documentations – our apparatuses of knowing. It is impossible to clearly tell one apart from the other. Thus, the *theory/practice* binary divide can be understood as totally dissolved. We materialise our notions as practices, and our practices and the materials involved mould our understandings of what is going on. Everything is intra-actions as inter-connections, interference and waves of diffractions without borders between theory/practice and discourse/material – *blurred entanglements*. Consequently, there can be no telling apart of discourse/matter (Barad, 2007). Barad writes: 'Knowing does not come from standing at a distance and representing something, but rather from *a direct material engagement with the world*' (2007: 49, original emphasis). This means a fundamental questioning of the belief in ontologically separate entities which an ontology of transcendence relies on, which I outlined in Chapters 1 and 2.

I will briefly re-activate this inherent split between the observer and the observed as I continue my further discussion on pedagogical documentation in relation to its immanent character. In resistance to this split or divide, we need to get rid of the Cartesian 'habit of mind', writes Barad (2007: 49), because it constructs a binary thinking and puts humans apart and separated from and on top of the material world, as has been described earlier. Hence, experience and what we see in the documentation cannot be explained from any privileged point: no being can be used to explain or order our existence. Rather, there can only be a univocal plane of being – *univocity* – with no ground or knower, *only the flow of experience itself*, writes Colebrook (2002), with inspiration from Deleuze's immanent philosophy. However, we document and make observations of our practices to be able to learn from the documentation and make it productive for subsequent learning events. In this way we can see ourselves as equal participants in the whole – *one-ness* – in a mutual engagement with all other organisms and matters in it. '*We are a part of that nature we seek to understand*', to put it simply (Barad, 2007: 67, my emphasis). In the last chapter of this book I will deepen this aspect of pedagogical documentation in relation to the questions of ethics and politics in early childhood education.

What does it mean to 'see' and observe?

We will now look at the apparatuses of knowing that we use in our educational practices and their productive effects. In schools and preschools these apparatuses have mostly been about observations made by a passive observer watching; for instance, the child's motor abilities and social skills, and/or listening to what is said. These mainly developmental psychological and behaviouristic practices can be understood as a parallel to classical physics, building on the Newtonian idea about distinct and inherent borders between the 'object' that is observed, and the 'observer': the observer has agency and is active, and the observed has no agency and is passive. This is an idea that quantum physics has challenged and proved very problematic (Barad, 1998, 1999, 2007). This idea also needs to be challenged in the scientific production of knowledge around children's development and learning. In the case of pedagogical practice we observe, for instance, the child's cognitive skills and development by determining the advancement of the child's conceptualisations in language, and assign stages of development to specific ages or stages of maturity.

The usage of pedagogical documentation that I have outlined above is working in resistance to the long tradition in Sweden, since at least the 1930s, of observing and documenting children in accordance with developmental psychological theories (Lenz Taguchi, 1996, 2000). During almost 100 years observational protocols and experiments have been used to judge children's development (Burman, 2007; Lenz Taguchi, 1996, 2000; Walkerdine, 1984). Educational observation methodologies have borrowed directly from the scientific practices of medicine and psychology. Valerie Walkerdine (1984) is one of the first educational researchers who has explicitly criticised what she called the *psychological–pedagogical* pair. This has produced a pedagogical model that has coded theory and practices in early childhood education since at least the 1950s. It was based on notions of a 'natural' inherent development and a spontaneous learning that can be observed, normalised and regulated by teachers.

One method, which was mainly used in training the preschool teachers in Sweden during the 1950s and 1960s, was the observation box and the one-way screen. I use the example of the box because it makes very explicit the problem of our trust in what we can see with our eyes as a reflection and representation of that which we understand as the reality or truth of practice. The box was placed in the middle of the floor or by the wall and was big enough to fit an adult sitting down and looking through a one-way screen to observe the children playing. Leading Swedish preschool teachers, as teachers in other Western countries, recommended using the observation box to observe all children with the goal of finding their imperfections so as to correct them (Boman, 1946; Lenz Taguchi, 1996, 2000).

It is important, however, to know that the main reason for such observations, which was quite benign, was to teach teachers to understand the natural development of the child, and so prevent them from forcing children to do or say things they were not mature enough to do or say (Lenz Taguchi, 1996, 2000; Ulin, 1946).

Hence, there has been and still is an idea of observing children to see what they 'really' are, so that we can treat them right and 'set them free' as developing, maturing creatures (Burman, 2007; Dahlberg et al., 2007; Lenz Taguchi, 1996, 2000; Walkerdine, 1984). Relating back to the contemporary question of how we deal with complexities of learning and difference among children of different gender, cultural backgrounds, etc., this kind of thinking is apparent in many of our current developmentally appropriate practices (DAPs). It can definitely be understood as a reduction of complexity and trying to make a complex world more manageable and controllable in order to know what to do with the children in our services (Lenz Taguchi, 2009a, 2008c). Many of the individual developmental plans that preschool teachers write for each child are based on the same kinds of development charts – for cognitive, emotional, social and motor development – as were used during the time of the observation box, although revised in line with more contemporary theories (Elfström, 2004). Plenty of critical research has noted the contradictions between granting the modern individual 'freedom' and equality or justice, and relying on 'normal' universal development, decided on by developmental psychology and the normative observational gazes of professionals such as teachers, psychologist and doctors (Burman, 2007; Hultquist, 1990, 1998; Popkewitz, 1998; Rose, 1989, 1999; Walkerdine, 1984). Nicolas Rose's early critique of the 'technologies of spaces and gazes . . . [which] entail opening spaces to visibility and locking each "free" individual into a play of normative gazes' (1996: 9) is still valid and perhaps even more so given the contemporary possibilities of digital surveillance.

To be able to actually see anything at all, we need to use our meaning-making, that is, our ways of conceptualising in spoken or written language. We use discursive notions and ideas already accessible to us as theories, notions or hypotheses based on our previous observations from our daily practices and lives in our specific cultural contexts. To be able to better understand how we come to know the child when observing it, I will turn to Barad again and her writing on experiments in science. When we use, for instance, the apparatus of a microscope, 'seeing' through it is not a matter of simply looking and passively gazing on something as a spectator. Rather, she says, it must be considered an achievement that requires a complex set of practices to be accomplished (Barad, 2007: 51). 'Seeing' in scientific experiments must be learnt by a *doing* and an iterative *practising*. To know if the child's language development is normal, you practise how to listen and look for deficiencies or lack in the language use, that is, what is not normal in relation to the criteria you have noted as normal – the statistical average – for specific age-groups. Such practice also involves learning how to discriminate that which is not important in relation to what you have convinced yourself to see. *Conviction* about what to see is thus a precondition for seeing in any scientific experiment. The theoretical discourses you have access to inform you about what to see. When the phenomenon is proved to be seen in a series of observations it is considered a truth.

But, as Ian Hacking writes, we must be aware that it is our 'large number of interlocking low level generalisations that enable us to control and create phenomena in the microscope', and no iteration is completely identical to the previous (1983: 209, in Barad, 2007: 51). This means that it is not possible, not even with a microscope, to actually see or observe on each occasion the exact and identical observation; rather, what we do is round our observations down or up in relation to our expectations and convictions of what to find. This is an inevitable part of doing scientific experiments, since no iteration can be totally identical to another. If observations through a microscope cannot be identical when performed by one and the same scientist, how can we expect observations of specific children in specific environments under specific conditions to be identical, and even worse, compared to observations with other specific children in other specific environments and circumstances?

It is exactly these problems connected to observation and documentation that Loris Malaguzzi and his co-teachers in the preschools in Reggio Emilia wanted to contest. Instead of using the observational tool to observe the normal development of the child, they turned the tool around for it to speak the voice of the multiplicity of differences of children's strategies and conceptualisations, and without any desire to categorise what it was they heard or seen. Giving voice to the child as a co-constructor of culture and knowledge was the main goal of their practices of pedagogical documentation; the second was to use it to further challenge children's processes of learning (Dahlberg *et al.*, 2007; Reggio Children, 2001; Rinaldi, 2006). What they started in the late

1960s and developed up to the present day has been and still is a resolute resistance against using observation and documentation as normalising and reductive strategies in early childhood practices.

How to understand *knowing* in an onto-epistemological perspective

So, how can we understand how we can learn from our observations and documentation based on an onto-epistemology, which takes the reversed strategies for using this tool a step further to include the agency of the material? Going back to the instant or moment of observation in a microscope or in an observation of a child, what we observe in this 'constructed cut' is what Bohr called a phenomenon. This observed phenomenon is what we observe as 'reality', which is really the image or sense of what emerges from the intra-activities taking place between the object, the 'apparatus' of knowing and the observer in their entangled state of being. Barad writes that '[p]henomena are constitutive of reality. Reality is composed not of things-in-themselves or things-behind-phenomena but of things-*in*-phenomena' (2007: 140, my emphasis). This means that phenomena are all about intra-actions and that which emerges from them: what we get when we look through the microscope and observe the intra-activity between the limitations of our biologically constituted eye (what it is able to see); the quality of the microscope (what it manages to show with the limitations of its construction by human ideas about what it should/can show); the matter/object we are observing in its uniqueness (and how it is affected by temperature, air, age, necessary sources of energies needed, etc.); and our discursively inscribed thinking (notions, theories connected to education, culture, languages, etc.); our previous experiences, and how much we have practised using the microscope, which also effects our discursively inscribed body (how we know how to use the body and relate it to other matters such as the microscope itself). Barad writes that '[t]he interaction between the object and the instrument or apparatus of observation form an inseparable interaction' and the *intra-action* taking place in-between them in this inseparability then becomes part of the phenomenon itself, which becomes that which we know – knowledge (1999: 4). Hence, phenomena are *not* the result of measurements of an observer epistemologically separated from what is observed. Rather, as Barad puts it:

> *[P]henomena are the ontological inseparability/entanglement of intra-acting 'agencies'.* . . . The notion of intra-action (in contrast to the usual

'inter-action', which presumes the prior existence of independent entities or relata) represents a profound conceptual shift.

(2007: 139, original emphasis)

In our observations through the microscope there is a cut right through the folds of all these inseparable agencies. This cut is agential and a result of the interdependence between multiple agentic matter, bodies, organisms, artefacts or, alternatively, between human subjects and material matter. Hence, and to repeat, it is not the more familiar Cartesian (or Newtonian) cut, which takes fixed distinctions between the subject and object for granted. Rather, intra-actions are material arrangements that put into effect an agential situated cut where meaning-making is constructed as a phenomenon: The cuts are agentially negotiated, writes Barad, and interdependent on other matter, as well as indeterminate (2007: 140).

To think in terms of agentially negotiated cuts is about us as teachers addressing a much wider scope of our practices. We soften, widen and expand our gaze and inter-connecting bodies with all of its senses, in relation to the whole of our pedagogical environments where the material objects, furnishing and architecture of the room is included. We change our focus from the perspective of the inter-personal – that which happens only in-between people – to the intra-actions between different organisms and matters. Here the human subject is just one such organism and her/his discursive constructs another, intra-acting with artefacts and things. The knowledge that is produced from these cuts, and that we understand as theoretical *concepts*, is understood as 'particular material articulations of the world', according to Bohr and Barad (Barad, 2007: 139). In other words, concepts are considered to be material and agentic in the same manner as agentic subjects and matter.

Materialising apparatuses of knowing and what they produce: two examples

In the discussions of the examples below, I want to show how our ways of using and understanding practices of observation and documentation have changed. The discursive convictions of what it is we think we can or will see when observing a child in a specific place or space are coded with different ways of thinking about children's development and learning. I will return to the example of the observation box, and then move on to a Piagetian experiment and to a water investigation with 1 year olds in a Reggio Emilia-inspired preschool outside Stockholm.

I will simplify the discussion by presenting three ways of observing and understanding what is or can be observed. The first two ways, when laid side by side, constitute a polarisation: a belief that we can observe nature and reality 'out there' is polarised against a belief that all we can observe and know is human constructions in culture and discourse. I will, however, as does Barad, focus especially on trying to go *beyond* such polarisations and divides in our understandings by suggesting a third way of observing in an intra-active pedagogy. These three ways of using observational apparatuses and producing knowledge from what we observe are connected to different ontological and epistemological understandings, and thus connect back to the theoretical discussions in Chapter 2. I use the first two ways of observing for the reader to be better able to identify the different usages of documenting practices from her/his own experiences, but also as a contrast to the third way of using observation as an apparatus for knowing. This way, I claim, goes beyond the ontological and epistemological divide and is based on an *onto-epistemology*.

'The child's language mirrors its cognitive development'

We will now return to our place within the observation box. What is it that we see when looking out of the box at the playing children and observing them? In the first case we think it is possible to know the 'true nature' of the child so we check our developmental protocol with its fixed age-related categories for motor, social, emotional or cognitive developments. In the second case we may simply write down what we see and hear, like an ethnologist, sociologist or social constructivist educational researcher and then try to understand it in terms of different cultural notions and discourses.

Looking closer at the first case, the practice of the observation box is done from within a representational and binary paradigm, where the observer is separated from the observed (a subject/object binary divide). Scientific knowledge is understood as an accurate reflection in language of a physical reality, and actually mirroring it (the discourse/reality divide). Now, we will look even closer at this way of observing and understanding by getting out of the box and performing a Piagetian experiment to check the cognitive development of the 5½-year-old girl Birgitta (Arvidsson, 1974). The experiment is arranged around the child being asked to make judgements of the weight of different matters, answering the question of whether an object can float or not, and then trying it out

Table 3.1 Birgitta's answers to the question of why the material floats or sinks

Material	Answer to if it can float	Teacher's notation	Answer to why it floats or sinks
Match	'floats'	Right	'It is made out of wood.'
Drawing pin	'floats'	Wrong	'It is made out of iron.'
Paper ball	'sinks'	Wrong	'It is made out of paper.'
Screw	'sinks'	Right	'I don't know.'

by putting it into a bowl of water in front of her. Lastly the child must answer the question of why it is floating or sinking. In Table 3.1 you can see the listed objects, the girl's answer when guessing if the object can float or not, the teacher's notation (right/wrong), and Birgitta's answer to the question of why the material floats or sinks.

In this book by Arvidsson (1974) on learning how to do child observations for students in early childhood education, used in Sweden far into the 1990s, Birgitta's cognitive development is commented on in relation to the findings of the Danish developmental psychologist, Rasmussen. According to his findings, 5 year olds generally manage to name things that can float as 'floaters' and those that sink 'sinkers', but they cannot derive an abstract and applicable rule to use. This is because children at this age are at a level in their cognitive development where observations such as these can only be singular and isolated experiences. They are, in other words, unable to construct an abstract theory of the connections between the object and whether it can float or sink. This is, however, possible for 7–9 year olds, who have developed their cognitive abilities to the extent that they are able to construct a rule based on their cumulative experiences. That Birgitta, who is only 5½ can at all express herself in terms of 'it is made out of wood' indicates a higher cognitive ability than is normal for a girl her age. This is an ability that children fully master at the age of eight or nine according to Rasmussen (Arvidsson, 1974).

If we read this example critically in terms of the underpinning epistemology and ontology, we can clearly see how language is expected to mirror and represent an event in the physical world outside of the child. Reality and discourse are separated. The use of conceptualisations in language determines the level of cognitive skills: the more advanced the language structure is in connection to what is observed, the more highly developed are the child's cognitive skills and abilities to understand the world in more abstract ways. The observational protocol is entirely based on these convictions and expectations, which means that this is what we will be looking for and what we will take notice of. The documentation instrument – our apparatus of knowing – determines what we understand as cognition and how it is materialised and understood in early childhood practice. What children are able to say, and how they connect their lived experiences to how they are able to express it in language is what we can observe and relate to our universal protocols of children's cognitive development. In other words, there is an intra-action taking place between the discursive expectations and theoretical convictions of the teacher materialised in the structure of the observational protocol. Thus, what the teacher hears and sees intra-acts with what she thinks and expects, which is structured in the categories of her protocol.

The practices of structuring human thinking and action can be analysed with the concepts that Deleuze and Guattari (1987) called 'striated' and 'smooth space'. Deleuze and Guattari use images of the city with its highly structured infrastructure to explain the striated space, and the desert or sea to explain the smooth (1987: 475–500). The streets and houses force our bodies to move in certain directions and follow streets and staircases the way they have been planned, structured and built. In the desert or on the sea, however, almost any direction or path can be taken or travelled. The space in the desert is not structured and striated as it is in the infra-structure of the city. In the pedagogical space the space is striated as we plan and organise activities at specific hours with specific materials to be used etc. Moreover, the space is highly striated if we as teachers view the actions and listen to what children say through the categories of an observation protocol such as the one above. In fact, the protocol structures what the teacher asks the child and what she sees and does in the event, and thus it also structures what the child is able to answer or do, more or less exactly. The protocol can be understood as a *performative agent* working on and actively imposing its categories on the teacher's thinking as well as on the child's understanding of itself being observed and talked to in this manner. Hence, the protocol is a performative agent in producing a striated pedagogical space in intra-action with the teacher using it to work with.

When using these concepts to analyse the pedagogical space, it is important to understand that striated space is not 'bad'. To put it simply, striated space is a way to understand the necessary structuring of our daily lives and practices, for us to be able to be social creatures without endless negotiations on what is the proper way of acting, talking and relating to each other in a specific culture, down to the simplest events of saying hello and goodbye. Smooth space, by contrast, is a space absent of such structuring habits. It can be created when we engage in questioning or dismissing taken-for-granted habits of doing and thinking in order to do or think differently (Colebrook, 2002; Deleuze and Guattari, 1987; Williams, 2008). Smooth space, as a totally unstructured and unplanned space, can be chaotic and even dangerous for a child (Davies and Gannon, forthcoming). I will discuss this more in a later analysis. What is central is to acknowledge and understand all spaces as a mixture of and constantly shifting between the more or less smooth and striated in the flow of the events taking place. It is sometimes difficult to determine what causes a passage from smooth to striated, and from striated to smooth. As shown below we must analyse the context carefully to better comprehend what can be understood as striated or smooth pedagogical space.

When we decide to categorise spoken language or bodily behaviours in an observation protocol, as in the example above, this constitutes an effective way of transforming our space of thinking and doing into a more striated space. For instance, the request for the simple answer of 'yes' or 'no' in the protocol above imposes on our thinking a strong binary categorisation. It forces Birgitta to an answer that cannot be anything in-between or beyond. It becomes impossible to say that first the cotton ball floats and then it slowly sinks. When, however, Birgitta is asked to describe *why* it is that something sinks or floats in the next instant, this constitutes a more open question and what we might conceive as a slightly smoother space to think in. Birgitta's answers seem suspiciously biased, though, by strong expectations of exactly *how* to phrase her answer to this question; she repeatedly refers to what kind of material the object is made out of, as if she knew what kind of answer was required of her – 'It sinks because it is made out of iron', etc. Her answers can be understood as given in a quite striated pedagogical space, in spite of the open-ended question asked.

'Discourse and reflexivity is what matters – the material world is unaffected'

As a contrast to this Piagetian experiment, another example also involves investigating floating and sinking objects in a bowl of glass. This example makes it possible to look a bit closer at the discursive, social constructivist and cultural approach to, in this case, what we see on our observations. This way of understanding differs from the Piagetian cognitive and constructivist learning theory in several ways, but the material is still seen as passive or the material stage on which humans are the only performative agents.

In the late 1990s I co-operated with a preschool outside Stockholm – Täppan – that enrolled a large number of 1 year olds. One of the preschool teachers, Malin Kjellander, decided to do indoor investigations with pairs of newly introduced 1 year olds. The idea was for them to learn to know each other and to experience their days at the preschool as challenging and interesting. She knew that most 1 year olds are interested in water. She arranged a small room for water investigations by pairs of children. In their diapers, a pair of 1 year olds at a time were presented with the opportunity of putting a variety of objects into large glass bowls of water, standing on towels besides a very low table. Throughout the weeks of these investigations Malin offered the children a vast variety of materials: small branches from trees, tree-cones and leaves from outside; paper, stones, balls of glass; screws and other things made out of metal. The teacher showed the children how some of the objects floated and some sank.

The children seemed amazed and started to investigate for themselves. They looked into their own bowl and the see-through bowl of the other child, trying out one object after the other. Some of the children stayed

Figure 3.1 Two children experimenting by the table. Photo: Malin Kjellander.

in the room for up to 50 minutes at a time totally absorbed in their water investigations. Malin photographed and then projected some of the photos on the wall while the children did their experimentations. The children then intra-acted with what was happening in the enlarged projection on the wall, as if there was yet another child in the room. They imitated what they saw – as in Figure 3.2, where the child goes up to the sink to turn on the water as does the child in the enlarged projection. Their engagement and focus in these investigations were amazing.

When the children were outside in the preschool grounds, other teachers were similarly amazed by how these 1 year olds seemed to know exactly what objects would sink or float in the puddles after the rain, gesturing to each other, talking, laughing and communicating what was going to or had just happened in the puddle. The teachers occasionally observed the children by taking notes of what they did, said or gestured. They agreed that these 1 year olds had a lot of knowledge about what objects would float or sink, although they were not able to say it in words like 'it is made out of wood'. It was obvious that these 1 year olds did not

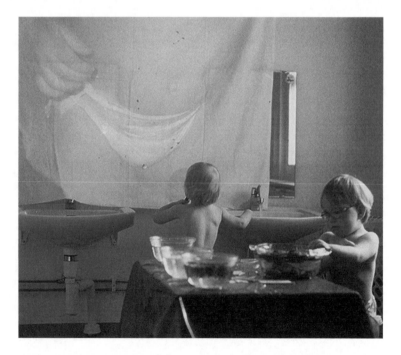

Figure 3.2 Two children and photo on the wall. Photo: Malin Kjellander.

simply experience singular and isolated events without being able to construct a rule. On the contrary, they seemed to be very aware of such rules based on their accumulated experiences, although they could not verbalise them yet.

How can we understand what cognitive development is in relation to the observations that Malin and her colleagues at Täppan did? When putting the experiences from Täppan besides the Piagetian experiment and the cognitive constructivist learning approach, we can see how cognitive development understood as what can be conceptualised in spoken language can be displaced and reconsidered. Malin's experiences thus challenged mainstream thinking on cognitive development. On the other hand, her experiences also showed us what was able to happen under the specific conditions she constructed – the apparatus of investigation with 1 year olds – and which may not have happened had she not set up such an experiment the way she did. In fact, she started out with letting three or four children experiment in the room at the same time, which she observed reduced their concentration, compared to the focus they achieved when there were only two children in the room at a time. By studying her documentation she could try out different ways of challenging the learning processes, such as showing the photo-slides to the children while experimenting, and actively choosing new materials and excluding old ones to investigate their qualities in the water.

Using Deleuze and Guattari's (1987) concepts of smooth and striated space to understand the example, this investigation of floating and sinking constitutes a much smoother space of operating, inventing and thinking for the children, compared to the structured and supervised Piagetian experiment. The space where knowledge could be constructed, based on lived experiences with the different matters and artefacts put into the bowl of water, was much smoother than in the case of the Piagetian experiment with Birgitta. However, the space for experimenting is nevertheless quite structured in terms of options of what to do in this space. That is, the child is expected to put things into the bowls and no place else, and stand still on its side of the table, and not run around or climb onto the table and into the bowl of water. In other words, the children read the codes in this striated space and basically behave accordingly. On the other hand, the learning processes of the teacher can be understood as constituting a smooth space, where her expectations and preconceptions are continuously challenged. This made her think, do and act differently when setting up the experiment the next day, based on what she had observed in the room or on the videotape. As a learner herself, the teacher's space of learning is open to variation and change.

With these two experiments in mind, it is interesting to quote Deleuze and Guattari (1987) as they write on the composing of music as a mixture of and communication between the two kinds of spaces, where the striated space in music is about mathematical counting in order to be occupied by structuring, but the smooth space can be occupied without such counting and rather goes beyond that practice of counting. What is interesting for us in relation to Malin's investigation practices with the children is that Deleuze and Guattari point to the possibilities of variation or alternation between the smooth and striated space, and the mixing of the two of them. They make visible the simplified difference between them when thinking about composing music:

> [T]he striated is that which intertwines fixed and variable elements, produces an order and succession of distinct forms, and organises horizontal melodic lines and vertical harmonic planes. The smooth is the continuous variation, continuous development of form; it is the fusion of harmony and melody in favour of the production of properly rhythmic values, the pure act of the drawing of a diagonal across the vertical and the horizontal.
>
> (Deleuze and Guattari, 1987: 478)

Hence, it is possible to understand how the smooth and the striated quality of spaces are dependent on each other and sometimes intertwined. It is also possible to understand Malin's water investigations with the 1 year olds as a parallel to how the invigorating effect of the smooth space of variation in a piece of music is in a sense *conditioned* by the counting of vertical harmonics and repetition of the horizontal melody. In other words, the smooth space that made it possible for the children to make hundreds of variations of experiences with different matters in a bowl of water was in fact *conditioned* by the striated space that structured and regulated the 1 year olds' behaviour in the room. That is, children were successfully reading the codes of the towels to stand upon besides the table, the bowl of water and the limited amount of objects to investigate with, etc. Hence, the striated space can be understood as being a familiar, safe and ordered space. Although the striated quality will limit the possibilities for change at some levels, it might condition and make possible a smoother space where change can emerge (Davies and Gannon, forthcoming; Malins, 2007).

At this point in the Stockholm project, our learning as teachers and researchers in the Reggio Emilia-inspired preschools in Stockholm did not engage in thinking in terms of making possible a smooth or striated space or creative shifts between them. Moreover, although the consciousness about how matter mattered in the learning processes of both children and teachers was very strong, we lacked concepts and language to discuss it. At this time, around the mid-1990s, our dialogues in the networks we had for discussing pedagogical documentation were mostly about exchanging experiences of material conditions for learning experiences. We discussed in terms of how the investigation was set up and what came out of different set ups. This constituted very important learning, especially in relation to the enormous impact and dependency on the material environment in the preschool. How the rooms were furnished and the attitude in relation to the access and usage of different materials changed drastically. The practices around how to organise, handle and exchange the materials in children's everyday environment was, and still is, a central topic of discussion (Åberg and Lenz Taguchi, 2005; Elfström *et al.*, 2008; Furness, 2008; Hultman, 2009; Nordin-Hultman, 2004). However, because of the lack of theoretical thinking that could actually help us de-code our previous understandings and re-code them in new ways, these exchanges most often resulted in a copying of each other's set-ups of investigational practices, to repeat them in our own practice, rather than constituting learning from our own practice.

As researchers we suggested to the teachers how to analyse their practice in terms of dominating or excluded discourses, along the lines of the social constructivist and discursive theories that dominated our work. This is what I have called the second discursive and cultural approach to observation apparatuses. When Malin showed her documentation from the water investigations, many colleagues could not believe it was possible to do such investigative work involving water and objects. First of all, from what they knew of children's development, children were not considered to be able to stay focused, stand still and perform the experiment in this way. Rather, and in line with a developmental psychology discourse, they were expected, at this age, to use the water to play with and splash around. Moreover, using water like this with 1 year olds was understood as upsettingly irresponsible. Children could stick their heads into the water and drown! The bowls were made of glass, which was another risk, not to mention the different objects that could make 1 year olds choke to death. Yet, what they saw in the videotapes were children who were totally focused on experimenting, and not putting things in their mouths or sticking their heads into the bowls of water. Hence, there seemed to be an absent or excluded discursive understanding of 1 year olds' abilities and development. They were obviously competent enough to do things that we did not find possible when relying on the developmental theories that most teachers took more or less for granted in planning and performing practices with 1 year olds.

With a discursive and social constructivist approach to understanding Malin's observations, what happened or did not happen could be understood as reflections of preschool culture and different discursive perspectives. The gain from such observations is that we are able to displace our understandings and understand things differently. Thus, in this case Malin's experiences strongly displaced a developmental psychological understanding of children's cognitive development. One year olds are obviously able to both concentrate on experimenting with water and make experiences that they can connect to new and other experiences, as when they translated what they learnt from the experiences in the bowls to what happened in the puddles outside. Teachers can, as reflexive practitioners, both contest dominant discursive thinking on children's development and learning, as well as produce and formulate new knowledge about children derived from their experiences from the practices they enact (Dahlberg and Moss, 2005; Dahlberg et al., 2007; Lenz Taguchi, 2000; MacNaughton, 2005; Olsson, 2009; Reggio Children, 2001; Rinaldi, 2006). In other words, discursive analysis helped us, and still helps us, displace our thinking around pedagogical practices and contest the discursive structures identified. Hence, doing discursive analysis proved to be, and will continue to be, of vast importance in the learning processes of practitioners as well as in teacher training.

Nevertheless, it is possible for us to supplement such analysis with the help of Deleuze and Guattari's ontology of immanence and with an intra-active understanding of the learning events. In this way we can also construct a language around how matter matters in our practices of learning. An important reason why this is absolutely necessary, as I see it, is that the discursive analysis resides in a paradigm of reflexivity. Barad writes that reflexivity is still founded on the idea that representations in language or on photographs, etc. reflect a reality, but in this case the cultural reality rather than nature (2007: 86–7). Reflexivity, she continues, holds the material world at a distance just as much as this idea of us being able to truthfully represent a reality, or that which is called representationalism. This is because reflexivity and the cultural or discursive way of thinking about the world states that all we have access to is language, rather than the objects themselves. In other words, staying with discursive analysis can be understood as enslaving us in our own language, and as excluding the agency of the material reality that we are unavoidably connected to and constantly intra-acting with if we think in terms of immanence and onto-epistemology.

An intra-active approach to make visible and possible the potentialities of the child

Again, using the concepts of striated and smooth space we can under-stand what took place in the water investigations in terms of a mixture and shifts between smooth and striated space. We can also understand that Malin's choices to change the learning situation relied upon her affirmative belief in what *might become* possible to think about children's learning and development and thus challenging the potentialities of 1 year olds. In relation to the third understanding of pedagogical docu-mentation, with an intra-active pedagogical approach, Malin can be understood to have documented what happened so as to be able to learn from her observations and be inventive in relation to what could become new possibilities of doing. What becomes a new pedagogical reality actualises the change in her imagination of what might be possible for the 1 year olds to do, that is, the not yet actualised and unexpressed potentialities of the child. What the child might *become* we can never know until it is expressed and actualised in the documentation. There are, however, limits to what a 1 year old can do based on the limits of its human body and mind, but no limitations to what, in an evolutionary sense, might be possible when it intra-acts and changes in relation to new

Figure 3.3 Child looking through two bowls of water. Photo: Malin Kjellander.

material and active circumstances. In this case, Malin could actualise in her documentation the 1 year olds' potentialities as they made connections and constructed knowledge about the relationship between water, material objects, density, speed, and concepts like sinking, fleeting, etc. These are learning-processes that no preschool teacher or developmental psychologist would have thought possible.

From what Malin saw in the videotapes and her notes, she could, to use Barad's line of thinking, identify in the constructed cuts of the documentation what the material conditions were that made specific learning with specific objects possible for each child. The documentation was used by her to work *machinically* as a part of the construction of her knowing – in the construction of phenomena. Phenomena as productions of knowing are constitutive of reality. That is, they actualise the learning event and make it real to Malin in a specific sense, which will then make it possible for her to make decisions on what new materials to bring into the event to change it. Hence, Malin identified in the constructed cuts, the intra-actions between numbers of matters that *mattered* in what happened in the learning event; for instance, the child repeatedly using one hand to drop objects in the water, then trying out using both hands to carefully lay the object on the surface of the water again and again, for the child to see the difference in the intra-action taking place in-between the object and the surface of the water as the object was not simply dropped. And later, putting objects in two bowls and watching the difference in speed and intensity of each of the objects as they sink, that is, observing the difference in the intra-activity between each of the objects and the water. The children observed that all the objects had their own specific agential qualities and potentialities, and thus agency as performative agents in the entangled intra-action with the water as they were put into it. Thus, what the child experiences and what we need to observe as the cut of the event is the intra-actions between the agentic quality of the water in this specific glass bowl, the agential qualities of the items and materials put into the water, the quietness of the room, and the size and the warm temperature of the room – all of which acted upon what happened in their different intensities and with faster or slower speed. Moreover, the lighting that cast shadows in specific ways and the height of the table in relation to the size of the children are also important to what can be understood as constructing the phenomena of learning observed in the cut of our observations, and in each of the repeated observations, which though repeated are never identical.

In the videotape and photos, we can observe the intra-action between what the child picks up from the image exposed on the wall, and its actions by the bowl. We can see how the child imitates what another child does in the enlargement on the wall. The documentation can be understood to *interfere* with what the children were doing. This interference seemed to open up more of a smooth space, and new possibilities of how to perceive what was happening while experimenting and simultaneously watching an enlarged friend on the wall. Again, the documentation was used *machinically* as a part of the production of new learning phenomena. All these bodies and matters intra-acted with each other, and constituted the specific conditions that made learning about floating and sinking possible for each of the children. Moreover, we can read the documentation from the perspective of the water in the bowl, or from the perspective of the objects put into the bowl, or from the perspective of the movements of the eye of the child, etc. The documentation actualises the learning event from these different performative agents by photographing only the surface of the water, or the focusing on the eye movements of the child while video-recording, etc. Studying different kinds of documentation of the learning events where an individual child is only one of the organisms and matters involved, we can unfold a multiplicity of intra-active learning experiences taking place, and make those visible in a subsequent documentation for the children or colleagues to take part in. In this sense pedagogical documentation as an apparatus of knowing focuses on 'differences from within and as part of an entangled state', as Barad put it (2007: 89).

In an intra-active way of understanding this learning event, the child and the objects put into the bowl, the bowl itself and the water, do not pre-exist as such and have no inherent borders. Rather, the subject and object *emerge* through intra-actions, as Barad has written (2007). They co-exist and are in a state of becoming-with each other. Hence, the child in this event becomes a *water-experimenter*, and the objects become 'floaters' and 'sinkers' of varying degree, speed and intensity experienced and perhaps conceptualised by the children and teachers together: they become different in themselves in this particular event of learning. Subjects and objects are not fixed entities/bodies but contingent, changing and in a mutual and entangled state of becoming.

To conclude on pedagogical documentation in an intra-active pedagogy

Using pedagogical documentation as an apparatus for knowing in an intra-active pedagogy shows how practice and matter come to matter in their materiality, that is, temperature, size, amounts, qualities, speed, time, but also, and very importantly, concepts. Concepts come to matter as '*material articulations of the world*' intra-acting with all other matters and discursive meaning-making (Barad, 2007: 139, my emphasis). For instance, when naming a stone a 'sinker', the concept as a material artic-ulation of the stone will make it become different in itself and take on discursive qualities and potentialities that might be further challenged. Focusing on differences, diffractions, interference and performativity, or on the concepts of Deleuzian striated and smooth space, is something very different from reflecting on representations of the world. This counts irrespective of whether such representations are understood as depictions of the real (what the child 'really' is), or discursive reality (culturally specific and changing discourses on children's development and learning).

Pedagogical documentation can be used in a way that makes it possible to understand it as making practice material for us to engage in further entanglements with and become different in ourselves as teachers – *being transformed in our new phenomenon of knowing and becoming-with practice, which makes practice real in a new way.* Thereby we not only engage in making ourselves aware of intra-activities in-between different matter, but also engage in enacting further intra-active processes from what we have learned. We can choose to resist the dominating ways of under-standing what it is we should be looking for in the documentation (as in the two first ways of analysing documentation), and instead read the event from its multiplicity – from the perspective of the water, or cotton balls, or the hand of the child. But what is most important is that we move our gaze from individual children as objects of intervention and their development 'from within', to the phenomena taking place in the intra-actions in-between the child and objects and matters around it. How can we understand what has taken place in the multiplicity of possible intra-active phenomena in-between the water, the tree cone, and the eyes and hands of a child? Where are the central turning points when children's strategies of doing things seem to be de-coded and re-coded and suddenly change, in the repetitive acts of putting things in the bowl of water? That is, when a new understanding seems to have taken place, because a new movement of the hand emerges, as it repeatedly drops things to the surface of the water.

Importantly, the observations and documentations can be understood as having agency of their own and in terms of their own materiality, acting upon us just as any other matter; for instance, as with the photo-slides projected on the wall as the children were active in experimenting. Concepts and words can in the same manner be understood as agentic matter that can give voice to the multiplicity of intra-actions and differences taking place. Hence, concepts we use to express things act upon us, and can thus be understood as material-discursive matter that are taking part in the ongoing reconfiguring of the world in relation to other matters. What we call *theorising* is a result of material-discursive experiences of intra-actions that we have from living in the world. Hence, there is no theory/practice divide when we think in this way.

Deleuze and Guattari suggest that a concept, which we use to theorise and think with, should be understood as 'an act of thought' (1994: 21). They go on to say that the image of thought, or what it means to think, is 'to *make use of* thought, to find one's bearings in thought' (1994: 37, my emphasis). This way of understanding concepts and thinking in terms of processes of becoming, corresponds very well to Barad's agential realist account when she writes about theorising:

> To theorise is not to leave the material world behind and enter the domain of pure ideas where the lofty space of the mind makes objective reflections possible. Theorising, like experimenting, is a material practice. ... [They are] dynamic practices of material engagements with the world.
>
> (2007: 54)

Theorising always contains the risk of determining, classifying and normalising – getting stuck in over-coding and strictly striated spaces, which might prevent opening up the necessary smooth space we need to think differently about what it is we are doing. We always risk forcing the materiality of practice into a state of representation and over-coding, when we document it in words and photographs, and when we theorise. Therefore, we must focus our work with pedagogical documentation on interferences and the differences that emerge in the constant flows of intra-activities taking place. In the next chapter I will show examples of this in a longer learning-project with 4 and 5 year olds.

Chapter 4

An intra-active pedagogy and its dual movements

> How we think about our world and how we live in it are entwined.
> Our ontology and our practical engagements are woven together.
>
> (May, 2005: 72)

In the example with the 1 year olds investigating sinking and floating in the previous chapter, the teachers experienced that learning events can be understood as *events of an intertwined material-discursive and embodied reality* in the intra-action between different kinds of matter and discourse. They saw that learning was not simply an individual cognitive process set in motion from within each individual child, but that the force of learning does not separate thinking and bodily doings from objects, matters, time, spaces and places. Teachers could see in their documentation how learning is a collaborative process of meaning-making taking place between human subjects, their bodies and things, in specific places and spaces around questions and problems arising in the moment or event of investigation, constituting important turning-points in the event. This would make the teacher – Malin – change the material conditions of her practice, sometimes in the midst of the process, and sometimes after having read and analysed the documentation afterwards. Hence, aspects of time and timing are important when discussing how we use pedagogical documentation when we want to use it to challenge and develop learning-processes among children and teachers.

This chapter deals with and exemplifies practising investigative learning-processes with children, using the tool of pedagogical documentation, as two different 'methodological' movements – a 'circular' and a 'horizontal' – in relation to a non-linear or progressive way of understanding time. Connecting to the above quote by Todd May, my aim is to show how thinking and living in pedagogical practices is an entwined material-discursive business which will make us think about and perform our work differently.

Introducing the dual movements in relation to creation, transformation and time

I will discuss the 'circular' and 'horizontal' movements in the usage of pedagogical documentation in a simplified way by connecting them to the word 'methodology'. I will do this to put emphasis on what a teacher needs to actively *will* or *desire* to be in a process of using pedagogical documentation in the fashion that I describe below. But it is *not* doing a method in the taken-for-granted sense of 'following a set of rules or fixed procedures, which if followed through will yield the desired result' (McQuillan, 2000: 3–4). On the contrary, it is 'methodological' in the sense of an active will of complicating what we know about our practices, to put ourselves in motion to be in a process of change and invention, not knowing the end state. This means that there is very little likeness with using developmental appropriate or constructivist learning practices, where we try to make real a desired result by following a set of predictive steps and rules for our practices. Moreover, it is not about evaluation in the dominant ways of thinking, or in a mechanical way trying to understand what it is we do in relation to a pre-set goal or promise or predict outcomes. And it is not a process of documenting to represent or resemble the real in order to critique it to bring about change. Lastly, it is not entirely the same as engaging in documentation of practice in order to do critical deconstructions, as in 'the ethics of resistance' that I have worked with and theorised on before (Lenz Taguchi, 2000, 2007, 2008d). However, the deconstructive analysis can be understood as being a part of what I will theorise, and shortly show, as the slowing down circular movement of working with pedagogical documentation. This new way of theorising from an ontology of immanence and an onto-epistemological perspective makes possible expanded and other ways of thinking and doing that I think are more productive for pedagogical practices.

The whole preschool should be impregnated with children's problems and projects

During my visit to the municipal preschools in Reggio Emilia in 1994, their pedagogical leader, Loris Malaguzzi, talked about doing learning projects with children. He described how these projects, if we use pedagogical documentation in a creative way, can become processes of an open-ended *duration* in time–space that impregnate the whole preschool: everything from its environment, materials, its children, staff and the society around the preschool. If, for instance, the children had been part of constructing a problem about understanding the neighbourhood around them and how to find your way (as in the project that will unfold in the second part of the chapter), this problem and project must impregnate and saturate all that is going on in the preschool – all the planning, organising of materials and contents, Malaguzzi said. What did he mean by this?

What he meant was that by taking very seriously the children's questions of how to find your way around the streets in your neighbourhood, by documenting what they do and say, and then re-visiting this documentation with the children and continuing to discuss, explore and re-enact different learning events taking place, the questions and problems arising around finding your way in your environment will spread out like a virus or an entanglement of a plant's complicated root-system in the organisation and activities that emerge. If the problems, questions and explorations are kept alive in the documentation put on the walls, tables or shelves of the preschools, and continue to be discussed at lunch, in assemblies and while walking to the park, all new and emerging questions and problems that come to children's minds will somehow relate to the first and transform it. Suddenly the playground or forest that the children visit also becomes a neighbourhood of streets, landmarks, signs and symbols, and a problem of architecture and design. Almost everything that the children play, draw or talk about will somehow connect to ideas of networks of streets, symbols or secret tunnels and hideouts, etc.

The project, which in the case below was named 'the Orientation project' by the teachers, is thus operating everywhere and has affected everything that is going on in the preschool. If you bake cinnamon rolls one afternoon, the children hide them in the playground and draw 'maps' for other children to follow and find them. If you do gymnastics, the children construct roads to follow on the floor to run around on and jump over rivers and fences that are in the way, etc. This is how the 'evolution' of learning works in an ontology of immanence, and can be made to work even better if we are aware of this and make use of our pedagogical documentation to strengthen this process of duration and permeation. Please note that impregnation here can be given the double meaning of a process of permeating but also fertilising. The whole preschool is in a state of 'pregnancy', if you will, as in holding within itself a potentiality of new invention, being in a state of duration but also of inventiveness and new becoming. You do not know what will happen, but yet everything is somehow related to the same set of problems about networks of roads, maps and finding your way around. This is an evolutionary-inventive process of learning, which, I would like to suggest, is what learning in a perspective of onto-epistemology, where learning and becoming are intertwined, is all about.

Pedagogical documentation as a state of 'inventive pregnancy'

As we move into an ontology of immanence (Deleuze and Guattari) and an onto-epistemology (Barad), pedagogical documentation takes on another meaning than if we observe and document to identify the development of the child's cognitive abilities or something of that kind, as shown in Chapter 3. It becomes, more than anything, an active process of transformation and creation in its different moves – from the observing and documenting itself, which is more than ever acknowledged as a material-discursive constructed cut (see Chapter 3, pp. 64–7), to the actualisation of the event in the documentation as a new creation. Yet, the actualisation of the event in the documentation is simply a fragment or splinter of its dense mixture. And still it encompasses both the temporal limits *and* simultaneously the infinite potentialities of the child and the other organisms and matter involved in the process, such as the limits in the qualities and possibilities of clay, sticks, paint, etc. in the events described in Chapter 1 with the children playing with sticks, or in Chapter 2 with the students making clay figures.

If we talk about it in a slightly different manner, pedagogical documentation is not to be used in a *reactive* way in terms of time, as in doing an evaluation and comparing outcomes with goals after an event. It is not, as it is often mistakenly understood, something *retrospective* – documenting what happened so we can judge and evaluate what 'was', and treating documentation as a representation of practice. Rather, pedagogical documentation is *pedagogical* because it is prospective more than anything else. However, using the concept of prospective is problematic, because it implies a progressive linear concept of time. Rather what we need is a concept of time that simultaneously encompasses temporal limits and infinite possibilities, which is a non-linear concept of time (Deleuze, 1990; Williams, 2008).

So, let us think of pedagogical documentation as a creative actualising of the event, making it 'material' in front of us, as we saw in the previous chapter. This makes thinking about the event and re-enacting it in our minds when we talk about it possible. We can even *counter-actualise* it, that is, read 'against' it, read it in reversal from another position, or read it differently to transform it. In this respect, pedagogical documentation relates strongly to what Colebrook has called Deleuze's 'active ethics' (2002: 55). Her way of putting it beautifully frames how we need to think about pedagogical documentation as something very different from the diagnostic tools we have been using and which are reappearing in different forms today. We are not psychologists, doctors or scientists as we practise pedagogical documentation; rather, we are collaborative creators and inventors of learning events with children and our colleagues. We are whole-heartedly engaged in a collaborative process of constructing new knowledge with and about specific phenomena and children and ourselves as teachers, and thus exploring our own limits and possibilities at the same time. Hence, this is about being *active* rather than *reactive*, to re-connect to the above.

All the teachers, practitioners and students who I have worked with during the last fifteen years have said: 'Once you get access to working with this tool in this way there is no turning back to practice-as-usual.' Once we have been a part of processes of desire for transformations and of willing events of learning and change, we discover the ethical aspect in this process. Deleuze has written on ethics as follows, which I will return to in the final chapter: 'Either ethics makes no sense at all, or this is what it means and has nothing else to say: *not to be unworthy of what happens to us*' (1990: 149, my emphasis). In a specific sense this is about awareness of, intra-acting with, and doing justice to *what is happening in each event* and being inventive of what is to come. It is about allowing yourself to become anew with each event, and to be affirmative of learning as a state of transformation.

In this way it is possible to see how the 'methodology' of pedagogical documentation in an intra-active pedagogy goes beyond the theory/practice divide, in that it embraces the interdependence of thinking and living. Thinking transforms living (practice), and living (practice) transforms thinking (Colebrook, 2002; Deleuze and Guattari, 1994; May, 2005). Thus, using pedagogical documentation in this way constitutes a strong resistance to the limiting and reductive learning strategies and practices imposed both on young children and on students in higher education today.

Reflections on time and duration

As indicated above, the dual movements in our practice with pedagogical documentation must be understood in terms of a non-linear concept of time. The dual movements that the rest of the chapter will be preoccupied with take place in the same space–time – the 'circular' slowing down and the horizontal 'speeding up' are operating more or less at the same time, so to speak. It is about duration – how something that was still is and will become although it becomes something new and different in itself (Deleuze, 1990; Grosz, 2005). Thus, space, time and matter are mutually constituted through the dynamics of iterative intra-activity. Barad writes about time in the following way:

> the past matters as does the future, but the past is never left behind, never finished once and for all, and the future is not what will come to be in an unfolding of the present movement; rather the past and the future are enfolded participants in matter's iterative becoming.
>
> (2007: 181)

The past is the condition of the present in both Barad's and also Deleuze's thinking. It is only through the past's pre-existence that the present can come to be, writes Grosz with reference to Deleuze (2005: 104). The past and the present co-exist. In every repetition we make of ourselves there is a new version of what was before that differentiates itself from the past, but contains and transforms it at the same time. This is like the image of 'pregnancy' as duration and holding within itself a potentiality of new invention and new becoming from what already is. The dual 'methodological' movements are, in line with this thinking, put to work while *being in the middle of things* in the duration of the mixture of what is present, past and future at the same time. In terms of action, you document what happens, and then you lay out the documentation on the table to re-visit, re-live or re-enact and unfold some of the multiplicities and differentiations of the event, but instead of thinking of such action in terms of a progression from past to present to future, we think about it as an ongoing *duration* of the event. This all might sound strange at the moment, but as the example below will unfold, you will see how a problem first posed to the 4-year-old boys in the example will linger and unfold in the duration of this learning event into a new one – tied to the first – much later.

To sum up the above: pedagogical documentation can be understood the way Williams describes Deleuze's philosophy in terms of a 'searching for the structural conditions for the real *and* for imagination' (2005: 56, my emphasis). In other words, we are in an interdependent relationship with what simultaneously already structures our thinking and doing, *and* with what might become infinitely possible. This, as you can see, relates to the concepts of striated and smooth space already put to work in the previous chapter. Here we could see how the structures in the striated space conditioned the smooth space where new inventions might be possible. The dual movement of 'methodologically' using pedagogical documentation is about making ourselves aware of both this inter-dependence in relation to our limitations *and* our unlimited possibilities of change and becoming different in ourselves and in our practices.

Two movements of pedagogical documentation: the 'circular' and the 'horizontal'

Although the two 'methodological' movements that I describe below in fact take place simultaneously, I will construct an imagined separation between them in my discussion. I do so to make it possible to identify the aspects where they do differ to some extent, although they are dependent on each other and always in a state of intra-acting. Moreover, I also separate them to make the provocative point that we are, in my experience, more inclined to will and enact the 'circular' movement of re-enactments and counter-actualisations. We seem to be more afraid to will and enact the 'horizontal' movements of invention and creation. To simplify things: we would rather discuss and reconsider what it is we see in the documentation – however painful that might be as we go against what first seems natural or taken for granted – than deliberatively expose ourselves to the risk of letting go of habits of thought and bodily habits. The letting go is in the centre of the 'horizontal' movement if it is to be inventive and creative, and for pedagogical practice to change. Any event can introduce change and difference in our practices, but our willingness to let that happen depends on how we think about learning and knowing and our relationship to that which we understand as reality.

My previous theorising on pedagogical documentation as an 'ethics of resistance' (Lenz Taguchi, 2000, 2006, 2007, 2008d) has sometimes had the practical consequences of getting stuck in aspects of the circular re-enactments and counter-actualisations that make us aware of how we think, but which does not explicitly include an inventive thinking that goes beyond what we have found in such deconstructive reflections to create something new. Moreover, an 'ethics of resistance' does not pick up on either the circular or the horizontal spaces that *children themselves* create in their investigations while doing them, but focuses solely on the learning of the adults for them to better organise practices *for* children. The teacher-centredness constitutes my biggest concern in my critique of my own earlier writings.

The 'circular' movement

What I will conceptualise as the 'circular' movement is about slowing down the speed of the movement in our work with children or with the documentation, to be able to re-enact (*re-live* – *live-again*) the event, and make counter-actualisations that can make new invention possible. (I will explain counter-actualisations below.) It is also possible to talk about this movement in terms of a *delay* between perception and action. Grosz (2005) writes about how we can understand that it is the human brain that constructs this delay between our perceptions and what we are then able to think or do. It is as a result of this delaying in the brain that we can engage in re-routing and re-organisation of what has happened in our thinking, which – and this is important – makes possible creativity and innovation (Grosz 2005: 98–9). This delay brings us away from the immediacy of our inevitably ongoing intra-actions with objects – the messy mixture of the present – and establishes a distance but also an important *indeterminacy*, which allows perceptual images to be assessed (p. 99). Grosz refers to Deleuze who states that this delay and indetermination can both enrich and complicate things, in that it makes possible re-enlivenment, re-enactments and thus counter-actualisations (p. 100; Deleuze, 1990).

I have chosen to use the Deleuzian (1990) concepts of re-enactments and counter-actualisations to frame the complexity involved in the process. First, the process entails a re-enactment as we write or talk about what happened, which makes reading against common sense and taken-for-grantedness possible. Second, it can make possible identifying how the pedagogical space is striated and thus the structural conditions in the event: how such striations are materialised as habits, routine behaviours, organisations of time, space and materials, and also in terms of thinking in hierarchies and binary oppositions, inclusions and exclusions. We can understand these striations as structural conditions in terms of discursive coding; for instance, how an activity or material is gender-coded or coded in relation to class, social groups, ethnicity, race, etc. Thus, we engage in processes of de-coding and re-coding our always somehow coded meaning-making of our world. Lastly, and not least, this delaying and slowing down 'circular' movement is about identifying the material-discursive intra-activity taking place, the inter-connections and inter-relations between matter, objects and human subjects and how they make themselves intelligible to each other (see Chapter 2, pp. 58–60). In this movement, however, we do not just engage in what from the above can be understood as critical and resistance analysis, or deconstructions (Lenz Taguchi, 2005, 2007, 2008d). Rather, the counter-actualisations always involve an opening up of new possibilities from what is or was; for instance, for us to think of the 1 year olds' water investigations in terms of developing an embodied (rather than expressed in language) cognitive understanding of what objects can float or which ones sink at different speeds, through iterative experimentations in intra-active processes with the materials, as in the example of the previous chapter.

It may also be productive to think about this 'circular' movement, paradoxically perhaps, in terms of a 'flattening out' of the actualised events; in laying them out in front of us on the table in their actualised materiality to prevent us from reading the event from a privileged position. Moreover, we flatten out the mixture of the pluralism and thickness of corporeality and materiality in the event that has been actualised as a splinter in the documentation, to be able to see it in some of its material-discursive differentiations and multiplicities (Barad, 2007; Deleuze, 1990; Williams, 2008). For example, how can we understand what happened from the point of view of the material, the furniture or floor, or the limited space of the room? How can we understand the intra-activity and connectedness between the hand and the clay from the point of view of the clay, or the hand of the child respectively? What are the time–space–place relations and conditions of the event of a child moulding a piece of clay or experimenting with water?

The 'circular' movement can also entail a process of 'mapping out' some of the structural *discursive–time–space–place–material* pre-conditions as well as the material-discursive turning-points in the events. The 'mapping out' is about the *emergence* of the event, that is, how what happened came to happen by means of the significant turning points in relation to the structural material-discursive conditions along the way. As in the example with the sticks in Chapter 1, the question posed by the student to the little boy playing with his stick as a gun can be understood as a turning-point that had material-discursive consequences in the next event that emerged. The 'circular' and slowing down movement is thus also a process of *tracing back* the event through what has been actualised in the documentation. And again, depending on what we focus on as we construct the documentation – by, for instance, taking the photo from the floor looking up – we will only actualise *one* of a multiplicity of aspects in the many folds of the thick mixture which makes up the learning event. The event can be understood quite differently if we were to take the photograph from the ceiling, or at the height of the children's eyes or from the viewpoint of children's hands. Irrespective of what it is that we might be able to trace back, this is done here and now to change future practices, that is, it must be understood in a dissolved conception of time.

The 'horizontal' movement

If the 'circular' movement is about slowing down, delaying and flattening out, the 'horizontal' movement is about speeding up the movement of the flow of events – as in *thinning* and *smoothing* out and creating a *smoother space* to enable transformation and change in a new event emerging (Deleuze and Guattari, 1987). As already pointed out in the previous chapter, the pedagogical space becomes smooth as we disengage and detach ourselves from habitual behaviours and habits of thought (Williams, 2008). The 'horizontal' movement can take place at any time. In a pedagogical space that is not heavily striated, coagulated or immobile, there will be shifts or fluctuations between the slowing down 'circular' and speeding up 'horizontal' movements all the time. The speeding up and smoothing out of the pedagogical space can take place right in the middle of the event in-between a child and a material in processes of experimentation.

In some of these instances, when there are no habits of mind or habitual ways of doing things, the pedagogical space is smooth enough to enable what Deleuze and Guattari (1987: 88–9) have called the 'line of flight' to become possible. It becomes the event of un-thought possibilities that leaps away from immobile over-coded striated spaces. The 'line of flight' is a state of 'in-betweeness' that works like a positive force or energy, creating new spaces of possible thinking that takes us away from our normalising habits of thought; as in the instance when the stick was transformed from a gun to a doll at the turning-point of the question posed to the little boy in Chapter 1. This is when we extend ourselves in creativity and are transformed as thinking and embodied beings. Hence, we might try to verbalise seemingly impossible ways of thinking or understanding something, or try out a new way of doing and organising something in our practices. Following Deleuze we can think of the event of the line of flight as being inventive of new experience, and as 'a form of experience itself' (Colebrook, 2000: 113). Deleuze and Guattari write:

> To think is to experiment, but experimentation is always that which is in the process of coming about – *the new, remarkable, and interesting* that replaces the appearance of truth and are more demanding than it is.
>
> (1994: 111, my emphasis)

I emphasise the last part of the quote above because what we experience in the line of flight demands that we think and live in new ways. Hence, this must have consequences for how we plan for future possible learning events. Or, to listen to Deleuze and Guattari again, the 'line of flight' is about 'extrac[ting] an event from things and beings, to set up a new event' (1994: 33). In other words, we are as teachers obliged to be attentive to and responsible for making use of the 'new, remarkable, and interesting that replaces the appearance of truth', as we go on preparing for new learning events with the children (p. 33). This is also a question of ethics that I will discuss further in the final chapter.

The 'horizontal', speeding-up movement can be desired and willed to happen, but, as we shall see in the example below, they can happen among children when they construct a space for themselves that is suddenly rid of striations; for instance, in imaginative play. As teachers we need to recognise when the pedagogical space opens up and speeds up into such lines of flight, for us to document them, acknowledge and maybe make use of them to further challenge learning. As teachers we can also use the 'circular' slowing down movement and our heightened awareness of how the pedagogical space is structured, striated and coded, and from this awareness try to speed up the movement and imagine new possibilities, as already indicated above. Children can partake in processes of re-enactments and counter-actualisations of the event, and join in de- and re-coding meaning-making while investigating or play takes place, as the example also will show. However, re-coding requires that the pedagogical space of thinking smoothes out to make invention and creation possible, that is, we need to really convince the children that they are allowed to think the way they want and not in proper, true or right ways.

It is difficult to let go of habits of thought and taken-for-granted ways of thinking and doing that make us feel safe. Developmental theories, universal standards and appropriate practice recommendations often make early childhood practice a highly striated space and seemingly coagulated or stagnant in its movements and repetitions. This is because it is built on structured and regulated habits of doing things and structured ways of thinking about what happens. Trying to set in motion the horizontal movement encompasses a de-coding of already coded and sometimes over-coded assemblages of understandings in pedagogical practices. But striated space can also, as indicated above, be understood as a safe place, where children recognise the routines and habits in our practices, which, if it is not understood as inhibiting striations, can be used as a 'platform' for speeding up and smoothing out the pedagogical space to enable new creations of thought or action (see also Davies and Gannon, forthcoming).

As with the striated and smooth space described in the previous chapter, the 'circular' and 'horizontal' 'methodological' movements are interdependent, and we should try to fluctuate in-between them. Too much of either one is not good. Either it will stop the investigative learning processes if we slow everything down too much, which is the most common experience I have had when visiting preschools doing learning projects. Or, taking off on lines of flight can go in directions that simply create chaos with no stability or focus in the learning processes. In my experience, the problem in both cases is that the project is not saturated and impregnated with the questions and problems of the children, which is what provides the uniting cord. We can use peda-gogical documentation to both slow down and speed up the movements in the pedagogical spaces we arrange. By immediately asking the children and discussing with them what it is they are doing, or showing them the documentation that was produced, we can slow down the movement and inspire the children to 'counter-actualise', de-code and re-code what it is they are doing. This in turn can speed up the movement and create a line of flight into a new construct of thought or embodiment.

To summarise the above discussion of the two movements when using pedagogical documentation in an intra-active pedagogy: the 'horizontal' and speeding up movement creates the smoother space necessary for the invention and creation of new becomings, whereas the 'circular' slowing down movement of re-enactments and counter-actualisations is neces-sary for us to make ourselves aware of the structural conditions, and the thickness and multiplicities in the learning events. What then follows from this can be a speeding up movement in the subsequent moment. The 'circular' movement can thus work as a precondition for a speeding up 'horizontal' movement and the creation of smoother space. Maybe now we can free ourselves from a habit of thought and be enabled to learn something new.

The Orientation project: an example of the 'methodological' movements and their enactments

In the example we will meet 4 and 5 year olds in a project about understanding and orienting yourself as a child in your most immediate environments – the Orientation project, which has been previously men-tioned. It took place during the spring of 1997 at Åkervägens preschool south of Stockholm. Three teachers, Susanne Hjelm, Michaela Sundberg and Solveig Åkerström, engaged a group of twenty-one children aged 3 to 5 years old in this project during five months as a part of their daily practices (Lenz Taguchi, 2000). The 5 year olds in this group mostly consisted of girls and the 4 year olds were mostly boys, although there were also a couple of 5-year-old boys and one 4-year-old girl. The discussion circulates around four groups of children; in the first similar learning events there were two pairs of children – one pair of 5 year olds (a boy and a girl) and one pair of 4 year olds (two boys). In the second learning events to be discussed below there were four 4-year-old boys in one group and three 5-year-old girls in the other.

I emphasise here that I have not chosen this example because it is an exemplary case of inventive and creative learning processes using pedagogical documentation. I have simply picked it because I have had access to this material, as it was a part of my doctoral research project (Lenz Taguchi, 2000). Moreover, I have been a part of this project myself as a collaborative researcher, which makes it easier from an ethical point of view to talk about it, and I have done some of the documentation and all of the photography myself. This project constitutes a complex series of events where habitual practice in striated pedagogical spaces can be identified, just as much as smooth spaces of invention. Moreover, I will not discuss the qualities of the learning taking place in this project. The aim is rather to use it to write about my thinking on an intra-active pedagogy and its dual movements in the usage of pedagogical documentation. I will not use the real names of the children.

Drawing your way home from preschool: the 5 year olds

Because the children had asked the teachers if they could walk to the homes of each of the twenty-one children in the group to see where they lived, the teachers decided to divide the children into smaller groups and ask them to answer a question, first in words and then on paper: 'Imagine that you have forgotten something at home. Can you describe your way home from the preschool?' The pairs of 5 year olds told detailed stories about what they saw on their way home to get what they had forgotten. When they made their drawings, they all started drawing the preschool first, and then continued drawing the streets, trees and other things they saw along the way. They finally drew their own house.

All these children stayed focused on the question of describing the way home from preschool and kept on adding things they had forgotten.

In Figure 4.1 the boy Olof reminded himself about the slide in the pre-school yard and put it in besides the preschool on the left-hand side of the drawing. He drew a car that he liked, which was occasionally parked outside his house in the right-hand corner of the drawing. Anna drew the café she passed and the grocery store. Then she needed to turn the paper around to be able to fit in the long distance to her home. She commented that the road was not really that bent, but having come to the end of that side of the paper she simply needed to turn it around to have it fit in. In the middle of her drawing she drew the big trees and the fence she had observed on her way home to her apartment. All the 5-year-old children were very concentrated on what it is they saw and took notice of in the environment. Olof was, for instance, very interested in the roof tiles, both on the preschool and on his own house, and put a lot of effort into drawing them.

We will briefly engage in a delaying and slowing down of the 'circular' movement and try to re-enact it, identifying some of the structuring

Figure 4.1 Olof's drawing with the preschool on the left and his house on the right.

striations, and look for material-discursive intra-activities in this very limited information we now have, including Figure 4.1. If we re-enact the event again from the point of view of the question and our seemingly taken-for-granted meaning-making of it, the children seemed to respond in accordance with our presupposed coding of the question and request from the children. That is, they seemed to pick up the codes informed by the expectations of the teacher, as well as a strong awareness of what the project was about, and that the drawings might be used as 'maps' in subsequent walks to their respective house. The pedagogical space in the room was comfortably striated with expectations that the children were going to be asked to make drawings of what they were thinking, seeing or observing. This had been done many times before in the different projects undertaken in this preschool.

The 5 year olds were already skilled in drawing. Because the children expected this safe habitual behaviour when asked to join the teacher in the atelier, they knew that they were probably going to be asked to start discussing a problem and then make a drawing. The children, so to speak, intra-acted intimately with the discursive codes of the situation in relation to this specific project in the pedagogical space, as well as with the striated habitual behaviour of talking first and drawing afterwards in the calm and safe environment of the atelier. Moreover, they were used to and comfortable with the tape recorder standing on the table and pho-tographs being taken. The routines and habits of working in investigative projects make up the structural conditions that striate the pedagogical space in specific ways, as would any other routines of pedagogical work. (As a parenthesis and to clarify, the problem is not if the space is striated or not, but whether or not striations can be contested and lines of flight and new invention can become possible.)

The discursive meaning-making and codes used when talking about what you see on your way to the preschool intra-acted with the materials available and the structural space–time conditions. The children liked to draw with the coloured pens with narrow points that made distinct lines (not too thick and not too thin) on bigger or smaller sizes of paper available to them. These papers were of high quality with a soft structure that absorbed the ink from the pens very nicely, as the pen and paper intra-acted to construct lines. But pen and paper also intra-acted with the discursively informed or coded hands of the child while drawing. Although almost all children chose the larger papers, the way they had planned their drawing did not always 'fit'. This is why Anna needed to turn the paper around to 'fit in' the distance by 'bending' the road back to her house. Anna's ideas about what to draw and the size and boundaries of the paper intra-acted in a way that would make her 'obey' or 'submit' to the size and limits of the paper. The children investigated what they thought a 'map' might look like by trying to actualise the concept of 'map' and/or 'the way to the preschool' on a piece of paper. It is difficult to identify, in this situation, any activity of de-coding and re-coding taking place or taking off on 'lines of flight'. On the contrary the situation seems to need some de-coding in relation to the obedient and habitual character of the event unfolding. As shown below, such de-coding and re-coding happened later as the learning events of the children turned out to move in more unexpected and less obedient, habitual or expected ways. But before discussing this, we shall look at another similar but different learning event based on the same problem of being asked to talk about and draw your way to the preschool, this time with a couple of 4-year-old boys.

The 4 year olds take a ride with their pens on paper

The 4 year olds in this group were both boys. One of the teachers worked with them in pairs and posed the same question to them: 'Imagine that you have forgotten something at home. Can you describe your way home from the preschool?' Both Anders and Eric seemed to find it hard to describe their way home in words. Anders asked the teacher why she was asking this question when she already knew where he lived and then simply stated: 'You just go straight home to me.' His friend giggled and asked: 'So, you just go straight ahead without turning then?' And Anders replied: 'Yes, you just go straight and then you come to a yellow house and that is my house!' The teacher tried to ask about other houses or things to see along the way, but Anders avoided all her follow-up questions carefully by answering with 'no' and 'I don't know' most of the time. As the teacher then turned her attention to Eric, his curious answers to the teacher's questions made both of the boys giggly and energised. Eric told a complicated story about how to get into his house through the open window because the door was locked, to get the swords he had forgotten. He had a lot of fun telling this story and his friend was greatly amused.

When asked to make drawings, both of the boys picked the larger papers and started to draw very eagerly, lying on the floor on their stomachs. Anders drew his own house first and then the straight road to it. He added a house in the distance that he passed on his road home, and Eric commented that it looked like a lighthouse. This comment aroused lots of amusement and both of the boys added one lighthouse after the other to their drawings. They started to talk intensively, making all kinds of different sounds and giggling a lot. The teacher asked the boys if they could really see a lighthouse on their way home, and Anders answered in a very serious tone of voice that the lighthouse is on the harbour far away and then continued to draw intensively. The teacher asked where the preschool was in their respective drawings. Anders stopped to think as if having been confronted with a new problem, and said that it is far away after passing many trees. He seemed to realise that to be able to draw the preschool he had got to have another sheet of paper. He taped on a smaller sheet to the first larger one. He drew more trees while making clicking sounds of heels hitting the pavement walking along the road. Then he stopped for a while looking, and added on another paper, and then a third using the tape. His drawing became very long on the floor.

Meanwhile Eric first drew his house and then water and an island, adding on several lighthouses. Then he drew a boat on top of the roof on a house with a chimney with smoke coming out of it. He too needed another sheet of paper but chose paper of the same size as the first sheet (see Figure 4.2). Yet another boat was added to the drawing. It had roller-skates under it so it could skateboard down the road when it was not on the water, he said. He showed how the boat skateboarded up and down in a serpentine movement on the road, drawing his pen across the paper, while making sounds of speeding up and slowing down. The boys had a lot of fun as this story emerged as lines on the paper and intensive sounds and bodily action, all in the space of the atelier.

These 4-year-old boys seemed to respond in a less pre-coded way to the question posed to them, both verbally and while drawing. It was as if the boys did not submit to the striations in this pedagogical space, coded with verbal and graphic expectations in relation to the teacher's question. Their ways of responding can be understood as a re-coding of the question on their own terms; letting it set them off into their imaginations as a line of flight away from truthful representations of the requested way home from preschool. This makes an interesting contrast to what happened in the pairs of 5 year olds. What kinds of events emerged as Anders and Eric responded to the teacher's request to tell about and draw their way home from preschool? The boys seemed to intra-act in-between themselves and with their imaginations, but just as much with the pens and papers at hand. In the act of drawing, Anders' intra-action with the paper was not about 'obeying' and keeping within its limits and borders. Rather, he decided to extend his drawing space by adding

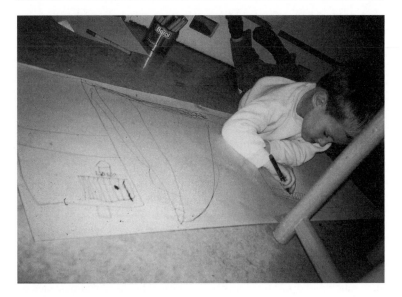

Figure 4.2 Eric on the floor drawing.

another sheet of paper, and then another one, while telling the story of having to pass all these trees along the way to get to his house. The road home became longer and longer and was actualised as a drawing constructed of an interconnected row of papers on the floor. He solved the problems as they arose while being in the middle of his telling and simultaneously drawing.

Reading this event from the intra-action taking place in-between the tip of the pen and Eric's imagination, the story of the house on roller-skates seemed to emerge as the wet ink was absorbed by the fibres of the paper actualising a clear line of speeding up movements of a roller-skating house. He was literally *on* the road in his telling about it. He was in a process of becoming-*with* his pen while drawing the road. The ink, the words, the imagination, the bodies of the boys intra-acted in this series of small inventive events with many turning points. The teacher's questions, posed from within the striated space, simply fuelled the speed of the movement and sometimes caused a turning-point, which in turn caused yet another event. The event of lighthouses in the water was in this way turned into an event of passing by trees alongside a successively extended straight road to Anders' home.

The papers, pens, hands and imaginations of the boys were immersed in a state of mutual becoming-with one another: what was what, and what came first or afterwards, is impossible to determine. Reading this event from an intra-active approach – from the non-spoken and silent point of view of papers and pens and the floor where the children were laying – we find events quite different from those we usually observe as teachers. We usually read these events in terms of developmental stages of maturity, cognitive and/or social, and evaluate whether or not these 4-year-old boys were able to concentrate on or perform the requested assignment. Instead, what we can see is creative and inventive intra-activity taking place, where joy, imagination and *matter* matters in processes of doing and thinking.

Teachers talking and actualising our habitual developmental thinking

As teachers we decided to meet to discuss how to understand what had happened and to study the documentation, that is, looking at the drawings, listening to some sequences from the tapes, and reading the written and drawn observations in our notebooks. We also needed to plan what to do next, based on what had happened. We spread out the drawings in front of us and tried to make ourselves aware of how we initially understood what it was we saw, read and heard. We asked ourselves very simple questions such as how the children had responded to the questions posed by the teachers. Immediately comparisons between the groups of children occurred. The 5 year olds, who were mostly girls, had seemed to know exactly what had been asked of them. They produced, we concluded, 'proper' drawings that could be used as a kind of map. The 4-year-old boys, on the other hand, we understood as not having been a bit interested in the question asked, or in the problem of the road between the preschool and their home. Their answers were meagre and their drawings preoccupied with other stories, about their imaginations rather than the road back home. Moreover, they had all started their drawings from the point of view of their own homes, being totally preoccupied with what it was that they had forgotten in the morning to bring with them, rather than starting from the point of view of the preschool and going home to get what had been left behind.

So in this first meeting, the way we understood what the boys had done was not picking up on their creativity and inventions. This is, unfortunately, what most often happens in practice-as-usual. We forget or do not know how to look for the horizontal movements, the smoothing out of the space that often occurs, but without us seeing it, identifying it or knowing how to challenge it further. Clinging on to our habits of thought and our taken-for-granted coding of developmental theories, we suggested that the 4 year olds were probably not mature enough to respond properly to our question and stay concentrated on the problem. And we were not surprised. They were, after all, boys, and thus less mature than can be expected of the average 4-year old. Maybe, we asked ourselves, they were unable to concentrate on anything not close enough to them? Being, we suggested, merely 4 years old they were still too much of an appendage to their parents and their home environment. Maybe this is why they started to draw their home first? The request to talk about the road or draw it was simply 'too difficult and advanced' for them, we concluded. Thus, these boys were still too immature in relation to cognitive development, that is, they were unable to make spatial and conceptual abstractions. Moreover, they were still being too ego-centric, that is, they were not able to abstract themselves from their own inborn and natural self-centredness at this age.

As a consequence of the above initial analysis, we decided on the following action. The 4 year olds were to talk about and draw what it looked like inside their homes – their immediate and closest environment. The 5 year olds would, however, be challenged as a next step to construct their way home with different kinds of construction materials on the floor of the atelier-room. In other words, at this point, we did not engage in any slowing down 'circular' movements of re-enactment to do counter-actualisation, de-coding of our thinking or reading the intra-actions. Rather we identified and re-confirmed our habitual thinking, coded with taken-for-granted developmental psychology and gender stereotypes, of boys being generally more immature than girls irrespective of age. We did not ask ourselves *why* it was that we would analyse what had happened in this way rather than another. We were in a hurry to decide what to do next, instead of slowing down. But what happened next would actually help us to slow down to re-enact, counter-actualise and de-code our initial analysis. Or, maybe what happened was that it was really the children that counter-actualised the previous events *for* us in their creative invention of the unexpected.

Things often don't turn out the way we expect them to . . .

So, what happened in the subsequent learning events? The simplest answer is that it was the reverse of what was expected. To summarise: a group of three 5-year-old girls, who we will look closer at below, built their homes and neighbouring houses and not the streets as we had expected. And a group of four 4-year-old boys turned their event around from the requested drawings of the layout of their houses and apartments, instead building on the floor a network of streets in their neighbour-hood. Figure 4.3 shows how the girls got into intense construction work and lay-outs of the inside of their houses on the floor.

The 4-year-old boys and the 5-year-old girls doing exactly the opposite to what we had planned, constituted in itself a counter-actualisation of the first events involving some of the same children. From what we had seen in the second learning event it was obvious that the 4 year olds were very interested in the road system; in fact, they constructed an almost perfect network of streets with construction materials on the floor. As for the girls, there was no mistaking the eagerness and joy with which they engaged in constructing plans of their homes, and then making up a play, dressing themselves up and, later on that afternoon, putting on a show related to their constructions. How did this happen?

The 4-year-old boys had discussed their different drawings of their homes, as had been requested of them. Although these discussions were very engaging, not least because their drawings showed very different and interesting strategies of drawing an outline of an apartment or a house, what would arouse their strongest interest was the question of what it was

Figure 4.3 Anna, Eva and Jeanette discussing their construction.

possible to see when looking out of their windows – the houses of their neighbours and the roads connecting the houses. This is when intra-actions in-between what is said, thought and done with concrete materials at hand simply explodes. The next event becomes an intensive flow of new meaning-making constructions in intra-action with pieces of papers, building-blocks and other materials.

The turning of the event leaped off as one of the boys jokingly started to imagine himself jumping out of his window, and wondering whether or not he would land on his own or his neighbour's lawn, or get stuck on the fence in between. This relates directly to the first event when one of these boys had to climb into his house through a window and then jump out of it again. With much giggling the boys described flying out of their windows, crossing lawns, neighbouring houses and streets. At this moment they all seemed to take off into an event of imagination – a *line of flight* taking them out of the arranged talk of the lay-outs of their homes lying in front of them on the table. And the teacher quietly awaited what was to come. In this event the boys co-operatively constructed and formulated a new problem of interest. What did the neighbourhood look like from above, if flying over it like a bird?

This became an important turning-point in relation to the previous question that had been posed to them some days before, about what they could see on their way home from the preschool. This question had lingered in the pedagogical space of the preschool where the Orientation project had slowly started to impregnate everything that was said and done among the children and staff. As an extended duration of the first event, and in close intra-action with new materials, another event with new questions emerged. Someone asked: if you live right beside some-one you're a neighbour, but if you live a few houses away, is this still a neighbour? How far away can you live and still be called a neighbour? And if you live on another street, are you a neighbour then? One of the boys picked up a few building blocks from a shelf to illustrate his view on these questions. A moment later the boys were on the floor starting to construct a network of roads and houses. In Figure 4.4 the construction work has just begun.

In our talk after this second session we immediately agreed that the pedagogical space for us to think inside had been hopelessly striated by our taken-for-granted ideas concerning children's cognitive and social development. The children had, in front of our eyes and attentive bodies, embarked into a new event, taking off from what had previously been done but transforming it into something else. The space was saturated and 'pregnant' with what had been and the potentialities of what might

Figure 4.4 The boys starting to construct their neighbourhood.

become. As teachers we had excluded the possibility of 4 year olds being able to construct an overview image of their close neighbourhood. Apparently these boys were able to think in more 'abstract' terms than we had thought possible, from a developmental point of view. Moreover, we could see how the available materials in the atelier had important agentic qualities intra-acting with the boys' imaginations and theorising. The things and materials in the atelier could be used as agentic tools intra-acting with the children's thinking and actions and making new important turning-points possible. What opened up in these new events were new possibilities for action, thinking and learning. These possibilities emerged in the speeding up into a 'horizontal' movement from the more striated space in which the boys had before been discussing their drawings and plans of their homes. The pedagogical space had broken lose from its previous striations.

In the group of three 5-year-old girls, the teacher had decided to let the girls use a vast range of different materials to prevent them, she said, from being 'good' and doing what the teacher expected them to. In planning the session she said that she thought the outcome of the first session might have been a result of the girls simply doing proper femininity and trying to please the teacher. In other words, she did not want them to remain in the safe and perhaps heavily gender-biased striated space that had been set up for them to work in the first time. Rather she wanted them to be able to perhaps speed up their processes into a horizontal, smoother and faster space of unexpected inventions. This kind of analysis done in relation to the teacher's planning of the upcoming work with the three 5-year-old girls can be understood as a slowing down movement of de-coding and identifying the striations in order to explore new possibilities. She tried to arrange a situation with an abundance of different materials, putting them out for use instead of sitting in their usual places in the shelves.

And her plan had the desired effect. The girls' imaginations exploded. Their play expanded to using materials collected from other rooms in the preschool as well. Their constructions emerged as complicated layouts of their own homes with different rooms, furnished with different objects and materials. They played out advanced stories inside their homes, often with complicated intrigues and arguments among themselves. Their play continued throughout the whole day and in the afternoon they invited other children to come and have a look at their home constructions.

When there is a speeding up in the horizontal movement of invention the forces are strong. Although these forces must be understood, as Grosz points out, as *inhuman*, because they have no intention or will, what drives them and keeps them going is most often affect. She writes:

> Pleasure and pain are the corporal registrations of the forces of the world, the visceral impact of forces that we use to struggle with and against, in order to become more and other. They are the most powerful aids to learning and the most direct and effective stimuli for action, and thus the expansion of force.
>
> (2005: 190)

Moreover, and very central to their process, was the girls' intense interest in the documentation produced by the teacher sitting at a table observing and drawing what she saw and commenting on the side. The girls ran back and forth to check out the documentation while it was produced. They compared, corrected the documentation or corrected their constructions in accordance with the documentation. They frequently asked the teacher to read out loud what she had written, laughed, or commented and made up new stories based on what they had just heard. Hence, the girls intra-acted with the documentation in their learning and playing process, as if it were a living and changing material artefact with agency of its own. The documentation materialised and 'flattened out' the events that emerged on the floor on a piece of paper, which, in its turn, intra-acted intensively with what would emerge next in their collaborative play (see Figure 4.5).

This process, on the one hand, slowed down and delayed the movement of the creative collaborative process, in order for a re-enactment of the event to take place, and reading against what just happened and commenting on what was going on. This inventive aspect of the slowing down movement simultaneously made possible a speeding up of the movement in the next instant, as a new leap or turning-point in the event emerged. When different points of view met in negotiations between the girls, this would also transform the emerging event.

In our subsequent talk we discussed at length the important role of the documentation, and how, in its materiality and presence, it came to exercise such strong agency in the learning processes emerging during these intense hours of play and learning. It indeed became a performative agent in the process, working upon the girls' next move in their construction-work and play. We realised how important the documentation was to the children, but in a new way. If the teacher had not used such a large sheet of paper to document on, but rather a small notebook, the same events would probably not have emerged. So, how can we produce documentation that constitutes an apparatus of knowing that has an even stronger agency than we first thought had been possible? Moreover, this example makes explicit that the documentation is not simply constructed in order for teachers to engage in 'circular' movement of re-enactments and 'horizontal' inventive thinking, but it is first and foremost a tool and apparatus of knowing for the children to make use of. The documentation process thus makes possible important feedback loops from within the emerging learning event taking place, either speeding up the movement or slowing it down.

We also discussed our contradictory gender biases that had emerged at length in our subsequent talks. We became aware of how problematic our coding of the boys' behaviour was as being generally more imma-

Figure 4.5 The girls reading and intra-acting with the documentation.

ture. But, on the other hand, we also problematised how, in the next instance, we understood the boys as more technically interested, as they constructed the neighbourhood on the floor. We would even ascribe to them a more humorous quality in comparison with the girls. The girls' behaviours had been coded in terms of being more dutiful and eager to please and being engaged in social play, and less inclined to engage in technical constructions. As the girls grabbed the chance to use so many materials, we initially understood this as typically girlish behaviour when starting to role play as they constructed overviews and plans of their homes. Irrespective of our way of understanding what the girls did, it always seemed to have less value compared to how we understood what the boys did. Such coding needed to be resisted for us to go against taken-for-granted power-production based on gender structures.

However, when reading against and counter-actualising these binary striations in our thinking, we could see that the girls had engaged in building advanced constructions, while simultaneously constructing a collaborative drama played out in these constructions. Intra-acting, not just with each other, but with the emerging story line, the materials to construct with, and also with the documentation that was simultaneously produced by the teacher, the girls engaged in a complex process of translations, de-coding, re-coding, creation and invention. We shamed ourselves for not having seen immediately these potentialities of the girls' enactments. Instead we had emphasised the brilliance of the boys as 'small engineers', constructing networks of streets on the floor without being asked to do so, as if having an almost inherent interest in such matters.

In conclusion

Spaces for intra-active agentic engagements in-between multiple materials cannot be planned ahead with fixed expected results, but can be prepared and hoped for in different ways by planning derived from our previous experiences from similar events and with similar groups of children. We need to make plans for our learning endeavours with the children. Plan ahead, but also always be on the edge and be prepared to immediately diverge from or let go of that plan when necessary. We must often simply stand back and wait to see what might happen next. Maybe taking off on a line of flight that just happened is something we can pick up on and make productive? This is why slowing down and delaying our movements in the pedagogical space is very important from time to time. And this is where the documentation can become an important agentic force. It can help us become aware of the striations in this particular space, so we can de-code and re-code our discursive meaning-making and how it intra-acts with other matter in the pedagogical space. This might make possible a speeding up of the movement again, for us to be able to think in new inventive ways.

Chapter 5

Going beyond binary practices in early childhood teacher education

> Pedagogy as a social relationship is very close in. It gets right in there – in your brain, your body, your heart, in your sense of self, of the world, of others, and of possibilities and impossibilities in all those realms. . . . It's a relationship whose subtleties can shape and misshape lives, passions for learning, and broader social dynamics.
>
> (Ellsworth, 1997: 6)

This and the following chapter aim to show how it is possible to go beyond binary practices in higher education at large and more specifically in teacher education. What do I mean when I talk about binary practices? I am talking about practices where we keep to the familiar but constructed idea that learning contents and skills are separated into limited academic or practical subjects, such as maths, reading and writing, history, biology, art, gymnastics and sports, art, etc. There have been discussions in education for more than a hundred years now on how to do trans- or inter-disciplinary teaching to connect to children's and students' lived and hands-on experiences, and relate to and pick up on students' various and different intelligences, skills and abilities (Dewey, 2004; Gardner, 1985). A major reason why developing such inter-disciplinary teaching and learning strategies has failed is the complicated power relationship in the binary divides that seem to master our thinking in education. These divides relate back to the time of the Western Enlightenment (Ball, 1994; Bauman, 1991; Hekman, 1990; Readings, 1996).

It is not just the theory/practice divide that constitutes a problem for educational practices to transgress and overcome. Theory has an almost self-evident higher value than embodied and practical knowing, and in addition there are several other binary divides with the same power relationship that seem to be even more problematic to deal with: mind/body, intellect/affect, objective/subjective, science/aesthetics, etc. We seem to get stuck in the trap of thinking that we need to choose either–or every time we discuss these binaries in relation to pedagogy and what kinds of practices they imply, as if one per definition excludes the other. Hence, we continue to do art separate from, for instance, biology or maths. What we need is a way to think otherwise and go beyond these binary divides and develop educational practices that understand how solving mathematical problems and constructing letters and words on a piece of paper is just as much a practical embodied and aesthetic activity, as dancing and drawing requires mathematical calculations and intellectual judgement. By documenting a learning practice, we can focus our analysis on the interconnections and the intra-activity in-between what we generally think about as the hand doing the practical activity of writing mathematical symbols on a paper, and the cognitive mathematical discursive activity. *Intertwined and in a process of interdependence* these will be actualised as mathematical figures on the paper. Thus, we can make visible that there is no divide between intellect and body: they are in a state of interdependence. If we can see this interdependence and interconnectedness between intellect and body, then moving the construction of a mathematical problem to a situation that takes its starting point in entangling the mathematics of a rock song or a break dance that the children or students are deeply involved with does not seem so far fetched anymore (Palmer, 2009a).

This chapter aims to show that it is indeed possible to go beyond the polarisations of the binary divides, and transform teaching and learning to create something new. Following from the examples in previous chapters, this and the following chapter show how it is possible to engage in educational practices in early childhood teacher education that are simultaneously both–and and neither–nor, and go beyond binary practices. To do this I will use an example from a ten-week course in interdisciplinary investigatory mathematics (Palmer, 2009a, 2009b) in a one-year reconceptualised teacher education programme in Stockholm (Lenz Taguchi, 2005, 2007, 2009b). In this course student-teachers also do a period of vocational training performing investigatory learning processes with children. The learning processes of the children and the students are documented throughout the course, and the documentations are used for writing an academic thesis, which is collaboratively supervised during the whole period of the ten-week course. This so-called 'hybrid-writing process' is the topic of the next chapter.

What binary dilemmas and other obstacles in education need to be transgressed?

As soon as we identify the binary divides outlined above that stratify and produce our understanding, we immediately risk going from one side of the binary divide to the other. When we get into learning processes that activate the personal, affective and emotional, the aesthetic, etc., we often end up under-emphasising or, worse, even dismissing theoretical work altogether, by, for instance, not asking the students to make connections to theoretical texts. We often fail to acknowledge the interconnections and interdependencies between the two sides of the divide, and thus make visible how theories are based on lived realities and how lived realities can be theorised to be understood in other ways. The resistance and construction of either–or keeps the binaries in place with emerging conflicts between the polarised practices as a result. Students are asked to write personal process diaries and log-books from their theoretical readings, but are not guided and supervised in how to analyse the personal with the help of theories or put the theories to work in relation to their own lived experiences. Moreover, they are asked to document children's activities in preschools and schools but are not supervised in how to read those documentations in ways that may also challenge a learning theory they are presently studying, or analysing practice with multiple theoretical perspectives, etc. Doing separate activities that keep the binary divided is problematic because one part of the binary will always be given the lower value and be underemphasised. Most often this is the feminine, aesthetic, affective, creative, etc.

Schools and universities are today increasingly interested in reductive methodologies that produce measurable and comparable learning outcomes. This means that trans- and inter-disciplinary teaching methods using arts, aesthetics and other embodied and alternative teaching methods lose out, partly because the outcomes of such learning are more difficult to assess and measure. At the same time there is an increasingly stronger focus on how to make education on all levels be more inclusive of children and students of non-academic backgrounds, and to make education more accessible and challenging for all. It has been a central question for critical and feminist pedagogy whether or not it is possible to dismantle the 'master with the master's tools' as Audre Lorde (1984: 112) once put it. Lorde refers to what happens when students with non-academic backgrounds learn or do not learn how to master traditional academic strategies. The question is whether or not mastery of academic tools and traditions is emancipating for students with non-academic backgrounds. Perhaps changing the academy itself may be more emancipating for everyone in the long run?

After more than two decades of critical anti-racist, feminist, post-colonial and post-structuralist research in education, it seems no loner possible to suggest that, for example, conventional academic writing can be employed without questioning the epistemological presumptions underpinning it. However, finding other tools for teaching, learning and academic writing that work in qualitatively new ways, but that are simultaneously accepted as scientific and valid, has proven to be complicated (Jung, 2005; Richardson, 1997). In order to really make *another* use of 'the master's tools' possible and transgress the binary divides that we create, we need strategies that are able to be involved in *simultaneously* becoming more complex, multiple, embodied and material, *and* finding ways to reduce complexity and aim for comprehension, receptiveness and some sort of validation. Moreover, such strategies need to be accompanied with tools of evaluation that take into account the inter-disciplinary and innovative character of such teaching methodologies.

We must also keep in mind and try to avoid some of the traps in our search for something new and innovative. Although, for example, experience-based teaching strategies have in many instances successfully undermined traditional academic norms that have oppressed gender, class and race perspectives and found new productive strategies for teaching and learning (Davies, 2000; hooks, 1994; Lather and Smithies, 1997; Malka Fisher, 2001; Mayberry and Rose, 1999; Richardson, 1997), we must stay clear of notions of true and 'authentic voices' of marginalised groups and children, and their always problematic essentialist implications as early feminist pedagogues have warned us (Ellsworth, 1992; Gore, 1992; Orner, 1992). The risk of romanticising children and making visible their own voices and strategies of thinking and doing, without simultaneously getting into in-depth processes of knowledge production and meaning-making, is disturbingly present and needs to be continuously contested for reconceptualised practices to be taken seriously. This is a continuing problem for feminist pedagogy, and no doubt also a problem for alternative early childhood education practices, including the Reggio Emilia-inspired practices in Sweden and the adoption of Reggio Emilia practices in other parts of the world as well.

On the other hand, experienced-based teaching *is* very often a successful methodology with students from a very young age, which the Reggio Emilia-inspired work has proven, to university-based education, which feminist, anti-racist and critical pedagogy has shown. This is because it is an undisputable fact that learning subjects pick up contents to be learned or mastered very differently, depending on a multiplicity of experience-based factors; these are especially related to how identity-constituting aspects of gender, ethnicity, race, sexuality and class intersect with each other in relation to the content and learning-situation (Bhabha, 2006; Blaise, 2005; Brown, 2004; Davies, 2000; Davies *et al.*, 2001; Ellsworth, 1997; Lather, 1991; Luke and Gore, 1992; Walkerdine, 1988, 1998). For example, and relevant to the upcoming example, girls and women in the Western world often have an ambivalent relationship to mathematics: although they perform well, they do not think of them-selves as mathematical (Mendick, 2006; Palmer, 2009a; Walkerdine, 1998). Pedagogy and learning is a relationship, as Ellsworth (1997) points out in the quote that opens this chapter, that gets close in and shapes the lives and identities of the learners. Learning a content or skill always also means a reconstructing of your identity/subjectivity. Teaching and learning is simultaneously also a process of subjectivity-construction on behalf of the learner. This is, unfortunately, a hugely overlooked conse-quence of education in educational research, which is still predominantly preoccupied with separating the production of knowledge as an individual cognitive process from the production of identity and subjectivity in contexts of teaching and learning.

Moreover, education is also a relationship that involves a hierarchical taken-for-granted power-production between the learner and the teacher. Ellsworth writes about the central concept of *understanding* – an inevitable concept whenever we talk about teaching and learning. It is the learner who is to understand what the teacher explains and already knows. That learning is a mutual and interdependent relationship, or can be a collaborative endeavour, where the teacher learns the content anew as well as learns about how students think and take up contents differ-ently, is not the way we generally think about it. To illustrate this, Ellsworth mockingly writes from the position ascribed to the learner in this hierarchical relationship:

> Yes, I have *stood under*. I have taken your perspective on myself, and now that we have established a common (your/the teacher's) ground for comprehension, disagreement and personal understandings on behalf of the students are allowed.
>
> (1997: 92–3, original emphasis)

So, how are we to teach being aware of all of this? How are we to teach when we desire equal power relations between learner and teacher, where they are understood as in a mutual and collaborative relationship of connections, intra-activities and learning from within an onto-epistemology? How are we to teach knowing that learning is not simply about a relationship with other humans but also with the non-human, and the material world around us? How do we teach when we know that learning is not just about cognitive 'mind' work, thinking, talking and writing, but also, as shown in the previous chapters, about the body, affects, the intensities and agency of the material objects around us, the environment, the organisation of time and space, and, moreover, involving multiple ways of expressions using different kinds of tools and aesthetic and creative means? And, how are we to teach when we know that learning always also involves a continuous re-construction of the learner's identity or subjectivity – a process of becoming?

How to go beyond and what it is all about

To be able to go beyond the binary divides and make possible new or other pedagogical spaces, we need to be involved in and displace both sides of the divides in order to find the inter-connections between them, and transform them into new creative ways of doing things. I want to turn to the concepts of striated and smooth space that I have introduced in previous chapters in this book to try to make this clearer.

Deleuze and Guattari write that the highly designed and structured space of the city is a good image of the striated space with its streets to follow, houses and doors to enter or exit, whereas the always-in-motion and changing sea or desert can be understood as smooth spaces. They emphasise, though, that it is possible to live smoothly in the city, and that 'even the most striated city gives rise to smooth spaces: to live in the city as a nomad' (1987: 500). Correspondingly, 'it is possible to live striated on the deserts, steppes, or seas' (p. 482). Hence, when the space is striated it is organised and structured, regulated or controlled, to produce specific movements and relations. Smooth spaces are less controlled by habits, schedules, architecture, etc., and make possible movements, connections, inter- and intra-actions and transformations. However, Deleuze and Guattari remind us that 'smooth spaces are not in themselves liberatory' and that we should not think that 'a smooth space will suffice to save us' (p. 500). The striations or 'structures' in the striated space should not be understood as fixed or unchangeable. Rather, as Williams (2008) suggests, we need to understand these 'structures' as the necessary conditions for the transformation of things, objects and subjects in the inevitable and ongoing events that constitute life and living. They simultaneously constitute a limit as something to resist and break loose from. The structures thus become the source of new becoming and change in an evolutionary sense, where things become different in themselves, rather than in a determining and exclusionary way (Williams, 2005, 2008).

Let us take the concepts of striated and smooth space and apply them to the question of how to be involved in reconceptualising pedagogical practices in early childhood teacher education in ways that can take us beyond the binary divides of theory/practice, mind/body, intellect/affect, science/aesthetics, etc. Striations are embedded in scientific concepts, stratifying and forcing our thinking into specific closed logics of thought. The over-emphasis on cognition and reading, writing and talking as a practice of learning, confines learning to stratified practices of using mostly books as tools for teaching and learning. Performing scientific or other experiments in a striated educational space means performing pre-planned activities in prescribed ways to achieve predetermined outcomes. The teacher guides the process by posing questions to which there is only one right answer and provides explanations. Bodily activities such as gymnastics, dance or drama are regulated and supervised, following specific rules and choreographies, with students divided in groups or pairs. All activities are usually highly regulated in time and space.

Now, what would be the opposite of a highly striated educational space? A totally unregulated anarchy of space and time, where students do unrestrained embodied aesthetic work, or what? In the Swedish educational debate there is often a polarisation between a traditional authoritarian teaching style and what is called a muddled, woolly and indefinable pedagogy with roots in the 1970s anti-authoritarian democratic movement. How do we go beyond such polarisations?

In my reading of Deleuze and Guattari, I understand that reconceptualised pedagogical work has to be about making possible a pedagogical space which *on the one hand* is sufficiently striated to constitute enough safeness and basic routine in terms of the students and teachers knowing where to find materials, having enough time and physical space to do things, etc.; while *on the other hand* making it possible for the students and teachers to enter into smooth space enabling them to go across stratifying thinking and habits of doing, into creation and invention of something new. Exactly how the pedagogical space should best be organised and stratified in a specific educational practice is impossible to know – it must be continuously examined and challenged in relation to the material conditions and what students and teachers are in the group. And again, this is when the tool of pedagogical documentation becomes inevitable also in higher education teaching. Working with collecting, reading and using our documentation in various ways, we can put in motion both the 'circular' movement of re-enactments and counter-actualisations that make us identify stratifications, binary divides or intra-activities taking place, and the 'horizontal' movement that precisely moves us into smooth space (see Chapter 4). The two 'methodological' movements of an intra-active pedagogy introduced in the previous chapter can be the tools we need to be able to be involved in these continuous shifts between striated and smooth space in our higher education and teacher education practices as well. Thus, we might be able to go beyond the binary divides that otherwise put us into choices of either–or, or one at the time. My aim with the rest of this chapter is to show some of the strategies we have been working with to be able to achieve this.

A reconceptualised teacher education in Stockholm since 1999

In constructing a reconceptualised early childhood teacher education our aim was to practise with the student-teachers the same teaching and learning practices that the students themselves were supposed to practise with children in their preschools and schools. This aim emerged out of the experiences from the networks in the Stockholm project with active practitioners, which I have described already in the introduction and in Chapter 1. These experiences clearly showed that the only way to do teaching and learning practices in new ways was for the teacher to try out and embody new experiences and construct new habits of thinking and doing (Lenz Taguchi, 2005, 2007). In this process pedagogical documentation had become a vital tool and made possible involvement in and learning from other teachers' practices. The collective processes and collaborative constructions of meaning in the network around documentation that we put in front of us on the 'table' or projected on the 'whiteboard' were key to pursuing reconceptualised thinking around learning and teaching in higher education as well.

Hence, we decided: a) to do trans- and inter-disciplinary investigative learning with inspiration from the practices in Reggio Emilia, using aesthetic expressions and tools (Edwards *et al.*, 1998; Lind, 2005; Reggio Children, 2001, Rinaldi, 2006); b) to use and practise a multitude of different kinds of pedagogical documentation in students' work with both their own investigatory projects and with the projects performed with children during vocational training; c) to develop a multi-genre academic writing practice that we would later call the 'hybrid-writing practice' (see Chapter 6); and d) to work with multiple theoretical perspectives, doing deconstructive work and multiple readings with inspiration taken from feminist post-structuralist work in education (Burman, 2007; Burman and MacLure, 2005; Canella, 1997; Davies, 2000; Davies and Gannon, 2005, 2006; Ellsworth, 1997; Gore, 1992; hooks, 1994; Lather, 1991, 1997; Lenz Taguchi, 2000, 2004; Orner, 1992; Walkerdine, 1998).

The reconceptualised teacher education aimed at going beyond not just the theory/practice divide, but also the science/aesthetics and mind/body divides. One of the central reasons for this was the experiences from children's learning in Reggio Emilia and in the Stockholm project of how meaning-making is strongly enforced by making inter-disciplinary 'translations' between many different kinds of expressions or 'languages' to make meaning and construct knowledge (Furness, 2008; Palmer, 2009b; Reggio Children, 2001). As in the example in Chapter 4, by first talking about what you see, hear and experience on your walk home from preschool, and then making a drawing, or constructing the 'road' with construction materials, you will come to know the road back home in many different ways, inter-connecting many senses, your body and cognitive thinking. The different means of expressing and actualising what you see, hear or experience will make your knowing more complex and simultaneously accessible for a collaborative process of meaning-making with others using the documentation. Three-dimensional constructions put on a table or floor can invite others to construct with you, and might re-negotiate your understandings. Drawings and designs can be collectively studied and discussed, refined and redrawn after subsequent discussions with others.

The theory/practice, science/aesthetics and mind/body divides are also transgressed in the different kinds of documentational practices used in the learning practices with the children or students. As was seen in Chapter 4, pedagogical documentation has agency on its own, in its very construction when children move back and forth to the documentation. When the children read the documentation it will alter what they are doing in their investigations. The apparatus and techniques of documenting enforce and produce different and specific actualisations of the learning events (Chapter 3). Moreover, if you decide to record on audiotape, the children and teachers will focus better on what is said. The focus is on constructing meaning by *talking and verbalising* something into existence. But we can also sketch or draw our meaning-making into existence in an observational protocol, perhaps accompanied by notes on the process or comments spoken. If we decide to videotape, bodily movements or refined strategies in the use of hands might be our focus. We videotape because we know that we will not be able to observe the situation from all the multiplicities going on in an event which can, to some extent at least, be 'caught' in the digital video-camera. You will always have to choose on what to focus, and maybe use a tape recorder to support or supplement your observation protocol if you want to catch the inter-connections to what is said.

As students do their investigations in teacher education, they observe and document each other in the exact same manner as they do with children, as you will see in the upcoming example. They might also take photographs during the learning event or afterwards. All kinds of documentation can also be constructed afterwards, by asking the children or fellow students how they constructed or drew something and let them show and tell. Photographs of constructions and drawings can be taken afterwards. Sometimes teachers also ask children (or students) to reconstruct a series of movements, playing, dancing, etc. The reconstruction of a learning event constitutes a re-enactment – *re-living the event* – that in itself becomes an important learning process, and is not simply done to get good documentation, as one might first think. On the contrary, the re-construction of a learning event constitutes the slowing down 'circular' movement of re-enactments and counter-actualisations that make visible the striations in the pedagogical space, and sometimes also re-lives the moments when space is smoothed out and maybe a line of flight emerges (see Chapter 4).

In what follows I will show how an intra-active pedagogy is materialised as learning-practices and strategies for teaching in early childhood teacher education, trying to achieve a practice of continuous shifts between the striated and smooth pedagogical space as well as going beyond some of the binary divides outlined above. I will do this by exemplifying from the practices used in investigative collaborative learning among students during a ten-week long mathematics course. I will also introduce the various and multiple 'texts' that students produce in their pedagogical documentations during their work, and examples of how these are analysed. These texts also constitute the multi-genre 'texts' used in the ongoing hybrid-writing process that I will describe and discuss in Chapter 6. Such texts are, for instance, process-writings, collective biography and memory writings, observations from investigations done by students or children in vocational training, and various photographed, filmed and audiotaped documentation from such activities.

'Making music from a room': an investigative and inter-disciplinary mathematics course in teacher education

This part of the chapter leads up to the learning event where the students were asked to '*compose or make music from a room*', using a vast array of musical instruments, their bodies in movement, mathematical concepts and different means of documentation (Palmer, 2009a). But first I will introduce some of the other practices and strategies that we have worked with to enable a reconceptualised understanding of teaching and learning, and which deal with the fact that learning and becoming a subject cannot be separated.

Learning and becoming cannot be separated: the construction of subjectivity in learning

To engage yourself as a student in an event of 'making music from a room' constitutes a highly inter-disciplinary process of constructing knowledge, which first and foremost challenges the mathematics/aesthetics binary divide, but also the mind/body divide. This work encompasses a reconstituting of your understandings of mathematics and sometimes also your own subjectivity as learner of mathematics. All learning contents are somehow also connected to how we understand what we are and can become. Being involved in processes of learning cannot be separated from processes of becoming a learning subject (Lenz Taguchi, 2004). My colleague Anna Palmer (2009a, 2009b) has done research on how students construct and reconstruct their mathematical subjectivities in the event of composing music and doing the mathematics of the room and similar events. In a survey, Palmer (2007) has shown that only a handful out of the 105 student-teachers surveyed expressed their own relationship to mathematics in terms of considering themselves to be a 'maths person'; 47 per cent explicitly said they did *not* understand themselves as 'maths persons', while the rest had more indefinite positions in relation to maths. Students were asked to write a story about a strong memory of doing mathematics, and a young woman wrote:

> I opened the door and felt irritated, nervous and tense. I knew that I needed to ask my father for help, but why should I? I knew that the same thing would happen as always happened in school. I showed my father the problem and he just gave me the right answer right away, without any explanations. 'I feel sad and incompetent', I told

my father. 'Lena, you are not a maths person, that's the way it is. You take after your mother and her family. You simply have to accept it.'

(Memory nb 2: collective biography work)

This is the kind of very simple stories and texts that we use in the course to analyse the dominant notions and understandings of students' mathematical subjectivity. When working with such stories it is, as Palmer (2009a) shows, also extremely important to make reversal readings – reading from an opposite or different understanding than we initially make – to try to find or construct stories which are positive and creative, or make visible the aesthetic qualities and good feelings involved when doing mathematics and in other aspects of everyday life. To be able to reconceptualise your understanding, not only of maths as a subject and content of learning but also of your own subjectivity, it is important to find ways of imagining and embodying new and other mathematical subjectivities. Palmer (2009a, 2009b) shows how this is in fact possible for students to do, but it requires teaching which works with and makes use of students' previous and ongoing experiences and actively challenging them with multiple theoretical perspectives and embodied hands-on experiences of alternative ways of teaching and learning, which I will illustrate below.

When students were asked to write down the first ten words they thought of when thinking about mathematics, the most common words were connected to bad or traumatic experiences with maths: 'stomach trouble', 'tests', 'problems', 'worried', 'difficult', 'complicated', 'headache', 'problematical', 'anxiety', 'fearful', 'cold sweat', 'shakiness', 'uninteresting' and 'boring' (Palmer, 2009a). As Palmer's (2009a, 2009b) research shows, student-teachers need a lot of practice and time to be able to perform reconceptualised inter-disciplinary learning processes in mathematics, reconstituting their subjectivities, but also to be convinced that these practices are really about learning mathematics. To address the difficulties that students have to reconceptualise mathematical learning and teaching, and understand that it can be something else than the school practices they have embodied as children and students in schools themselves, the course always starts with deconstructing the dominant discourses about mathematics in teaching materials, media, movies and experience-based memory writing of different kinds. Students are encouraged to write their personal 'mathematical history', but also to write memories of specific situations when they were learning maths, such as the one above. Making visible how you have been positioned and positioned yourself in relation to maths, made legitimate the fear and negative experience of maths that was predominant among these mostly female students (Palmer, 2007, 2009a).

Mathematical thinking is understood in terms of rationality, logic, intelligence and 'smartness', which is considered predominantly male. Valerie Walkerdine (1998) has written that when girls are good at maths it is generally, and specifically by teachers, considered a result of hard work and basic learning, rather than of intelligence or 'smartness'. Being good at maths and simultaneously enjoying it can for women also be a sign of deficient femaleness, and/or not being a part of the female collective in correct ways, where conforming to consensus and the lowest common denominator is important (Lenz Taguchi, 2005). It is, however, very curious how such constructions of subjectivity in relation to the content and subject of maths is related to ethnicity and culture, writes Palmer (2009a). Self-doubt in mathematical competence is predominant among white Western European women; it is not a problem among Asian and East European women. This is because notions connected to mathematics in Western countries are tied to technique, physics and other hard sciences that have a long tradition of male dominance, whereas in other countries maths is connected to the humanistic disciplines (mainly philosophy and poetry), which in the Eastern part of the world have not been understood in gendered terms as they have in the West (Gallagher and Kaufman, 2005 in Palmer, 2009a). These circumstances are also reflected in the large and sometimes higher percentage of women professors in mathematics in Eastern European and Asian countries.

Below I offer two text examples from the maths course, which I have analysed in previous writings, that make visible the dominance of negative subjectivity constructions in relation to maths (Lenz Taguchi, 2005). The first shorter extract is from a process-writing by a student after the first maths session with the maths teacher. It is followed by my own process-writing as participating co-teacher during the same session. Students and teachers alike continuously write and exchange process-writings from any learning event over the internet on a routine basis for evaluation and collaborative learning. Typically we divide the paper in at least two columns: one for what happened or took place as a material event, and one for what reflections and theoretical connections, etc. we make. Sometimes personal reflections are separated from theoretical analysis, sometimes not. Below I will only provide personal reflections. First, though, the student's reflection:

> I finish in less than 30 seconds, and I have that wonderful feeling of getting it! The feeling of being able to solve the problem, and very

quickly. But in the same moment I realise that there is probably another much better solution to the problem than there was last time. There has to be, since I am bad at maths. I feel so frustrated that I cannot come to the best solution, the right way to think.

(Student's process-writing notes, 15 September 2003)

My reflections as co-teacher:

The mathematical discourse really showed its powerful face today. It is so obvious how Lisa [the maths teacher] is constructed as someone who knows or has got the answers, and that the students feel stupid, in some cases inferior or submissive. It seems as if they think Lisa can give them an exact answer or formula. When she won't give the answers, but tries to displace giving answers and herself, by asking the students, I can feel seconds of disbelief in her competence as maths teacher, rather than a questioning of the mathematical discourse. It seems unthinkable when Lisa states that not even within the maths discourse is it possible sometimes to give an exact answer. There cannot be something wrong with mathematics, it must be Lisa or us! . . . Even when Lisa wants to give us a problem without a correct answer, the notion of 'true maths' is hanging like a thick grey cloud over our foreheads. And it is in our bodies to the extent that we hesitate when given the hands-on material to work with. It feels as if we were afraid of being cheated. The few students who seem to like maths have another attitude in their body. They seem certain they will soon find an answer to the problem, so that they can climb over the fence of power to the side of Lisa, the maths teacher. . . . The maths discourse is like a knight on a white horse coming to rescue us from what we cannot solve ourselves. I got that feeling when one of the students said that she had to go home and ask her husband, who is a maths genius. Yes, he and mathematics can solve all problems. Another student said she felt deceived when she understood that there is no mathematical formula to solve the correlation between area and circumference. Who had deceived her? Lisa or Mathematics, or her own notion that mathematics can always give an answer?

(Lenz Taguchi, process-writing notes, 15 September 2003)

All the columns in a process-documentation can be analysed in various ways. When analysing these personal reflections it is easy to see how the pedagogical space of maths teaching and learning is rigidly structured by simply analysing the emotions at work and how they discursively position the subject in different ways. Most students, and even myself as a co-teacher, put ourselves in positions of inferiority, submissiveness and self-doubt in relation to our own competences in relation to maths. When the maths teacher tries to move us into a smoother space, and hence disrupt and displace our positionings in relation to maths by giving us problems with no right answers to them, this is not done without resistance. Some of us would rather doubt her competence and position as teacher than reconceptualise and displace the authoritarian position given to maths. We resisted understanding maths as indefinite or having multiple answers and many different logics for a long time, until our hands-on experiences made us embody another understanding. The maths teacher needed many hours of class time to convince the many doubtful students, including myself as the co-teacher, to make us re-construct our subjectivities as being 'mathematically competent'. In the smoother pedagogical space provided by the maths teacher we would slowly come to know our own mathematical logics and strategies of solving mathematical problems and thus become more confident in our own abilities to do maths.

During the course all students, and teacher-educators as well, continuously produced process-writings from what was going on in classes, collaborative work and practical investigations, such as the one shown below. As teacher-educators we used the students' processes as a basis for planning the next learning situation in the course. From time to time we collaboratively analysed excerpts of the processes with the theoretical concepts being worked with in class, whether it was gender, constructivist teaching and learning practices or power. When analysing their own or each others' process-writings and stories, students engaged in the slowing down 'circular' movement of re-enacting the events that had taken place. We practised posing counter-actualising questions such as: What are the structures that striate the pedagogical space in this piece of process writing? Are there any power-producing binary polarisations at work here that temporarily position the subject of the story in specific ways to other subjects, or to the materiality of the maths book or maths problem with its strong agentic oppressive or liberating qualities intra-acting with the subject? Or, how can I read this process or story in terms of reversed positionings? How do I read it from an angle where I look for the aesthetic rather than the mathematical? What is it that will emerge when power-production and striations are disrupted, displaced and undermined?

In this way a 'horizontal' speeding up movement could sometimes be put in motion, where power-producing hierarchies are, if only temporarily, flattened out. The speed and intensity is increased and students are able to think themselves away from, or out of, the striations and embodied habitual ways of understanding maths, and thus displace or disrupt their relationship to maths. To think *out of line* might invoke a 'line of flight' (Deleuze and Guattari, 1987). Suddenly the story of an oppressive maths practice can be read with empowering qualities and with a humorous and joyful twist.

Here is a brief example. The story below can be read in many different ways depending on the discourses you have available or use and how you make visible the material-discursive intra-action taking place in-between the student and the material objects in a specific environment. From a critical pedagogical and feminist perspective this story can be read by identifying a classical authoritarian teaching style with the teacher in total control, which directly and indirectly has oppressive effects on students in the framing of problem-solving. A heavily striated space orders and controls the bodies and relations of students that are saturated with power-production in relation to who knows and who does not know how to solve the problem on the blackboard.

> I know I can solve that problem. My body feels suddenly hot and impatient. I raise my hand and straighten my whole body so that the teacher can see me, but he lets someone else give the answer. I feel the disappointment drain my body. Now he writes a new problem on the blackboard and asks if anyone wants to solve it for him. I raise my hand again and hope to get picked. He points at me. I walk the short path between the seats up to the blackboard and it feels infinitely long. I choose a piece of chalk. It is perfectly rounded and well-used not to squeak when you write with it, but the feel of its dryness shoots an involuntary shudder through my body as I start printing with it on the board. I don't take any notice of everyone watching me and write the numbers of the solution carefully and neatly and I know it is going to be right. My back feels straight and proud, yet I lower my eyes and look into the floor as I walk back. Back in my seat I am pleased to recognise my own handwriting on the blackboard. It looks nice and I feel good.
>
> (Collective biography in a maths class, August 2006)

It is, as you probably immediately sense while reading this story, also possible to understand it from an emancipative perspective, where the mastery of maths and aesthetic aspects of writing on the blackboard work upon this specific student's subjectivity in empowering ways. Consider the inter-connections in-between the blackboard, the chalk and the student's hand thoroughly printing the numbers: in this intimate and dense affective moment of quiet intra-activity, the student proudly and humbly enacts her mathematical knowing and mastery in her writing on the blackboard and through her body-language. Maybe the feelings that are actualised are connected to her gendered position, or maybe they intersect with class or ethnicity, or simply with her own relationship to mathematics. Although we have no information on these aspects and possible intersections and intra-actions at work, the story can make us consider all the possibilities that might be at work here. As 'becoming teachers' the students can identify themselves as both students and teachers while analysing this story. They can take on and try out different positionings and relate to the intra-activities taking place. They can consider the discursive power-production in-between students, and students and teacher. Relating to my discussion in Chapter 4 about aspects of time in relation to the 'circular' and 'horizontal' movements, the students can relate to the *duration* of such a memory from childhood as it continues to produce power and meaning many years later as the students consider their own future teaching-practices.

Moving into smoother spaces: 'making music from the room'

Bringing with us our mathematical concepts, tools and strategies, and an awareness of our shifting, conflicting and changeable mathematical subjectivities, the next event was engaging in investigational inter-disciplinary mathematics. We had hired a musician who is also very knowledgeable in maths – Andreas Fantuzzi. He let the students play around with and try out a vast range of musical instruments, listen to music (ethnic folk music of different kinds, jazz, blues, classical, modern) and analyse the mathematics of different music styles. Students played around with the instruments, sounds and beats, learning as well as un-learning how to play the instruments in the 'best' or in different ways, to make music in many various ways, and in line with different kinds of mathematics. This first session was about discovering the material-discursive intra-actions in-between maths, music, your own body and the physical playing of specific and different material instruments of different size and character, and each with their unique qualities, limitations and possibilities.

Music has specific striations related to the mathematical aspects of counting and rhythms. Deleuze and Guattari write about the striated in music as that 'which intertwines fixed and variable elements, produces an order and succession of distinct forms' and organises the melodic and the harmonic (1987: 478). Music is, in their way of thinking, a combination of striated and smooth space, where the smooth is about continuous variation and development of form in the fusion of harmony and melody. The smooth space goes beyond and across the striated in the music (1987: 478). Moreover, there are habitual ways and routine behaviours in how to use each and every one of the musical instruments more or less embodied in each of the students. Some know how to play well, or a little and some do not know how to hold and handle a specific instrument at all. This can be understood as the space being stratified, when students have an already embodied relationship to an instrument or try to submit to the right ways of playing a specific instrument to make it sound right. On the other hand, an undoing of such habitual ways of using the instruments can constitute an emergence of smoothness of the space in the playing of the instruments. In the intra-action emerging in-between the students' ways of physically handling the instruments, making sounds from them and their discursive conceptualisations of what the maths in the music was all about, strange and familiar sequences of music emerged during this long session. Using pen and paper or writing on the whiteboard, some students tried to document these sequences of music, making up their own signs and using numbers and mathematical formulas.

In the next meeting students were divided in smaller groups. Ebba Theorell, a dancer and *atelierista*, which is the name given to a pedagogue who is educated to do investigative learning using different forms of aesthetic expression, came to the class to challenge and supervise the groups (Reggio Children, 2001; Rinaldi, 2006). Mathematics can also be connected to dance choreography, and choreography can also be drawn artistically or with signs and mathematical symbols, using pen and paper. After working with what can be understood as translations between music, dance choreography and mathematics, Ebba gave the students the problem of making music from the architecture of a specific room. The students engaged in discussing the different geometrical shapes, angles, lines on the walls, patterns on the ceiling, the placing of windows and doors, etc. They identified circles, squares, rectangles, triangles, rhombs, length, height, distances, areas, regularities and irregularities, which could all be translated into mathematical problems, which in their turn could be translated into music (Palmer, 2009a). The relationship between mathematics and aesthetics is very strong, writes Palmer with references to other research (Rothstein, 2006; Sinclair, 2006; Sinclair et al., 2006, in Palmer, 2009a). She quotes from the hybrid-writing of a student who was in the group making music from the hallway (see Figure 5.1):

We talked about mathematics. It's in your body although we are not always aware of that. Such a simple thing as that stairs need to have standardised measures of length and height so that we don't tumble when we walk the stairs. We don't think about that but the body remembers distances, gaps and spaces. It's not only in our thinking that we make generalisations and search for rules. The body needs regulations and classifications too.

(No. 6, 2005 in Palmer, 2009a)

Having been assigned a room to compose its music and find out its mathematics, the students began a long day of investigative practices that

Figure 5.1 Making music from the hallway.

were thoroughly documented in different ways: photos, audio- and videotapes and constructing music-sheets with pen and paper or on whiteboards. How can one make music from this huge hallway with staircases running high into the light, with the tools of your body, musical instruments, pen and paper, and mathematics? All these have their specific limitations and potentialities and striate the pedagogical space in different ways. What will happen in the (im)possible inter-connections and intra-actions in different constellations? What will emerge as infinite (im)possibilities? The students ran around in the hallway, up and down the stairs, listening to their breath becoming increasingly faster and heavier while running up and down the stairs. They found the music in the movements of their bodies, first energetic in a high key and then slowing down to a lower key, while their breath simultaneously was speeding up. The students' shoes hit the stone with specific sounds depending on the material of their soles, hard and clear or muffled and quiet. And then stopping to listen to the silence of the dust slowly moving through the cold air in this huge room with a soundless glittering through the rays of light beaming in from the top windows nearly ten metres up in the air. What instrument is this dust, my breath, my bodily movements? How can I draw that movement of my arms and legs moving back and forth while climbing the stairs, and what sound does it have? How do I catch the height of the ceiling and the rays of sun into the music?

What is taking place here is a multitude of connections in-between different material-discursive elements at work. What are the discursive associations in relation to height, light, darkness and conceptions of the size of space translated into numbers, rhythms and sounds from instruments? And how can we put into music the stamping feet or breathing heavily and regularly or irregularly and randomly? The space shifts between striations at work and smooth space emerging and occupying the room and the bodies of moving, dancing and playing students in endless improvisations. There is a confrontation between the smooth and the striated passages and alternations (Deleuze and Guattari 1987: 482). This confrontation becomes materialised and audible in this work with making music from the room. Then there are the trans- lations to paper and a construction of mathematical schemes. This kind of documentation has contradictory qualities. On the one hand the mathematics stratifies the music, but on the other hand the scheme can be read in various ways every time the piece of music is repeated. Playing the maths from the paper or whiteboard – a re-enactment – the difficulties in the translations into music turn the space into smoothness of joy, laughter and improvisations again. Every time they play their piece something new is created. In every repetition the music becomes different in itself (Deleuze, 1994).

In this learning event all different kinds of materials, space and place, human bodies and discursive conceptualisations are put in motion in relation to each other in a process of mutual transformations: transformations of music, of mathematics, of space and place and of the multiple subjectivities of students. Learning is a material-discursive intra-activity where there is an intertwining of the conceptual and the physical dimensions at work (Barad, 1999): the room, architecture, artefacts, instruments, the materiality of sound and music, light, temperature, dust, words, signs on paper, pens, breath, discursive understandings of music, maths and yourself as a musically or mathematically embodied subject. All these human and non-human organisms, performative agents or matters have agency and potentialities of their own, potentialities that will be challenged and emerging in the intra-actions taking place in this event. We cannot know how. This is a process of infinite experimentation, where the 'new, remarkable, and interesting' will replace the appearance of truth (Deleuze and Guattari, 1994: 111).

On teaching and learning beyond binary practices: in conclusion

If we embrace an onto-epistemological perspective of immanence and *one-ness*, then learning in a pedagogical space cannot be isolated to a simple cause and effect relationship. We cannot think that if we do exactly *this*, *that* is what will be the learning outcome which can then be correctly measured. This is because *this* material that we use, or *that* way of explaining or talking, is never isolated from a lot of other things going on *in-between and through* other things in the learning event in a specific moment. The 'reality' in the pedagogical space can thus be understood in terms of a thick and dense mixture of different kinds of material-discursive 'structures' that structure pedagogical spaces, and a pluralism and multiplicity of events that happen and run together or against each other – connect and disconnect – in all different kinds of directions and with different kinds of intensities, force and speed in the pedagogical space. With the tool of pedagogical documentation we gain access to some of these constructed cuts of the thickness of what is going on (see Chapter 3, p. 86), so we can 'read' the event in different ways to identify some of the many things that are happening. This has also been shown in the previous chapter in the example of the Orientation project.

If this is the way we choose to understand pedagogical practices we will become interested, not in cause and effects and learning outcomes, but rather in what is happening in the actual events taking place and what we can learn from them, as well as in formulating continuously new questions and problems to be investigated. By engaging in trying to read from the documented learning event – a cut in the splinter or fragment that has been actualised in the documentation – we can learn about some aspects of the multiplicity of what took place, which can also become the starting point for inventing a new problem or event. We can come to learn something about what happened in the inter-connections between the students conceptions of maths, music, the musical instruments, the room, the mathematical symbols; or between the child, its hand, the clay, the stick, the water and the matters, conditions of temperature, light, etc. in the space of the learning event, as in the examples from the previous chapters. The documented event is re-enacted and embodied as material-discursive knowing that can make teachers plan and arrange the pedagogical space in ways that were previously unimaginable.

I will conclude by connecting back to Ellsworth's quote at the beginning of the chapter and put her words in relation to the example unfolded above. The example of working with an inter-disciplinary and investigational approach to mathematics, involving your mathematical subjectivity as learner, shows how pedagogy is a relationship that gets 'very close in', and can 'shape and misshape lives, [and] passions for learning' (1997: 6). We cannot, however, determine exactly how and when this happens for each individual student or child. But from this repertoire of embodied learning experiences and experiences of constituting and re-constituting your subjectivity as learner in relation to different learning contents and learning and teaching practices, we can accumulate knowledge and awareness of the complexities and unpredictabilities of learning and, not the least, of the infinite possibilities and potentialities of the students we work with.

Chapter 6

The hybrid-writing process

Going beyond the theory/practice divide in academic writing

> [H]ow contexts effect our writing and how our writing affects
> ourselves are complex and multilayered.
>
> (Richardson, 1997: 5)

How do you write in a way that goes beyond the theory/practice divide? That is, how do you write so that the reader can see not only how theoretical notions and habits of thought have become materialised as habits of doing and routines in everyday practices, but also that learning from children's strategies can challenge and alter theory? Moreover, how do you write to do justice to the complexities of children's and students' strategies and thinking, and the multiplicity of different texts involved in your learning process as student-teachers?

The multiple texts produced in the reconceptualised teacher education, as shown in Chapter 5, consist of memory and narrative writing from students' personal experiences, high theory literature and research, documented learning processes with children, students' documented investigations in science, mathematics and other literature in the educational field. Is it possible to connect and interweave all these different kinds of texts that are involved in learning? In other words, is it possible to perform academic writing processes from an onto-epistemological perspective, where being is a state of interdependent becoming, and where learning and knowing takes place in-between different agencies that are trying to make themselves intelligible to each other? How does one piece of text – a series of photographs for instance – make itself intelligible to a piece of theoretical text on children's identity construction – and how does this text on identity make itself intelligible to a series of photographs of children in investigative play? And lastly but not the least: How do you put in motion writing processes that constitute emergent learning and processes of becoming in material-discursive intra-action that simultaneously meet the academic requirements?

This chapter focuses on writing processes in our reconceptualised teacher education course work as a part of the early childhood teacher education programme developed and performed since 1999. I want to show how it is possible to go beyond the theory/practice divide by using what I have called the *hybrid-writing process*. This entails making both practice and theory *material* as text, that is, being involved in materialising processes as a transformation of thinking and doing in a form of writing where theory/practice are inter-weaved in a way that also makes the text qualify as well-written scientifically coherent academic writing. In the second half of the chapter I offer a discussion of how this writing process was taken up and understood based on my research on four classes making up a total of eighty students and their open-ended written evaluations from this one-year course. They were written and handed in after the course was finished and graded, when they had gone on to new and other courses. I include these research results in this chapter because they also constitute an evaluation of this reconceptualised teacher education that has been introduced as a practice of doing an intra-active pedagogy, with examples in Chapters 2, 5 and now in this chapter. The analysis was done with a focus on how the hybrid-writing practices can be understood to be inclusive and/or exclusive of students' diverse and multiple subjectivities taking into account the vast majority of students with non-academic backgrounds that constitute the larger body of teacher education students in Sweden today (Lenz Taguchi, 2009b).

Binary thinking and writing in teacher education

The theory/practice binary divide is a very difficult obstacle when dealing with writing processes in teacher education. It is easy to see the divide between what students as teachers-to-become write about their own personal experiences and observations from vocational training in terms of lived practice, and what they are required to write from theoretical literature prescribing what teachers and practice ought to achieve. Moreover, student-teachers are also required to observe and analyse practice from a 'scientific' point of view, taking the position as researcher, just as any student in any other academic discipline. Increased academic requirements in Swedish teacher education have made visible the pre-existent divide between conventional academic writing on the one hand, and experience-based forms of writing that focus tacit knowledge on the other. These latter forms of writing have taken their inspiration from resistance modes of scientific research practices emerging from critical, feminist, post-colonial and post-structural perspectives in different fields during the last thirty years, as I have already pointed out in the previous chapter.

Laurel Richardson (1997) has been one of the most successful researchers to describe the divide between different practices of writing in the academy, and has also suggested new forms of writing. She writes on the dominant way of understanding scientific writing, in a way that we recognise from the discussions in previous chapters, as being an observer and separate entity putting her- or himself outside of the world. When writers see themselves as separated from the world, writing has the following requirements and qualities according to Richardson:

> [S]cience writing is neutral and transparent. Like a clear pane of glass, science writing presumably neither distorts nor smudges reality but aims to let the 'audience see the external world as it is' (Gusfield, 1976: 17). Reality is conceived of as standing outside and independent of any observation of or writing about it. The 'conduit' between 'thing' and 'thought' is unobstructed. This modernist belief in the externality of 'facts' and the neutrality of language, however, is out of step with contemporary *scientific* though about science and its construction.
>
> (1997: 41, original emphasis)

We recognise this way of thinking from Chapter 2 on understanding learning, where language in dominant ways of thinking is understood as representing the world as it is 'out there', but also from the discussion in Chapter 3 on pedagogical documentation discussed from different ontological and epistemological perspectives, where observations or photographs of children are sometimes understood to be representations of an aspect of the 'truth' of the child separated from the observer and the tool of observation.

In the literature on academic writing, the constructed binary divide puts forward a dominant thinking that sets norms of 'correct' academic writing – in terms of objectivity, rationality, neutrality, transparency and reference to research data – against writing that is rooted in the subjective, the personal, embodied experiences (Jung, 2005; Richardson, 1997). This divide is, in its turn, based on binaries such as mind/body, thinking/feeling, rational/affective, objective/subjective, neutral/personal, transparent/opaque, binaries that have been mentioned in different contexts throughout this book. They all, as pointed out in Chapter 1, implicitly refer to a more general binary divide between masculine/feminine and male/female. The dominant way of understanding what academic writing should be all about mostly finds its self-evident expression in positivistic writing trying to produce logical, coherent and comprehensible texts, but is also taken for granted in the academy in general as the only thinkable way of doing scientific writing (Jung, 2005: 8–9). The dominant understanding can be understood as a practice of *complexity reduction* aiming at clarity and comprehension in the writing, which is an important and indisputable quality for all writing.

In the course of the 1980s, far-reaching critiques of the notion of representation challenged the idea that language can represent or depict social reality – the paradigm of representation. The 'totalising vision' of conventional academic writing was replaced by 'concerns with contextuality, exceptions, indeterminants, and the meanings of participants' (Richardson, 1997: 13). The 'blurring of genres', advocated by Clifford Geertz in the 1980s, was one strategy that tried to undermine conventional notions of academic writing by encouraging academic disciplines to borrow ideas and methods from one another (Richardson, 1997; Jung, 2005). From a feminist perspective, dominant writing represents dominant masculine practices that exclude personal experience, emotion and the body from academic 'serious' writing. Where personal experience is actively used, it only discloses the 'recitation and revelation' of oneself is the critique from the dominant advocates (Lu, 1999, in Jung, 2005: 58). That is, writing something that is personal has nothing to do with doing science or writing scientifically. Conventional academic writing practices have rendered all writing that does not fit its standards at the same time both unscientific and feminine (Jung, 2005; Richardson, 1997). The subjective and personal interventions developed by feminist and critical pedagogies since the 1980s can hence be understood as a resistance to the normativity of masculine academic writing (Richardson, 1997).

Resistance writing, where we make use of students' experiences, voices, and different writing genres – such as personal recollections, narratives or diary entries – can be understood as a *complexity increase* in the writing process as opposed to the prevailing reductive strategies (Davies and Gannon, 2005; Ellsworth, 1992; Gore, 1992; hooks, 1994; Jung, 2005; Malka Fisher, 2001; Mayberry and Rose, 1999; Orner, 1992). One has to be careful, however. If we do not firmly work against all binary oppositions in the writing process, and especially the theory/practice binary divide, resistance writing can easily lose its complexity and indeed become reduced purely to the revelation of personal experience. An analysis and resistance of the binary logic is needed if we are to be able to perform writing that goes beyond the theory/practice binary into another way of understanding and practising academic writing.

The strategies of hybrid-writing: going beyond prevailing binary oppositions

Trying not to fall into the trap of binary thinking, the hybrid-writing process presented here constitutes a process that works with interdependent, fluctuating and disruptive movements and forces between, within and beyond the 'objective/neutral' and 'subjective/personal'. Moreover it aims at going beyond the divide between the discursive/material. Since 1999, I have developed and used the hybrid-writing process in collaboration with my colleagues in the one-year reconceptualising course that forms part of the undergraduate teacher education programme in Stockholm, which has also been described in the previous chapter. In what follows I will outline the different strategies we have used in the hybrid-writing process.

A first step to familiarising the students with the hybrid-writing process was to do readings of several text genres, such as personal recollections/memories, narratives, newspaper and journal articles, observation notes, academic and methodological texts. Our goal in the writing process has been to make active use of and work with the students' diverse subjectivities, perspectives and experiences as central contents to be theoretically analysed in relation to other contents. The readings were done from different theoretical perspectives in order to understand the production of meaning and the didactic consequences when operating within different discourses; for instance, a constructivist, behaviourist, developmental psychologist or post-structuralist discourse (Lenz Taguchi, 2006). Our objective was to 'disclose' and disrupt the belief systems underpinning these discourses, and the forms in which they materialise as practices and learning activities (Barad, 2008; Burman and MacLure, 2005; Davies and Gannon, 2005; Hekman, 2008; Lenz Taguchi, 2005, 2007, 2008d). Furthermore, the power-producing aspects of gender, class, sexuality, ability, race and ethnicity that intersect in complex ways were analysed in relation to specific teaching and learning situations and activities, from instruction in mathematics to free play (Lenz Taguchi, 2005, 2006; Palmer, 2009a). The next move was to interweave the different texts and the analyses made, to make visible how they connect and inter-connect, and how they intra-act with each other to produce new theoretical thinking or implications and consequences for practice.

In the feminist post-structuralist discourse that guided our work, the 'personal' and 'subjective', that which is 'experienced', is not excluded from what is constituted by discourse and must hence be deconstructed (Burman and MacLure, 2005). Moreover, it is not excluded from intra-activity with the material environment around the subject (Barad, 2007). This means that even when the reading and writing subject speaks/writes in line with feminist emancipatory theory, she needs to position herself as a material-discursively constituted reader and writer at the same time. Thus, 'personal' experience can neither be treated as 'self-evident', 'real', 'authentic', or 'true', nor can it be situated prior to or outside discursive practices and the way they produce meaning (Lu, in Jung, 2005: 58). Personal experience is, in the often-cited words of Joan Scott, 'not the origin of our explanation, but that which we want to explain' (1992: 38). Scott also proposes that 'experience is at once always already an interpretation *and* is in need of interpretation' (p. 37, original emphasis). Following a similar line of thinking, Davies writes:

> My authority must be reconceptualised as authority, with emphasis on *authorship*, the capacity to speak/write and be heard, to have a voice, to articulate meaning from within the collaborative discourses and beyond. This capacity does not stem from the essence of the person in question but from the positions available to them within the discourses through which they take up their being.
>
> (2000: 68, original emphasis)

Thus, the personal, the subjective and experience, in such a feminist post-structural discourse, becomes just another discursively constituted data source in need of being deconstructively analysed (Burman and MacLure, 2005).

From a material feminist perspective, discourse and material phe-nomena – such as pedagogical practices and the use of matter in such practices – are not external to one another; rather, the material and the discursive are mutually implicated in the dynamics of intra-activity. It is a relationship of 'mutual entailment' (Barad, 2008: 140). Accordingly, we understood language neither as a representation of 'truth' nor 'authentic' experience, but as a discursive materialising process that constitutes an interdependent and fluctuating movement beyond binary oppositions such as discourse vs matter or objective vs subjective. Identifying how the material is discursively constituted and how discourse is constituted by material agency in intra-activities in-between ourselves and the materials we handle constituted an important aspect of the analysis done in the writing performed.

To be able to engage in these kinds of analysis we needed to slow down the movements in the writing process by letting several readers read and comment on a text and re-write parts of it together in the collaborative supervision process. Julie Jung describes a similar process in terms of a 'revisionary rhetoric' that works with multi-genre texts, which in the juxtaposing of different text genres constitutes a writing that *listens* and constructs *delays* in the understanding and clarification of meaning, so that differences and disruptions can be heard and explored (2005: 3). For the individual writer this is about identifying how different kinds of texts from different genres intra-act with each other and observing what is produced in this intra-activity while writing and trying to interweave the different texts. For instance, this can be about trying to find the connections between a series of photographs of a preschool environment and a couple of theoretical passages on understanding how power is produced in pedagogical practices (cf. Chapter 1, pp. 24–8). When other readers of the text provide their ways of reading the different texts in the collaborative supervision, this provides delays and spaces of duration in time that open up possibilities of re-enactments, displacements, resistance but also understanding anew, creation and maybe even taking off on a line of flight.

This connects to what I have described as the dual movements of an intra-active pedagogy and its usage of pedagogical documentation: the 'circular' movement, which is about slowing down the speed of the movement or a delay imposed on our thinking-writing on different texts and events taking place in the text, to be able to re-enact the event, make counter-actualisations, identify striations, de-code; and perhaps speeding up into a 'horizontal' movement, which is creative and inventive of new possibilities (see Chapter 4, p. 99).

In relation to the material handicraft of writing, we aimed at making the writing as visible, tangible, material and accessible as possible. In order to do so, we made use of different writing models to demonstrate not only how different text genres intersect and how they produce contradictions and disruptions, but also how they merge and inter-connect in producing meaning in similar ways. During processes of collaborative supervising and re-writing of texts, the discursive production of meaning and learning was conceived as a *collaborative responsibility* rather than an individual one, that is, the text became a collaborative process. Moreover, the re-writing process was understood as materialised 'differential play' during which sentences and paragraphs took on different meanings in different contexts, in relation to other texts, or by different readers. It was like working on a quilt or patchwork of different pieces of text or fabric with different patterns that are laid out to connect to each other in different and infinitely possible ways (Deleuze and Guattari,

1987: 476). Later, they were 'stitched' or 'sewn' together by theoretical threads specifically picked up and chosen by the writer to connect the pieces in a specific way in order to construct the text. In this process, referencing was very important, to all kinds of texts and sources of information and understood as tracing inter-textual learning and intra-activities, bringing them into the open through specific theoretically driven storylines.

Our approach to formal and conventional academic composition with its required organisation of contents, etc., was ambivalent. On the one hand, we saw it as representing a long tradition of dominant modernist discourse; on the other hand, we understood it as a very concrete guide-line into which we could fit our hybrid 'text patchworks' to make them readable and understandable. With a Deleuzian and Guattarian under-standing of striated and smooth space, we can understand the formalities of academic writing as the striations that make the text a more or less familiar or safe space where you can recognise some of the trails to follow (1987: 475–8). On the other hand, hybrid-writing constitutes a process that can indeed be seen more as a 'rhizomatic' process of virus-like inter-connections and differentiations, where from time to time the space of writing becomes smooth in its inventive lines of thought, and not at all following the logic of academic taken-for-granted composition. However, what comes 'out of' the smooth space or lines of flight is then subjected to the striated space of the academic writing-composition format in order to produce a comprehensible text for others to read.

Summarising the hybrid-writing process

To perform writing processes from an onto-epistemological view we need to understand what it is to write when production of knowledge in writing is understood as different texts making themselves intelligible to each other, and achieved in the processes of living in an inter-dependent relationship with every one and everything else (Barad, 2007: 185). I have tried to 'capture' such transitory and fleeting process in the following way:

- Writing is a process of producing inter-connections and differen-tiating different meanings produced in the space in-between different kinds of texts or matter in the rhizomatic patchwork that makes up the hybrid; and simultaneously adhering to a conventional academic form, so that they can eventually become actualised in a text-production that qualifies as academic text.

- Writing is a collaborative process that takes place in the intra-active relations we have with everyone and everything in the world around us. This means that meaning is produced in material-discursive intra-active processes, rather than in the head or cognition of a single writer, and that what materialises as text production in the computer software is a result of such collaborative and negotiated material-discursive processes. Thus, the whole environment of teaching and learning, but also the context of living, can be understood as active and 'responsible' for what is produced as text.
- Writing is a continuously ongoing process that takes place also when you are not actually writing, when you talk your understandings into existence, when you negotiate your understandings with others, when you read and communicate with other texts around you – when you are in the process of living your life. The text is never finished but goes on operating even after the text is formally finished.

What are the necessary stratifications of the space of writing the hybrid, that is the practical consequences to which we inevitably needed to submit the students and ourselves as teacher educators and supervisors?

- All students are formally responsible for their own text as an end product to be graded. In this text they are supposed to describe and analyse their own learning process throughout the course period using all available texts produced during the course.
- The text consists of a mixture of or patchwork of different texts that are to be interwoven and intertwined as the writing progresses, foremost by producing theoretical analysis in the inter-weaving of different texts. Doing multiple readings from diverse theoretical positions and comparing the consequences for thinking and practising has to be a part of the analysis to show understanding of material-discursive intra-actions and materialisations.
- All the different texts have equal value in this process. But students are required to produce and interweave pedagogical documentation from practice placements as well as make use of the compulsory theoretical literature from which they are required to pick out central concepts to discuss and use throughout their analysis.
- The problem for investigation and questions to discuss or answer must be established during the vocational practice placement period at the latest, when a topic for investigation is chosen with the children and/or responsible teachers. It is the investigation with

the children that will become the main aim and topic of the thesis, although it is written as a learning process of the individual student in intra-active processes with others and the world around her/him.

- All students write 'their own' thesis but belong to a smaller group of three to five students that collaboratively 'supervise' each other's texts during the whole period. Discussions in the group, suggestions or reflections from others and reflections on what the supervision from the group did to the text are also treated as texts to make visible their impact on the learning and altering of the text and should be referred to.

- Supervision is provided by one to three teacher educators with different views on things to trouble, destabilise and challenge the student's thinking and theorising in different ways.

- The thesis takes on the form of a conventional academic composition with introduction, aim, questions, methodologies, theoretical tools, analysis, discussion of pedagogical consequences and conclusions.

The hybrid-writing process as understood by the students: evaluation analysed

In the second half of the chapter I will discuss how the students understood and took up the hybrid-writing process in different ways, using the analysis from my research made from eighty evaluations from four groups of students during the years 2003–2006 (Lenz Taguchi, 2009b). What is interesting to learn from this analysis is that the hybrid-writing process was differently embraced by different groups of students depending on their familiarity with formal academic writing processes. Some of the students who had already successfully performed writing in line with the dominant academic style resisted the process of the hybrid-writing to some extent, as shown below, whereas all students with no prior or bad experiences with academic writing whole-heartedly embraced this kind of writing process. I will focus especially on aspects of how it was possible to make use of marginal subject positionings in this writing process and non-academic texts, and the inclusive effects this kind of writing can have.

Going beyond polarisations

The long writing process during the spring semester was amazing. I got to use my own experiences *and* got the chance to comprehend the fundamentals of how an academic text is composed and written. I have become so much better at analysing and reflecting. It doesn't feel strange to write anymore. It has stopped being the burden it was when I constantly doubted my own ability as a writer. It has become fun!

This quote summarises the strongest aspect of the hybrid-writing process: the possibility to revert to personal experience while learning the fundamentals of academic writing at the same time. By stressing this 'both–and' aspect of the hybrid-writing process, we were able to overcome the binary oppositions in which these processes are usually caught. The following analysis attempts to further explain and exemplify this.

There were basically three ways in which the students distinguished the hybrid-writing process from conventional academic writing. We can best demonstrate this by the following juxtapositions:

- 'Using your previous personal experiences to learn' (this was by far the most regular general description that the students gave the hybrid-writing process) vs 'using data as representation of reality; reporting theories and facts from books'.
- 'A challenging and never-ending writing process of collaborative giving and taking' vs 'an isolated and definite individual writing process'.
- 'Acquiring skills through practice' vs 'unspoken, non-visualised knowledge'.

These phrases are the result of a deconstructive analysis of the most frequently used words and expressions in the students' open-ended evaluation questionnaires (Burman and MacLure, 2005). Here are some examples of the exact words and expressions that were used that were often constructed as a polarisation distinguishing between two ways of writing. I have chosen to call the diffuse 'other' way of writing, which was not the way we did it in this class, a 'conventional academic writing practice', in line with the above discussion:

Conventional Academic Writing Practice	Hybrid-writing Practice
'writing has no effect on me'	'writing changes me'
'lack of feeling'	'emotional', 'euphoric'

'no connection to the personal and emotional'	**'a tumbling trip through my life's history'**
'no reference to experience'	**'using experience'**
'solitary process', 'on your own'	**'participating in others' learning'**
'independence'	**'interdependence'**
'mediating practice and theory'	**'theory and practice walk hand in hand'**
'referencing theorists' thinking'	**'reflecting on your own and other students' thinking'; 'understanding things from within new discourses'**
'no analysis of power'	**'understanding and analysing the discursive production of power'**
'confirming your thinking', 'stating your opinions'	**'changing your truths'**

It is important to avoid a possible misunderstanding here. Despite the students' distinctions between what I have called a conventional academic writing and the hybrid-writing, they do not re-create a binary opposition. Especially when describing the hybrid-writing process's interdependent character in relation to theory and practice, and the relationship between the material and discourse, the students clearly went beyond a mere binary opposition between the 'objective/neutral' and the 'subjective/personal', as I will show below. This is further confirmed by the emphasis they put on how their own learning is intertwined with that of other students, how important the mutual support in these processes is, and how complex ('non-binary') the relations are that consequently follow. Hence, we need to understand that the opposites used in their evaluations were purely didactic as a result of answering questions about shifts in perspectives caused by partaking in a practice. Thus, I am tempted to suggest that it must be understood as 'natural' for the student to answer in this way, since this is also how they are taught to write evaluations.

Most students emphasised that the hybrid-writing process helped them '*understand the academic writing process*' better. This is of particular importance in relation to a study by Hultqvist and Palme (2006) that confirms that success in higher education is often a result of comprehending and mastering 'hidden agendas'; in other words, the non-verbalised and non-visualised cultural competence of students with academic backgrounds. They specifically state that, in order to allow students with non-academic backgrounds to uncover and demystify academic language and text, it must be possible for these students to revert to their own experiences as well as their motives for becoming teachers – while being challenged to confront these within academic norms at the same time (Hultqvist and Palme, 2006: 60).

The most important realisation conveyed by the hybrid-writing process seemed to lie in tying, or making connections between, personal–practical experiences and theoretical reflection. The pedagogical consequences for children in everyday practice made these connections, in a sense, material and tangible to the students as they were discussed in the slowing down movement of collaborative re-enactments. The two following quotes demonstrate this:

> It's been difficult to think from within new discourses and relate them to practices in preschool. But I've gained a lot of experience from doing things in new ways, and I see what I did before differently now – also in terms of the consequences it had for the children.

> [I]t isn't possible anymore to look at children by using essentialist categories like 'a typical 6 year old'; I have to look at all children through the contexts they are in, pay attention to the various ways in which they communicate, and need to be aware that a child is in a constant process of change.

These quotes show how students began to understand practice, reality, even the children themselves, as constituted by discourse and material-discursive intra-actions. They began to understand that discourse and theory have material consequences for children; for example, in the form of pedagogical practices, that is, in the ways that children are taught, related to and cared for (Lenz Taguchi, 2006, 2008d).

In the following quote a student writes about how she constantly challenged her own thinking throughout the continuous re-writing in the hybrid-writing process and about the re-constituting effects this had on her:

> The writing has become easier and more difficult at the same time. I have really been affected emotionally by the process of doing yet another reading of a text, which has had consequences for my own writing and so on. The writing has become a tool for both developing and complicating my own thinking. Every time I read or write I am left unsatisfied. I want to re-read and re-write again and again. I want to change through writing, because writing turns me into something new/different.

In talking about writing as a 'tool' and a process that turns you into 'something new/different', this quote illustrates the materialising aspects of the hybrid-writing process. The student goes beyond conventional notions of learning as 'progressive development' by emphasising the notion of complication and transformation within the learning process. Jung notes that 'revisionary writing' must be understood as an epistemological process that occurs within individual writers – a process that constitutes a 'writing-to-discover', rather than a 'writing-to-make-clear' (2005: 4).

Sometimes, the line we want to draw between personal writing and academic/theoretical writing is thin. In our study, all students stressed the importance of using diary entries, notes from observations, narratives and newspaper and journal articles alongside academic/theoretical texts. It helped them overcome notions of abstract, coded writing (Davies and Gannon, 2005). Whether the use of the personal was understood as a *reduction* or *increase* of complexity depended on the shades of *interdependence*, that is, the extent to which the students managed to do inter-textual and discursive analyses while weaving together their multi-genre texts. Not a single student considered either personal writing or theoretical writing satisfying by itself.

It is, however, very interesting to say something about the differences in the take up of doing personal reflections, memory writing and narrative writing. The few students with prior academic experience (one to three in each group had taken a year or more of different courses) said they enjoyed writing personal texts, but considered this mainly a separate activity that they obviously valued less than the theoretical texts they insisted on focusing on, regardless of what the rest of the group was doing. In fact, they very much questioned the idea of combining different text genres and in some cases forcefully maintained the importance of separating the 'subjective' from the 'objective'. Judith Butler (2000) describes the antithesis between the subjective and the objective as a defining moment of Western thought. It creates a logic in which theory precedes practice, and the abstract the concrete. Butler writes on Hegel's challenge to Kantian thinking when he uses the example of a person who thinks that he can learn to swim by learning first what is required before entering the water. She goes on:

> The person does not realise that one learns to swim only by entering the water and practising one's strokes in the midst of the activity itself. Hegel implicitly likens the Kantian to one who seeks to know how to swim before actually swimming, and he counters this model of a self-possessed cognition with one that gives itself over to the activity itself, a form of knowing that is given over to the world it seeks to know.
>
> (2000: 19)

Butler writes that we need to go beyond the dominant logic of knowing before doing and theory preceding practice by suggesting we engage in performative action where meaning is materialised as performance, and, at the same time, constructed through performance. This corresponds to the material feminist notion of a 'performative metaphysics', that is of meaning as an ongoing 'material-discursive . . . intra-active performance' of the world (Barad, 2008: 139). Students with prior academic experience were also particularly eager to 'understand' new theoretical concepts in 'correct' ways. But at the same time they were more anxious concerning their 'achievements' than other students. One of these students wrote:

> It is distressing – even if challenging – for me to write now, mostly because I struggle with understanding and using post-structuralist theory. I think I have improved my writing a little, but I struggle with the same problem over and over again. I am constantly frustrated because I forget and lose my understanding of concepts and theories and am worried that I can't exactly write what I want to say. I have to re-write my texts over and over again. It is very tiresome.

This quote talks about theory as a separate domain, without relation to practice, experience or even other students' texts. The struggle that is expressed here concerns the incapability to formulate one's thoughts in a way that communicates them well or correctly. This stems from an understanding of writing that finds itself in conflict with the notion that writing itself produces and materialises meaning. Instead, writing is understood as a process in which certain thoughts and things are to be represented 'as they are'. This stands in stark contrast to one of the previous quotes in which a student described writing – in line with Barad's (2008) intra-activity between matter/text, subject and learning – as a process that turned her 'into something new/different'.

The collaborative dimension of the hybrid-writing process and the inclusion/exclusion of subjectivities

In order to move beyond *either* 'subjective' *or* 'objective' writing, almost all students emphasised the importance of the collaborative dimension of the hybrid-writing process, most notably the collaborative supervising and re-writing processes mentioned above. Both the intellectual challenge and the collaborative responsibility involved were commonly welcomed, in particular as an improvement to the writing experience of the isolated individual in conventional academic writing.

Of particular importance for our project, however, was the fact that the collaborative dimensions of the hybrid-writing process allowed the inclusion of students that identified their positionings as often being marginalised: students with ethnic backgrounds other than Swedish, students with ability limitations, homosexual or bisexual students. Making difference visible and productive in the learning processes, and an element of the general learning process, encouraged students of, for instance, different ethnic and/or cultural backgrounds to talk and write about dissimilarities in their everyday school experiences, in their ways of perceiving and educating children, in their experiences of learning and learning environments, and in their approaches to writing. The following quote reflects the dual burden that minority students often have to carry: being reduced to a member of the minority they represent; and being expected to educate others about being marginalised.

> As a homosexual, I have shared my experiences with regard to issues of homo-, bi- and trans-sexuality. This has not always been without problems. Yet, others have said that they were really happy to have me in their group since they now read literature about queer perspectives, cultural studies, etc. This feels both good and scary. Like, what would have happened if I had not been there? And what happens in groups when there is no one like me?

This quote painfully demonstrates our failure to displace the 'normal' in order to make it as 'strange' as the marginal. It also demonstrates our failure to show that we all find ourselves in marginal positions at times, irrespective of class, race, ethnicity, sexuality, gender or ability. As a consequence of the analysis of these evaluations, this has been a topic for intense discussion in the teacher-educator team.

When students call the experiences they have gone through in the course of our study '*bewildering*', or describe them as '*a tumbling trip through life's history*', I believe that we can interpret this as a success of critical/ feminist pedagogical practice. Students make 'themselves visible', and are 'defining themselves as authors of their own world', as Ellsworth puts it (1992: 100). And this is not reduced to simple 'emancipation'. The students also become aware of the discourses that construct them as subjects, and they begin to perceive themselves differently. One student made this explicit by stating that she went from feeling 'in the hands of the teachers' and 'not being able to make a difference [in class]' to the understanding that,

> language and text constitute us here and now . . . depending on how we position ourselves and how we are positioned by others as 'agentic' subjects. This realisation has really made a vast difference for me in all areas of my life.

The following quote reveals another transgression of the binary opposition of 'objective/neutral' vs 'subjective/personal':

> What has been most challenging and rewarding for me have been the collaborative processes, in which I got to analyse my own words and thoughts and those of others. . . . I have learned not to take anything for granted, that my truth is mine, and that I can change and transcend it.

We can interpret this as a realisation that individual learning is the result of a collaborative process. Dependence on others for individual learning carries an important 'both–and' aspect that goes beyond the 'either–or' aspect implicit in the binary opposition of 'the subject vs the collaborative'. This 'both–and' aspect also reminds us of the process of subjectification, analysed by Foucault and embraced by feminist post-structuralism (Butler, 1997; Davies, 2000; Foucault, 1982). The process of subjectification describes how 'we are made' and 'make ourselves' into a subjectivity within or against the dominant discourses in a particular socio-historical context (Davies, 2000). Davies has used the metaphor of a '*textual weave*', indicating that we are woven into, and weave ourselves into, the social fabric. Mostly the weaving goes *with*, but sometimes also *against* the grain. In my opinion, this correlates to learning as an intra-active process between different subjects that involves thought and speech as much as physical and material interaction.

As shown above, the hybrid-writing process proved successful in terms of including students with ethnic minority, non-academic and working-class backgrounds. They finished their courses and degrees. The common feature in their evaluations was that they felt that they had mastered a kind of academic writing that gave them access to many positions within and outside academia. About half of the students considered doing graduate studies. (Even though many remained unsure about whether this was something they really wanted to do.) Another important aspect for many students was that they had been able to develop a self-understanding in terms of encompassing multiple subjectivities – this is reflected in the following quote:

> During this class I have had the possibility to learn so much that has helped me understand myself and others better. In the documentary work [with multi-genre texts] I have been able to make myself and others visible, which has been a euphoric experience. My subjectivity has changed and grown, and I have discovered concepts and tools for being different in different contexts. I am multiple!

The feminist post-structuralist notion of multiple subjectivities makes it possible to be both working class *and* academic. Jung writes that 'because genre is inextricably tied to the construction of social identity . . . and because multigenre texts juxtapose more than one genre, they can be studied to enhance our understanding of identity (dis/re)formation' (2005: xiii). In a similar fashion, the hybrid-writing process makes it possible for students to write themselves 'anew', 'revise' their positions, and get access to multiple subjectivities, without the necessity to 'escape' or 'surrender' their *minority subject* positions in order to become an *academic subject* (hooks, 1994).

Exclusionary tendencies within the hybrid-writing process

Unfortunately, we cannot deny that the hybrid-writing process has its exclusionary tendencies too. These concern mainly students with an academic family background and/or prior academic experience. When students with such academic backgrounds entered the programme, some of them were confident writers within the 'objective/neutral' dominant academic writing-discourse. They soon felt that the hybrid-writing process challenged their position. In the following quote, one student questions the notion of the hybrid-writing process in a way that echoes the views of many established academics:

> I agreed to participate in an open long-term writing project, but I found it difficult and odd to write on a thesis before you even know what you will be focusing on and what your aims will be. . . . I hope you don't think that this method of writing [the hybrid-writing process] is absolute or that it is perfect for everyone.

This quote comes from a student who wanted to write along conventional academic lines and who did not want to partake in collaborative supervising and re-writing. In the context of our study, this made her feel excluded and marginalised. Nonetheless, she continued to refuse 'weaving texts' and kept on working on her – very good – conventional academic writing instead. One of her quotes also reveals the shaky self-confidence that is characteristic of many students with academic backgrounds and/or experiences:

> I feel frustrated that I am on this low level in the teacher education program. 'Intellectually' I feel ready to start a Ph.D. programme now! However, sometimes my self-confidence wanes and I am convinced that I won't be accepted into any programme, that my teacher education will go to hell, and that I will end up sorting mail at the post office.

It is often the case that students with academic backgrounds – who generally possess a high level of self-confidence when it comes to writing – express strong fears about not succeeding in their studies or about being criticised by their teachers or other students. This became particularly pronounced when these students were confronted with the hybrid-writing process. After they had mastered conventional academic writing practices to a point where they felt like 'competent writers', they obviously felt challenged by this new approach and were reluctant to abandon the skills they felt they had earned. They definitely valued the hybrid-writing process less than conventional academic writing. Some might have even seen it as inferior 'feminine' writing, judging from their comments on it in various situations.

When these students decided to participate in the collaborative supervising and re-writing process, they proved much more self-conscious than others. They took all the questions and comments very personally.

It seemed like they had more to 'live up to' and to 'defend'. These experiences can be related to Valerie Walkerdine's conclusions about British middle-class girls' complex and fragile self-confidence (1998). Walkerdine shows, for example, that no matter how good these girls' grades in mathematics were, they did not think of themselves as mathematically talented. For a middle-class girl, being a 'good student' seems to be taken for granted and appears to be a 'must'. As a result, there seems to be an ever-present risk of failure. For a working-class girl, however, not doing well academically matters little because nothing else is expected of her anyway (Walkerdine, 1998).

The problems that the hybrid-writing process created for students with academic backgrounds reveal that, irrespective of what kind of pedagogy you employ, it will establish its 'rules of reason' in the classroom (Ellsworth, 1992: 90) – rules that imply certain norms and hence the danger of excluding those who do not fit in. Particularly from a feminist perspective, we must recognise that, in this sense, experiences of students always take place within a context of asymmetrical power relations that emerge through the flow of events taking place in one way or the other. No order that is temporarily constructed is ever entirely symmetrical. In order to avoid exclusion we must prevent the establishment of orders by constantly trying to make them visible and contest them.

Summary and conclusion

The hybrid-writing process can be understood as able to dismantle the borders between 'normality' and 'marginality' in terms of positionings in relation to the handicraft of academic writing and understanding yourself as an academic. One way of understanding this is that dismantling borders is achieved by integrating marginal positions of both human subjects and non-academic texts instead of silencing them, and by allowing all multiplicities of texts and subjectivities to be at work in the hybrid text. From an onto-epistemological perspective I understand this in terms of our managing to flatten out the hierarchal positionings in the writing that previously was stuck in asymmetrical power-producing binary divides, such as theory/practice, mind/body, objective/subjective etc. In the flattening out of the multiple-genre texts that were used, as well as the shifting and complex subject positionings in the collaborative supervision and meaning-making processes, there is no true or privileged position from which to read a learning event.

This also means that the stratifications that are always present in the space of writing an academic text – everything from writing from left to right or constructing words into sentences, to following a scientific storyline of aims, questions, methods, theories and analysis – are simultaneously productive and at work to achieve a comprehensible text, as they from time to time are smoothed out as new inter-connections between different texts are identified or invented. The stratifications at work supply to the students a sense of safeness around which to negotiate the multi-genre texts with all their multiplicities of intensity of detail, affect and theoretical complexities. This has led, as we have learnt from evaluations, to increased self-esteem and self-confidence, especially amongst non-academic and marginalised students. In turn, their overall academic performance increased and these students did not drop-out of the teacher education programme.

Although we reached our objective in this sense, we cannot deny that the hybrid-writing process implies exclusionary potential too. This reminds us that all practice produces power in different ways and that the answer to exclusionary aspects of conventional academic writing cannot lie in establishing new exclusionary norms of writing, or for any other pedagogical practice for that matter. Much rather we must engage in continuous processes of transformation as suggested by so many feminist writers before me (Ellsworth, 1992; Gore, 1992; Grosz, 2005; Hekman, 2008; Lather, 1991, 2007). This leads up to the last chapter of this book, which aims to discuss the politics and ethics of an intra-active pedagogy. How can we think about ethics in relation to these kinds of practices based on an ontology of immanence and an onto-epistemology where we grant all agencies in the intra-active processes equal value?

Chapter 7

An ethics of immanence and potentialities for early childhood education

> An ethics committed to univocity is therefore an ethics of potentialities.
>
> (Colebrook, 2002: 99)

I will turn to questions of ethics in this last chapter and ask: what are the ethical consequences of different theories of learning and development that belong to different ontologies and epistemologies? Such questions are, I think, not discussed enough in the field of education at large and especially not in early childhood education. In my feminist philosophical and post-structural theoretical readings I have been confronted with this question a number of times in relation to my teaching and research practices. The material feminist researchers Alison Jones and Kuni Jenkins (2008) have asked a very specific and interesting question that has inspired me in writing this chapter: *what reality* is invoked and materialised before us depending on what ontological and epistemological position we take?

Picking up on Jones and Jenkins's (2008) question, I will continue to use practical examples to analyse them from different learning and developmental theories belonging to different epistemologies and ontologies, but this time will provide discussions on the ethical implications. Before I do that I will introduce yet another couple of concepts from Deleuze and Guattari (1987, 1994) that I find helpful in relation to the question of ethics and how ethics relates to some of the general aims of education. In the second part of the chapter I will provide an example of how different ways of understanding pedagogical practices produce different ways of planning and different actions with very different ethical implications. The chapter ends with outlining in more detail what I have chosen to call an *ethics of immanence and potentialities*. The concept of an ethics of potentialities is borrowed from Claire Colebrook from one of her writings on Deleuzian philosophy (2002: 99).

The politics and ethics of going beyond binary divides in education

In what follows, I would like to say something about how an onto-epistemology and intra-active pedagogy challenges the contemporary reductive, universal, goal-oriented and outcome-based practices. Going beyond the dominant power-producing binary divides in education can mean that we can be seriously concerned with challenging the *possibilities and potentialities* of children, students and teachers, instead of putting the energy on reproducing knowledge and measuring outcomes. An intra-active pedagogy based on an ethics of immanence and potentialities is focused on the inter-connections and intra-activities between and beyond the binary divides of science/philosophy, science/aesthetics, language/material, objective/subjective, rational/affective, masculine/feminine, adult/child, etc.

Here I will use science/philosophy as an overarching divide when discussing the ethics and politics of going beyond the divides. If I allow myself to simplify somewhat, I think it is fair to say that in the context of education, science has been given a higher value and status over critical reflection and, if you will, philosophy and the art of thinking. This is materialised in terms of philosophy and critical reflection being given significantly and increasingly less time – space in the schedules of schools. In other words, educational practices can be understood to have become increasingly reductive and simplified, in terms of measurable knowledge goals and even increasingly closed off as systems, rather than having evolved in the direction of giving more attention and value to openness, complexity, difference, multiplicity and creativity in our thinking and acting (Biesta, 2008; Osberg and Biesta, 2009; Semetsky, 2008).

Deleuze and Guattari (1994) describe how science and philosophy depend on each other, but are different and accomplish different things. They invented a new concept to show this difference. When they talk about concepts in science, they call these *functives* instead, whereas the word 'concept' is ascribed to philosophy. Well-known functives are, for example, 'molecule' in chemistry or 'cognition' in psychology. In science the object of interest is functions of the words used. These functions are presented as propositions in discursive systems, such as botanic systema-tisations of plants or different stages of maturity in the development of the child. In these systems all functives are organised in such a way as to refer to each other in a logical and thus predictable way. This enables science to communicate from within its system of functives, and thus we all know what it is we are talking about. In education, children are taught systems of functives in different sciences and can build increasingly more abstract and scientific knowledge constructs. Constructivist learning theorists from Jean Piaget and Lev Vygotskij to more contemporary theorists have shown how children pick up scientific functives generally starting on a lower abstract level and can be challenged with an increased level of abstraction, according to constructivist learning theories (Marton and Booth, 1997). Ideally, science does not explicitly depend upon philosophy to uphold these systems of references and functions of functives, according to Deleuze and Guattari. However, science is, in their thinking, totally dependent on what they understand as a philosophical way of thinking in order for the scientist to think 'outside of the box' and the agreed upon discursive system, and invent new ways of thinking that might alter or create new scientific discursive systems. In the practice of philosophy on the other hand, we are dealing with inventing new concepts and lines of thoughts that are not part of already established systems of thought. Moreover, philosophical concepts, according to Deleuze and Guattari (1994), are not about finding representations of an 'essence' of reality as functives in science, but of assembling knowing as complexities of affect and material-discursive embodied lived experiences. This means that philosophical concepts are simultaneously connected to actual reality of experience and possibilities and potentialities that have been previously unimaginable. Or, in other words; philosophical concepts derive from the experiences of lived as well as imagined and invented life.

If we put functives and concepts in the context of education, we must of course be teaching the systems of functives in the different sciences of physics, biology, literature, etc., since these systems are those upon which we build scientific production and progression. These can also be fairly easily measured and evaluated, because of their logic and referential character. To be able to achieve this, constructivist learning theories can be understood as adequate methods of teaching and learning. But for children and students to practise thinking from their lived and possible experiences, and to practise being inventive of concepts as well as functives in the different sciences, education needs to entail more than reproduction of functives in scientific systems. In short, education needs also to provide philosophy and the practice of thinking, reflecting and being inventive. So far these practices have been kept apart, or philosophical thinking is not practised. This happens in education at large, although we know that science would not have been able to progress at all if scientists had not repeatedly gone beyond the divide between science and philosophy and engaged in philosophical thinking.

In terms of politics then, it seems important that our civil servants and politicians consider how education can entail more critical thinking and philosophy, not the least if they are interested in improving educational results and scientific achievements for society at large.

In this perspective, how can we teach going beyond this divide, which entails simultaneously dealing with the systems of functives and creating new concepts? How can we teach in a way that make children and students simultaneously think critically and inventively in collaboration and by themselves in intra-action with the material environment, as they learn key functives in different disciplines and sciences? And lastly, how can we teach both of these things and be aware of the ethics involved in teaching – an ethics that is inclusive of children's and students' different strategies, experiences and thinking, as it simultaneously challenges their potentialities?

Pedagogical and ethical consequences of different theories and ontologies: an example

In the following section I will provide an example from the Orientation project which was also referred to in Chapter 4. The three teachers involved in this project were Susanne Hjelm, Michaela Sundberg and Solveig Åkerström, who I have understood as collaborative learners in my doctoral project on pedagogical documentation (Lenz Taguchi, 2000). I will unfold different ways of reading the drawings made by the children from different learning and developmental theories in the realm of an ontology of transcendence, and then move on to read the event and drawings from the perspective of an onto-epistemology and an intra-active pedagogy.

The example taken from the Orientation project involves a group of 5 year olds and concerns changing places at the table, which is used as a combined table for work and eating lunch. At lunchtime, these particular children sat in a group of ten, always at places assigned to them. Over a period of several days, two girls repeatedly asked to change places with another child at the table. The preschool teachers decided to incorporate this request into the on-going Orientation project. They wanted to ask the children to draw a map in order to show who to change places with. On this particular morning, the 5 year olds were asked to perform the following task: 'Please draw a map of the person you want to change places with. Don't tell anyone who it is while you are working, so we can guess later.' The children enthusiastically agreed to this request, although, as you may see, the task was very problematic. Was it actually a map of a person, the table or the room that was requested of the children? Below I will briefly outline the multiple readings from different developmental and learning theories that the teachers and myself as a participating researcher made, to be able to discuss the different consequences they provided for our choice of action and the ethical implications that arose in relation to such choice.

A developmental psychological reading: taken-for-granted and laying most readily at hand

The initial comments and questions about the drawings were very much in line with a developmental psychological perspective. This is simply because these were habits of thinking that in 1997, when this happened, were most available to teachers. In traditional Swedish ECE practices, but also and in line with some of the (then) current thinking on DAP, children's drawings have been seen as expressions of their inner psychological and cognitive development through essentialist and universal stages. According to this line of thinking, the quality of the work will naturally improve as the child matures mentally, psychologically and physiologically. Preschool children will be able to draw in characteristic preschooler ways, limited by the cognitive abilities expected for their young age and stage of development. Because of our taken-for-granted ideas about expected 'limitations' in preschoolers' abilities to represent their ideas graphically, we were all surprised and fascinated that two of the drawings were from what we regarded as aerial perspectives (Olof, Figure 7.1 and Irvin, Figure 7.2). One teacher commented that it is difficult for a small child, or even an adult, to draw a room from above, imagining oneself simultaneously at and above the table. According to Piagetian and constructivist learning theories, both abstract thinking and representational drawing develop around the age of seven or later, so these aerial drawings by 5 year olds quite understandably seemed 'unnatural' to us at first.

What does sticking to a taken-for-granted discourse on developmental psychology do to our thinking and actions? If we were to follow the system of these Piagetian functives and their logic of reference, we would very likely start to judge the performances of the children according to this system of thinking. We would treat the drawings as representations of each child's developmental stage and state of maturity. This was what happened as we started to compare the different map-drawings to each other.

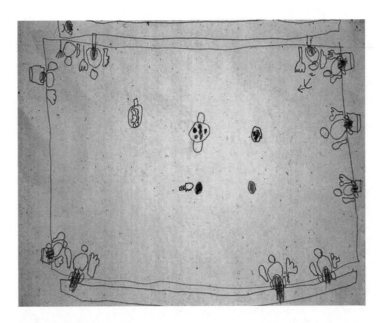

Figure 7.1 Olof's drawing.

Figure 7.2 Irvin's drawing.

Figure 7.3 Vanessa's drawing.

As we listened to the tape with our initial analysis we could hear that we all thought that the boys, who made drawings from above (Olof) or almost from above with profile (Irvin), had actually drawn maps, whereas the girls (Vanessa, Margret, Juliette and Ann) had addressed the task in various ways, but had *not* drawn maps, which we believed at the time they had been asked to do. We talked about Vanessa's and Margret's drawings as 'problematic' and 'lacking' as adequate responses to the question the teachers had put to the children. When reviewing the tape of the drawing session we heard the teacher describing the task: 'Please draw *a map of the person* you want to change places with. Don't tell anyone who it is while you are working, so we can guess later'. The teacher's instruction to 'draw a map of the person', if considered separately, actually made little sense, even if the children were familiar with maps, since maps typically represent place locations, geographic features or routes; they do not, as the term is commonly used, represent people. To make sense of the teacher's instructions, Vanessa's drawing obviously focused on '*the person*'

Figure 7.4 Margaret's drawing.

and '*who it is*', so she simply drew the face of the person she wanted to change places with. As Vanessa later explained, she wrote the name of this boy 'as a whisper beside his ear, since we mustn't tell anybody who we want to change places with'; so it became obvious to us that Vanessa had, indeed, followed the teacher's directions as she heard them.

Organising our practice from an essentialist developmental psychological theory would probably have meant that we would have thought that, because the child matures naturally from within, we must be careful not to try to demand more of the children than their current level of maturity permitted. To stay with such an essentialist view on children's development and learning would, in my view, mean that we would abandon the children after judging them in relation to their developmental progression and status as normal or lacking. This produces a pedagogical practice that normalises children in accordance with dominant views on universal development, with no room for collaborative meaning-making with children.

A constructivist reading of logical and spatial correspondence

Eager to challenge our initial readings, however, we continued with reading the event from a constructivist epistemological perspective based on Marton and Booth's (1997) theories on children's map-drawing. This constructivist learning theory states that a map drawn by children must include, at least to some degree, both *logical and spatial correspondence*. Logical correspondence means that all the objects in the mapped area must be present in the drawing. The larger the number of objects, the higher the degree of logical correspondence required. Spatial correspondence refers to the map drawer's awareness of the relative space between the objects in the drawing and how this corresponds to reality. The higher the degree of spatial correspondence, the more the map represents actual spatial relationships in the real world. According to Marton and Booth (1997), children typically develop logical correspondence first and spatial correspondence later. Logical and spatial correspondences are not well developed until about the age of 7. According to the theory, a drawing that has neither logical nor spatial correspondence is not a map.

Applying this definition, then, we looked at the drawings again and could see that Vanessa's and Margret's drawings did not qualify as maps, and Juliette's and Ann's drawings included little evidence of logical or spatial correspondence. However, both Olof's and Irvin's drawings had a high degree of both logical and spatial correspondence. It was clearly the boys who drew maps that we prized most highly, either in terms of a naturally inborn talent or a highly developed technical skill using logical and spatial correspondence. We saw the girls' drawings as typically (for girls) focused on relationships (faces, chairs with hearts), or simply 'plain' or 'unelaborated' and generally 'lacking' compared to the boys' drawings.

Again, if we would have followed the logic of the constructivist system of functives, this would have meant judging the drawings in accordance with the functives of logical and spatial correspondence. Thereby some drawings would qualify as maps and some would not. Asking the children to read each other's maps, we could have made the children aware of what drawings could be more easily considered a map and the reasons for this. After analysing all the drawings with the children, we could have asked them to make new drawings from what they had learned, guiding the children to understand that an aerial overview with logical and spatial correspondence would make the better map for other children to be able to read. Eventually all the children might have understood how a map is best drawn, whether they learn it by practising or as they mature from within. The constructivist learning theory is close to the essentialist developmental psychological theory in some ways. It allows for an identification of the child's strategies in order to direct the child to choose the best strategies and learn the system of logic with its central functives. Such a strategy is very much in line with the emergent learning theory called 'learning or lesson studies' (Marton and Tsui, 2004).

In terms of ethics, both these theories will entail a strong element of judging and valuing the drawings in relation to pre-formulated criteria, goals or scientific functives such as logic and spatial correspondence. Such judgement generates children's success or lack in relation to what is required for the assignment or content to be learnt. The best ways of drawing maps are known beforehand in the consciousness of the adults, and the aim is to try to make children aware of what are the specific qualities of a map drawn the right way. Marton writes in the preface of his colleagues' book that: 'This book contains a number of studies where adults (pedagogues, teachers) *help* children to learn something *pre-decided* that the adults consider good and important for children to learn' (Marton in Pramling Samuelsson and Pramling, 2008: 1, my translation and emphasis).

A discursive and social constructivist reading

It was our resistance to judging and valuing the drawings in any way, and especially with strong gender biases, that made us move on to a social constructivist or discursive reading of the drawings. As already outlined in the introduction of this book social constructivism, or social constructionism, as it is sometimes also referred to, is basically a social science theory in anthropology, ethnology and cultural studies, whereas constructivism generally refers to psychological and cognitive and social constructivist learning theories (Steffe, 1995). Inspired by the practices in Reggio Emilia, the three teachers were very aware of the importance of making visible differences in the strategies of children as part of how they have been culturally 'coded' and not attempting to value one strategy over the other, in line with the way they thought about collaborative learning, democracy and inclusion with inspiration from Reggio Emilia. As the teachers incorporated their reading of the book on maps by social constructivist historian Dennis Wood (1992), they could see that the drawings had a particular social function in this theory: to convey the specific information that each child wanted to communicate. In line with a social constructivist perspective, they tried to focus on the general idea of a map and on these children's drawings as a construction of the social world as each child experienced it. The teachers began to see each drawing as an expression of a particular child's understanding of the task and of map construction, and we were able to do more elaborated gender readings of the drawings (Lenz Taguchi, 2006, 2008d).

The social constructivist reading would have consequences for planning the upcoming work. The plan for the next activity was in fact chosen in line with this theoretical perspective. The teachers assembled the children to ask them how they understood what a map is (as a cultural and discursive construction), and also to make them aware of different cultural expressions of maps historically, as well as identifying what cultural symbols and signs can be used in map drawing. The children then suggested inviting children from another group to 'read the maps' to see what happened. To the surprise of the adults, these younger children knew exactly how to read the drawings of Vanessa and Margaret, because they knew of the social relationships between all the children at the preschool and could thus make correct guesses.

As you can see from this example, a materialisation of practice from different theories of learning and development such as developmental psychology, constructivist learning theory and social constructivist theory has very different consequences for what teachers do and say next in their work. Our epistemological frame of mind, so to speak, will make us address the children and plan the learning activities very differently, which will also have different ethical consequences. Note that all of the three theories used above are based on an idea of a clear-cut separation between the child and the adult in the learning situation, as if all the learning takes place inside of the child although culturally coded, etc. These theories also take for granted a separation between what the children drew and their emotional desires to switch places with a specific person, and the material reality where this particular table is a central matter. This brings me to imagine this map-drawing event from an onto-epistemology.

Re-living the event anew from an onto-epistemology and an intra-active pedagogy

How might we understand this event from the onto-epistemological perspective that this book has tried to outline and from an intra-active pedagogy? What happens if we try to read this event anew, re-live it and try to imagine the different map drawings as materialised actualisations of the question posed to the children? What happens if we try to imagine and re-live the event in the inter-connections between the children and the different matters involved in this event? Jones and Jenkins ask a very interesting question about how to imagine and re-live what we can understand as a new reality:

> Can a new *reality* appear when we read between the lines – or must we only see multiple discursive, speculative, 'realities'? Can new actors *materialise* in texts, and become real in the past when they were not there before – or can the actors only be discursive subjects?
>
> (2008: 126, original emphasis)

Transferred to this event, we can ask ourselves about the possibility of a new reality and of new actors materialising in the drawings and the documentation of this event. When listening to the tape of the drawing event and realising that what the question really asked for was a 'map of the person' and not of the room or table, we realised that we had not discussed with the children what the concept of map might be all about during the weeks that had passed on the project so far. Nor had we as adults in-between ourselves discussed this, or even considered if it was really a map that we wanted the children to draw, and if so, what such a map might look like. Becoming aware of this with the help of the documentation of the videotape and audiotape, we realised that what went on during that event of drawing might in fact be a *totally different reality* from what we had thought it was.

There was nothing in the discursive-material preconditions that would have made the children draw what we as adults might consider a map. Thus, this realisation evokes the reality of a totally different learning event, which was actually *not* about drawing maps. Hence, no maps were actually drawn that day, if we think about it critically. This was because there was no common discursive idea about a map and how it might materialise as a drawing, other than the taken-for-granted and totally unproblematised way that each of the adults encompassed. Rather, what the children actually drew was an answer to the reality of the material-discursive preconditions at play in the learning event of that morning. This is what needs to be analysed for teachers to do the practice in line with the reality of the children in intra-action with the material preconditions in the environment of the preschool, and thus making the practice more ethical.

Practising an ethics of immanence and potentialities by becoming-minoritarian in the event as child or as pen . . .

If the teachers and I, as a participating researcher, would have looked more closely at the reality of the material-discursive preconditions at work that day, what we would have observed was the thickness, pluralism and multiplicity of the actual event. We would have experienced and sensed the event in many different ways. Here I want to introduce another concept from Deleuze and Guattari (1987) – *becoming-minoritarian* – to discuss the ethics involved when we engage in the process of re-living and re-enacting a pedagogical event with the help of pedagogical documentation. In this discussion I will take the idea of reading the event from the point of view of the child or pen a step further, which has stronger ethical implications in Deleuze and Guattari's way of understanding these things philosophically. What do I mean when I say that we should read the event from the point of view or perspective of the child? Do I mean empathy? Or do I mean taking the role, acting and being the child? When en-acting or re-living the event anew through the documentation, we *don't* want to simply make a reading from the children's lesser valued position and give them voice. Instead, what we want to do is to *re-install* ourselves in the event and as teachers engage in a process of becoming in the event as child – *becoming-child*. Contrary to taking a position of someone else, or trying to become the other, this is about re-installing yourself in the event to become different *in yourself;* that is, to put yourself in a process of *change and transformation* to be able to experience the event differently.

Deleuze and Guattari (1987) show how what they conceptualise as the *majoritarian* refers, not to a greater relative quantity as you might first think, but to the determination of a state, standard or norm: a state of domination and habits of thinking and doing things. *Becoming-minoritarian or minor* (which is another translation to English) is about a process where we as, for instance, teachers put ourselves in a state of *becoming-other* – becoming-child, becoming-pen or becoming-clay, etc. Contrary to taking the position or role, acting or *being* the child, pen or clay, the focus of becoming-minoritarian is about *change and changes in ourselves,* and also changes in the clay becoming softer when being moulded, or the pen being used, etc. Processes of change are what *becoming-minoritarian* is about, Deleuze and Guattari write, and they clarify by saying that each process of change and becoming *is* a *becoming-minoritarian* (1987: 291). May and Semetsky (2008: 152) clarify, with reference to Deleuze, that this is about becoming *other in ourselves – becoming transformed*. Hence, I am not acting or taking the position or role of the child, which would mean that I could at any time step out of this position and act or take the role or the position of the adult teacher again, as if these were separate and distinctly different from each other. Moreover, it is not about *being* the child, because then the question arises if I am no longer an adult, when I am being the child? Rather, as an adult becoming-child or becoming-clay means that I am still an adult but change and become different in myself, as I re-enact an event where the child for instance moulds the clay. I am activating my imagination of what clay might feel and how it changes, and what the child might think and feel and how the moulding of clay affects her or him depending on the material-discursive intra-actions taking place in the room at this moment. Moreover, I take on the affective experience of moulding clay in intra-action with hands, other materials and the discourses that are at work in the pedagogical event, and it will make me become different in myself as an effect of this affective experience of imagination. Becoming-child and becoming-clay might then make it, in a sense, easier for me to read an event from the perspective of the child or clay. However, this is done from an *enlivened change in myself*, where I actively reconstitute and transform myself, rather than temporarily acting, taking on a role or taking a position, which are not necessarily actions that will make me change and become different in myself.

In the context of education and early childhood education, both children and adults can re-enact the event and become other in ourselves, as we put ourselves in a state of becoming-child as adults, or becoming-ethnically, religiously, racially or sexually other, or becoming-clay or pen, etc. We can also become aware of the mutual intra-activities taking place in learning events between children and matter in the pedagogical space. Again, this is not simply about making another interpretation or understanding something from another discourse, position or role, but *becoming-other* in the material affective event that is re-enacted and actualised anew in the documentation. This is about using the documentation to actively *re-live* the event as a material-discursive body – re-installing myself as the pen as it is intra-acting with the child's hand when drawing – and thus understanding the event in a completely new way and becoming different in myself. This change in ourselves has ethical and perhaps even political consequences for early childhood practices.

To return to the example of map drawing, had we worked from a perspective of immanence and onto-epistemology we would probably have tried to engage the children directly in collaborative processes, where both a slowing down 'circular' and a speeding up 'horizontal' movement could have been productive in different ways (see Chapter 4, pp. 96–101). Slowing down the movement to reinstall ourselves in the event, we would probably very quickly have become aware of how the children in different ways intra-acted with the question posed to them, and their different strategies of answering it in different ways. Maybe we would also have become aware that the children were already enmeshed in long discussions on concepts of directions and place, such as the different meanings of 'across the table' and 'the other side of the table'. (We learnt this only several days later in the subsequent group discussions around the drawings.) Moreover, the children may have made us aware of, or even told us about, their individual experiences of the force and agency of the pen and hand while drawing, and how this may have made the drawing turn out in the specific way it did, maybe even taking off on a 'line of flight' after having been stuck for a long while, not knowing how to answer the request of the question, as in the case with Margret and the chairs' drawing (Figure 7.4). It took her a lot of solitary thinking to decide upon what to draw that morning.

In this re-installing in the event we could have put ourselves in a state of becoming-minoritarian that makes it possible for us to imagine how, as Jones and Jenkins write, 'new actors materialise' and become real (2008). It is, for instance, possible to imagine the chairs with hearts above as *performative agents* (Barad, 2007) that actualise the event of switching seats with the person you are in love with. Moreover, it is possible to actually put or re-install yourself as an adult in the state of *becoming-chair* in this event, to understand the intensity at work as Margret makes her drawing. If you cannot, you can at least recognise the chairs and the hearts as agents in the material-discursive intra-action in the drawing itself, and how they actively act upon us and give us information to understand who Margret wants to change places with. Hence, you can imagine the force of love intra-acting with the two chairs – both the ones in the drawing and those materially present in the room – charging them with affect and actualising the event of Margret switching seats with the one she is in love with.

When we re-install ourselves in a pedagogical event with a perspective of immanence this also means that the inter-connections that take place in the event are 'flattened out'. This flattening out and becoming-child in the event means that we cannot read the event from any privileged position or from an idea of truth. Instead of analysing how the children have understood the question in relation to a pre-determined idea or goal as in a constructivist epistemology of for instance making a map, the re-enactment of the event can make the adults aware of how different children intra-act differently with the question and the material-discursive reality at work when they make their specific drawings. Thus, the adults are *not* in a position of defining the problem and judging the success or lack of expected result. Instead adults understand themselves as simply one other (important) organism intra-acting in the re-enactment of the event. Hence, there are profound ethical consequences if we understand the mutual responsibilities at work, when you think and act within an onto-epistemological framework and an ontology of immanence, rather than a constructivist framework, where the learning goal or content is the ground from which to understand the event. Every organism in the intra-activities taking place can be understood as acting from their own agency and responsibility. As pointed out before, this makes it impossible to value or judge the individual child's performance as separated from everything else. Any evaluation must include identifying the intra-activities taking place in-between other matter in the event including the physical environment and the questions and input of the teachers.

Moreover, the above way of re-enacting this particular learning event is simultaneously about knowledge production and invention and creativity. It is simultaneously about making 'sense' of words, concepts and drawings as material-discursive pre-conditions and performative agents in the pedagogical space; and it is about imagining yourself becoming-chair. The teachers do not choose to help the children to see which is the better map drawing in terms of functives, such as logical and spatial correspondence, as in the constructivist epistemology. Instead, they let the children discuss their different understandings, strategies and knowledge constructs that emerge in the complexity of the material and embodied event at work. Relating back to the earlier discussion about the goal of education in terms of science (functives) and philosophy (concepts); this example shows how it is possible to focus on the intra-activity between both scientific functives *and* philosophical concepts – learning logical systems of reference *and* inventing new concepts for thinking and doing things.

An ethics of immanence and potentialities

In an ethics of immanence, the teacher cannot understand the student, the content or the methodology in terms of being a fixed entity apart and separated from everything else. An ethics of immanence in education is concerned with the inter-connections and intra-actions in-between human and non-human organisms, matter and things, the contents and subjectivities of students that emerge through the learning events. It is concerned with students and teachers in processes of *mutual engagement and transformation*. This means that we have to view ourselves in a constant and mutual state of responsibility for what happens in the multiple intra-actions emerging in the learning event, as we affect and are being affected by everything else. The flow of events thus becomes a collective responsibility on behalf of all organisms present, whether they are human or non-human. Responsibility is thus built into the immanent relationship between all matter and organisms. Thus, responsibility is nothing we can chose to have or take on, rather it comes with living, which is about affecting and being affected (Deleuze, 1988). In the slowing down 'circular' movement of re-enacting the events, we can re-live and critically analyse what happened to such affect, forces and intensities at work in the intra-actions taking place. This makes us aware of the forces of what we call responsibility, so that we can ask ourselves what it is we *can* do *here and now* to affect something or someone in a different way in line with an affirmative thinking of unknown potentialities, rather than what we *should* do in line with the transcendent idea of a higher value to be strived for.

Colebrook writes that ethics for Deleuze is about a 'love for what is', and not an ethics of knowledge and a search for some truth, justification or foundation beyond, outside of or transcendent to what is (2002: 71). Rather, what we are interested in is what an organism, a child, a teacher, a preschool, a learning event can *become* in its intra-activity with the surrounding world. A pedagogy that deals with becomings basically means that we move – simultaneously – between what is (the actual), and what might become (the virtual). What Deleuze (1988, 1990) calls the virtual is the reality of the potentialities of all organisms in the inter-connectedness with everything else around us. Drawing upon Deleuze, we strive for the *virtual* potentialities of a child, an organism or an event, which allows for the child (and yourself as teacher) to reinvent herself or himself with each event, and to be affirmative of learning as a state of transformation. This has the consequences that we must extend and expand ourselves to that which is not yet. Moreover, we are not interested in defining an organism by its limitation, separatedness or form, but by its capacities for affecting and being affected in relation to other organisms in the world (Deleuze, 1988: 123–5).

So, an ethics of immanence and potentialities addresses life, pedagogy, knowing and learning in an affirmative, evolutionary and creative way, in that it always looks for the virtual possibilities and potentialities in the child and in learning, and does not look for lack or deviance from truths, norms or pre-set learning paths. If we believe that the child in learning is a process of transformation and becomes anew in intra-actions and inter-connectedness with the rest of the world, then it becomes impossible to exclusively adhere to pre-formulated stages of maturity or learning specific contents, as in the case of constructivist theories of learning and developmentally appropriate practices. In other words, our focus as teachers should not be with what we think is the right or correct thing to do in relation to such norms or truths, and being exclusively fixated with learning-goals and outcomes. Instead, we should learn to look for the differences in and evolvement of strategies and thinking in the investigation of a learning content. We should learn to look for how the material is productive of what children do and say, and how the intra-activities between the material conditions and the actions of the children alter their understandings and strategies. We should try to make ourselves aware of what happens in the events of the present and look for what *might* be possible, what emerges, and what *can* become. This way of addressing the child or student and our pedagogical practice constitutes, in my understanding, a fundamental shift when we think of ethics and justice in education.

To conclude: practices that perform an ethics of immanence and potentialities go *beyond* the prevailing divides in education, such as science/art, intellect/body, rationality/affect, etc. and become transgressive and affirmative of change and development in a perspective of human beings in a mutual state of co-existence with everything else. Such an ethics might be able to transform educational practices so that they can be about challenging children's, students' and teachers' potentialities and capacities to act and be inventive in processes of collaborative experimentation and production of concepts and knowing. Moreover, it doesn't treat pedagogical work as being exclusively about trying to get children, students and teachers to reach pre-set goals of pre-set learning contents as in contemporary developmentally appropriate practices, constructivist learning theory and learning studies (Bredekamp and Coople, 1993; Gestwicki, 2006; Marton and Tsui, 2004; Pramling Samuelsson and Pramling, 2008).

And to end this book . . .

I write this last chapter in a time when a globalised economy has proven to us how every organism, human and non-human (i.e., money), intra-acts agentially and can build up strong forces and intensities that act upon everyone and everything in very destructive ways. This can be

compared with the immanent force of diffractions of ocean waves building up over many years to become the tsunami, with effects on almost
everyone and everything all over the globe. As I have quoted from
Deleuze before, ethics is about 'not to be unworthy of what happens to
us' (1990: 149). How are we to understand this in relation to these events
and our very lives as a result of immanent forces and intensities?

At this time I want to ask of you as a reader to actively go against what
I see as the dominant reductive and simplifying and limiting forces in
education, at least temporarily while reading this book, and seriously ask
yourself the overriding question: 'What *can* I do?' What can I do to set
another wave of diffractions in movement and in other directions? How
can I slow down the movement and re-enact and counter-actualise it,
and then maybe speed it up again and take it someplace else? In this way
we can be worthy of what happens to us in the development of the field
of early childhood education and in relation to a lot of other areas and
matters as well. We can ask ourselves again and again the question posed
from within an immanent worldview: 'How *might* one live?' instead of the
moral and transcendent question of 'How *should* one live?' (May, 2005:
1–4, original emphasis).

In this complex world I find it an impossible task to ask of ourselves
how we *should and must* all live in order to live justly and ethically. This is
because, first, such universal ethics will not be understood as universally
ethical by all, and, second, such questions exclude the possibilities of
asking ourselves how *can* or *might* we all live in different or other ways?
The philosophical approach to education that I find necessary today
cannot be found in an approach where a formulation of an ethics *precedes*
with ideals and goals understood to be beyond our capacity to actually
achieve them in our very living and being, such as true justice or
true democracy. That is, we should not think that we can know what
is right and wrong *before* living and knowing about the complexities of
life. Rather, the approach we need is an ethics that *derives from living
and lived life in the process of living it* (Smith, 2003). This is an ontology that
is an ethics, because it is derived from the immanent 'relation of beings
to Being at the level of their existence', writes Smith (2003: 63). This
is about ethics and ontology becoming one and the same, and not
separated and kept apart. And to bring us back to the beginning
of this book, Karen Barad's thinking, and her merging of ontology
and epistemology, what we get is an *ethico-onto-epistemology*. I want to
conclude this book with Barad's definition of such an ethico-onto-
epistemology as

an appreciation of the intertwining of the ethics, knowing and being – since each intra-acting matters, since the possibilities for what the world may become call out in the pause that precedes each breath before a moment comes into being and the world is remade again, because the becoming of the world is a deeply ethical matter.

(2007: 185)

References

Åberg, A. and Lenz Taguchi, H. (2005) *Lyssnandets pedagogik: Demokrati och etik i förskolans lärande* [Pedagogy of listening: Democracy and ethics in preschool learning practice]. Stockholm: Liber.

Ahmed, S. and Stacey, J. (eds) (2001) *Thinking Through the Skin*. London and New York: Routledge.

Alaimo, S. and Hekman, S. (eds) (2008) *Material Feminisms*. Bloomington, IN: Indiana University Press.

Albrecht-Crane, C. and Daryl Slack, J. (2007) 'Towards a pedagogy of affect', in A. Hickey-Moody and P. Malins (eds) *Deleuzian Encounters: Studies in Contemporary Social Issues*. New York: Palgrave Macmillan.

Apple, M. (1982) *Education and Power*. Boston, MA: Routledge and Kegan Paul.

Aronowitz, S. and Giroux, H.A. (1991) *Postmodern Education: Politics, Culture, and Social Criticism*. Minneapolis: University of Minnesota Press.

Arvidsson, T. (1974) *Barnobservationer i förskolan* [Child observations in preschool]. Stockholm: Liber.

Ball, S. (1994) *Education Reform: A Critical and Poststructural Approach*. Buckingham: Open University Press.

Barad, K. (2008) 'Posthumanist performativity: toward an understanding of how matter comes to matter', in S. Alaimo and S. Hekman (eds) *Material Feminisms*. Bloomington, IN: Indiana University Press, pp. 120–54.

Barad, K. (2007) *Meeting the Universe Halfway: Quantum Physics and the Entanglement of Matter and Meaning*. Durham, NC: Duke University Press.

Barad, K. (1999) 'Agential realism: feminist interventions in understanding scientific practices', in M. Biagioli (ed.) *The Science Studies Reader*. New York and London: Routledge.

Barad, K. (1998) 'Getting real: technoscientific practices and the materialization of reality', *Difference: A Journal of Feminist Cultural Studies*, 10(2): 87–126.

Bateson, G. (1979) *Mind and Nature: A Necessary Unit*. New York: E.P. Dutton.

Bauman, Z. (1991) *Modernity and Ambivalence*. Cambridge: Polity Press.

Bhabha, H. (2006) *The Location of Culture*. London and New York: Routledge.

Biesta, G. (2008) 'Five theses on complexity reduction and its politics'. Paper presented at the *Chaos and Complexity SIG Symposium of AERA*, New York, 24–8 March.

Blaise, M. (2005) *Playing it Straight: Uncovering Gender Discourses in the Early Childhood Classroom*. New York and London: Routledge.

Boman, E. (1946) 'Barnpsykologisk forskning – Seminarieutbildning av förskolepedagoger', in Ulin, C. (ed.) *Från spädbarn till skolbarn: Utvecklingspsykologiska studier i barnens egen miljö* ['Research in child psychology – The preschool seminar teacher education', in Ulin, C. (ed.) *From Infant to School: Child Developmental Psychological Studies in Children's Environment*]. Stockholm: Natur och Kultur.

Bonta, M. and Protevi, J. (2004) *Deleuze and Geophilosophy: A Guide and Glossary*. Edinburgh: Edinburgh University Press.

Braidotti, R. (2006) *Transpositions: On Nomadic Ethics*. Cambridge and Malden: Polity Press.

Braidotti, R. (2002) *Metamorphoses: Towards a Materialist Theory of Becoming*. Cambridge: Polity Press.

Braidotti, R. (1994) *Nomadic Subjects. Embodiment and Sexual Difference in Contemporary Feminist Theory*. New York: Columbia University Press.

Bredekamp, S. and Coople, S. (1993) *Developmentally Appropriate Practice in Early Childhood Programs Serving Children from Birth Through Age 8* (NAEYC series #234). 10th edn. AECA Specialist Early Childhood Publishers.

Bredekamp, S., Coople, C. and Neuman, S.B. (2000) *Learning to Read and Write: Developmentally Appropriate Practices for Young Children* (NAEYC series #161). National Association for the Education of Young Children.

Brown, N. (2004) *Gender Equity in the Early Years*. Maidenhead: Open University Press.

Bruner, J. (2004) 'Reggio: a city of courtesy, curiosity and imagination', *Children in Europe*, 6: 27.

Buchanan, I. and Colebrook, C. (eds) (2000) *Deleuze and Feminist Theory*. Edinburgh: Edinburgh University Press.

Buchanan, I. and Lambert, G. (eds) (2005) *Deleuze and Space*. Edinburgh and Toronto: Edinburgh University Press and University of Toronto Press.

Burman, E. (2007) *Deconstructing Developmental Psychology*. London and New York: Routledge.

Burman, E. and MacLure, M. (2005) 'Deconstruction as a method of research', in B. Somekh and C. Lewin (eds) *Research Methods in the Social Sciences*. London, Thousand Oaks, CA and New Delhi: Sage Publications, pp. 318–25.

Butler, J. (2004) *Undoing Gender*. New York and London: Routledge.

Butler, J. (2000) 'Restaging the universal: hegemony and the limits of formalism', in J. Butler, E. Laclau and S. Zizek (eds) *Contingency, Hegemony, Universality: Contemporary Dialogues on the Left*. London and New York: Verso, pp. 11–43.

Butler, J. (1997) *Psychic Life of Power: Theories in Subjection*. Stanford, CA: Stanford University Press.

Butler, J. (1993) *Bodies that Matter: On the Discursive Limits of 'Sex'*. New York and London: Routledge.

Butler, J. (1990) *Gender Trouble: Feminism and the Subversion of Identity*. New York and London: Routledge.

Canella, S.G. (1997) *Deconstructing Early Childhood Education: Social Justice and Revolution*. New York: Peter Lang Publishing.

Ceppi, G. and Zini, M. (1998) *Children, Spaces, Relations: Metaproject for an Environment for Young Children*. Milan, Italy: Domus Academy Research Centre.

Colebrook, C. (2006) *Deleuze: A Guide for the Perplexed*. London and New York: Continuum.

Colebrook, C. (2002) *Gilles Deleuze*. London and New York: Routledge.

Colebrook, C. (2000) 'Is sexual difference a problem?', in I. Buchanan and C. Colebrook (eds) *Deleuze and Feminist Theory*. Edinburgh: Edinburgh University Press, pp. 110–27.

Dahlberg, G. and Bloch, M. (2006) 'Is the power to see and visualize always the power to control?', in T.S. Popkewitz, K. Petterson, U. Olsson and J. Kowalczyk (eds) *'The Future Is Not What It Appears To Be': Pedagogy, Genealogy and Political Epistemology*. Stockholm: HLS Förlag.

Dahlberg, G. and Lenz Taguchi, H. (1994) *Förskola och skola: Om två skilda traditioner och om visionen om en mötesplats* [Preschool and school: Two different traditions and the vision of a meeting-place]. Stockholm: HLS Förlag.

Dahlberg, G. and Moss, P. (2005) *Ethics and Politics in Early Childhood Education*. London and New York: Routledge/Falmer.

Dahlberg, G. and Theorell, E. (2009) *Barns dialog med naturen* [Children's dialogue with nature]. Stockholm: Stockholm University Press.

Dahlberg, G., Moss, P. and Pence, A. (2007) *Beyond Quality in Early Childhood Education and Care: A Postmodern Perspective*. London and New York: Routledge/Falmer.

Daston, L. (2007) *Things that Talk*. New York: Zone Books.

Davies, B. (2000) *A Body of Writing 1990–1999*. Walnut Creek, CA and Oxford: Alta Mira Press.

Davies, B. and Gannon, S. (eds) (forthcoming) *Pedagogical Encounters*. London and New York: Routledge.

Davies, B. and Gannon, S. (eds) (2006) *Doing Collective Biography*. Maidenhead and New York: Open University Press.

Davies, B. and Gannon, S. (2005) 'Feminism/poststructuralism', in B. Somekh and C. Lewin (eds) *Research Methods in the Social Sciences*. London, Thousand Oaks, CA and New Delhi: Sage Publications, pp. 284–92.

Davies, B., Dormer, S., Gannon, S., Lenz Taguchi, H., Laws, C., McCann, H. and Rocco, S. (2001) 'Becoming school-girls: the ambivalent project of subjectification', *Gender and Education*, 3(2): 167–82.

Deleuze, G. (2001) *Pure Immanence: Essays on A Life*, trans. Anne Boyman. New York: Zone Books.

Deleuze, G. (1994) *Difference and Repetition*. New York: Columbia University Press.

Deleuze, G. (1990) *The Logic of Sense*. New York: Columbia University Press.

Deleuze, G. (1988) *Spinoza: Practical Philosophy*. San Francisco: City Lights Books.

Deleuze, G. and Guattari, F. (1994) *What is Philosophy?*, trans. Graham Burchell and Hugh Tomlinson. London and New York: Verso.

Deleuze, G. and Guattari, F. (1987) *A Thousand Plateaus: Capitalism and Schizophrenia*, trans. Brian Massumi. Minneapolis: University of Minnesota Press.

Dewey, J. (2004) *Democracy and Education: An Introduction to the Philosophy of Education*. London: Aakar Books.

Doveborg, E. and Pramling, I. (2000) *Att förstå barns tankar* [Understanding children's thinking]. Stockholm: Liber AB.

Doveborg, E. and Pramling Samuelsson, I. (1999) *Förskolebarn i matematikens värld* [Preschool children in the world of mathematics]. Stockholm: Liber AB.

Edwards, C., Gandini, L. and Forman, G. (1998) *The Hundred Languages of Children*. Greenwich, CT and London: Ablex Publishing.

Elfström, I. (2004) 'Varför individuella utvecklingsplaner? En studie av ett nytt utvärderingsverktyg i förskolan' ['Why individual developmental plans? A study of a new tool for evaluation in preschool']. Masters thesis, Stockholm University.

Elfström, I., Nilsson, B., Sterner, L. and Wéhner-Godée, C. (2008) *Barn och naturvetenskap* [Children and science]. Stockholm: Liber AB.

Ellsworth, E. (1997) *Teaching Positions: Difference, Pedagogy, and the Power of Address*. New York and London: Teachers College Press, Columbia University.

Ellsworth, E. (1992) 'Why doesn't this feel empowering? Working through the repressive myths of critical pedagogy', in C. Luke and J. Gore (eds) *Feminisms and Critical Pedagogy*. New York and London: Routledge, pp. 90–119.

Fausto-Sterling, A. (2000) *Sexing the Body: Gender Politics and the Construction of Sexuality*. New York: Basic Books.

Fendler, L. (2001) 'Educating flexible souls', in K. Hultqvist and G. Dahlberg (eds) *Governing the Child in the New Millenium*. London: Routledge/Falmer.

Foucault, M. (1990) *The History of Sexuality. Volume 1: An Introduction*. New York: Vintage Books; London: Penguin.

Foucault, M. (1982) 'The subject and power', in H.L. Dreyfus and P. Rabinow (eds) *Michel Foucault: Beyond Structuralism and Hermeneutic*. Hertfordshire: Harvester Press.

Freire, P. (2001) *Pedagogy of the Oppressed*. 30th anniversary edn. London and New York: Continuum.

Furness, K. (2008) *Rådjurets återfödelse till toner av mögelmusik: Förskolan Äventyret i Skarpnäcks stadstel hösten 2005–våren 2006* [The rebirth of the deer to music made by mould: Äventyrets Preschool in the municipality of Skarpnäck autumn 2005–spring 2006]. Stockholm: Reggio Emilia Institute.

Gallagher, A.M. and Kaufman, J.C. (2005) *Gender Differences in Mathematics*. Cambridge: Cambridge University Press.

Gardner, H. (1994) 'Foreword: complementary perspectives on Reggio Emilia', in C. Edwards, L. Gandinin and G. Forman (eds) *The Hundred Languages of Children: The Reggio Approach to Early Childhood Education*. Norwood, NJ: Ablex.

Gardner, H. (1985) *The Mind's New Science: A History of the Cognitive Revolution.* New York: Basic Books.

Gatens, M. (1996) *Imaginary Bodies: Ethics, Power, and Corporeality.* New York: Routledge.

Gestwicki, C.L. (2006) *Developmentally Appropriate Practices: Curriculum and Development in Early Education.* 3rd edn. New York: Delmar Learning.

Gore, J. (1992) 'What we can do for you! What *can* "we" do for "you"? Struggling over empowerment in critical and feminist pedagogy', in C. Luke and J. Gore (eds) *Feminisms and Critical Pedagogy.* New York and London: Routledge, pp. 54–73.

Grosz, E. (2008) 'Darwin and feminism: preliminary investigations for a possible alliance', in S. Alaimo and S. Hekman (eds) *Material Feminisms.* Bloomington, IN: Indiana University Press.

Grosz, E. (2005) *Time Travels: Feminism, Nature, Power,* Durham, NC: Duke University Press.

Grosz, E. (2001) *Architecture from the Outside: Essays on Virtual and Real Space.* Cambridge, MA: MIT Press.

Grosz, E. (ed.) (1999) *Becomings: Explorations in Time, Memory, and Futures.* Ithaca, NY: Cornell University Press.

Grosz, E. (1995) *Space, Time and Perversion: Essays on the Politics of Bodies.* New York and London: Routledge.

Gusfield, J. (1976) 'The literary rhetoric of science: comedy and pathos in drinking driver research', *American Sociological Review,* 4: 16–34.

Hacking, I. (1983) *Representing and Intervening: Introductory Topics in the Philosophy of Natural Science.* New York: Cambridge University Press.

Hansen, M.B.N. (2000) *Embodying Technesis: Technology Beyond Writing.* Ann Arbor: University of Michigan Press.

Haraway, D.J. (2008) *When Species Meet.* Minneapolis and London: University of Minnesota Press.

Haraway, D.J. (1997) *Modest_Witness@Second:Millennium.FemaleMan_Meets_Onco Mouse: Feminism and Technoscience.* New York and London: Routledge.

Haraway, D.J. (1991) *Simians, Cyborgs, and Women: The Reinvention of Nature.* New York and London: Routledge.

Hartley, P. (1999) *Interpersonal Communication.* London: Taylor and Francis Ltd.

Hayles, K.N. (2002) *Writing Machines.* Cambridge, MA: MIT Press.

Hekman, S. (2008). 'Constructing the ballast: an ontology for feminism', in S. Alaimo and S. Hekman (eds) *Material Feminisms.* Bloomington, IN: Indiana University Press, pp. 85–119.

Hekman, S. (1990) *Gender and Knowledge: Elements of Postmodern Feminism.* Cambridge and Oxford: Polity Press.

Helm, J.H. and Katz, L. (2000) *Young Investigators: The Project Approach in the Early Years.* New York: Teachers College Press.

Hickey-Moody, A. and Malins P. (eds) (2007) *Deleuzian Encounters: Studies in Contemporary Social Issues.* New York: Palgrave Macmillan.

Holmqvist, M. (ed.) (2006): *Lärande i skolan: Learning study som skolutvecklingsmodell* [Learning in school: Learning study as a model for school development]. Lund: Studentlitteratur.

Honan, E. (2004) '(Im)plausibilities: a rhizo-textual analysis of policy texts and teachers' work', *Educational Philosophy and Theory*, 36(3): 267–81.

Honan, E. and Sellers, M. (2008) '(E)merging methodologies: putting rhizomes to work', in I. Semetsky (ed.) *Nomadic Education: Variations on a Theme by Deleuze and Guattari*. Rotterdam, The Netherlands: Sense Publishers.

hooks, b. (1994) *Teaching to Transgress. Education as the Practice of Freedom*. London and New York: Routledge.

hooks, b. (1981) *Ain't I a Woman, Black Women and Feminism*. Cambridge, MA: South End Press.

Hultman, K. (2009) 'Children's gendered subjectivities and becomings in relation to places within pre-school'. Paper presented at the *International Feminist Methodology Conference*, Stockholm, 4–6 February.

Hultqvist, K. (2001) 'Bringing the gods and the angels back? A modern pedagogical saga about excess in moderation', in K. Hultqvist and G. Dahlberg (eds) *Governing the Child in the New Millenium*. New York and London: Routledge/Falmer.

Hultqvist, K. (1998) 'A history of the present of the Swedish welfare child', in T.S. Popkewitz and A. Brennan (eds) *Foucault's Challenge to the Knowledge, Curriculum and Political Projects of Schooling*. New York: Teachers College Press.

Hultqvist, K. (1990). *Förskolebarnet: En konstruktion för gemenskapen och den individuella frigörelsen* [The preschool child: A construction for collectiveness and individual emancipation]. Stockholm: Symposion.

Hultqvist, E. and Palme, M. (2006) '*Om de kunde ge en mall.' En studie av lärarstudenternas möte med lärarutbildningen* ['If they could only give me a guide.' A study of teacher students encounter with teacher education]. Dept. of Society, Culture and Learning, Stockholm Institute of Education and The Research Group of Educational Research and Cultural Sociology at Uppsala University.

Jablonka, E. and Lamb M.J. (2005) *Evolution in Four Dimensions: Genetic, Epigenetic, Behavioural, and Symbolic Variation in the History of Life*. Cambridge, MA: MIT Press.

James, A., Jenks, C. and Prout, A. (1998) *Theorizing Childhood*. Cambridge and Oxford: Polity Press.

Jones, A. (1997) 'Teaching post-structuralist feminist theory in education: student resistance', *Gender and Education*, 9(3): 161–9.

Jones, A. and Jenkins, K. (2008) 'Indigenous discourse and "the material": a post-interpretivist argument', *International Review of Qualitative Research*, 1(2 August): 125–44.

Jung, J. (2005) *Revisionary Rhetoric, Feminist Pedagogy, and Multigenre Texts*. Carbondale: Southern Illinois University Press.

Katz, L.G. (1998) 'What can we learn from Reggio Emilia?', in C. Edwards, L. Gandini and G. Forman (eds) *The Hundred Languages of Children: The Reggio Emilia Approach: Advanced Reflections*. Norwood, NJ: Ablex, pp. 27–45.

Lagerroth, E. (1994) *Världen och vetandet sjunger på nytt: Från en mekanisk världsbild till ett skapande universum*. [The world and the wisdom enchant anew: From a mechanistic worldview towards a creating universe]. Göteborg: Korpen.

Lather, P. (2007) *Getting Lost: Feminist Efforts toward a Double(d) Science*. New York: State University of New York Press.

Lather, P. (1991) *Getting Smart: Feminist Research and Pedagogy with/in the Postmodern*. New York and London: Routledge.

Lather, P. and Smithies, C. (1997) *Troubling the Angels: Women Living With HIV/AIDS*. Boulder, CO: Westview/HarperCollins.

Latour, B. (2005) *Reassembling the Social. An Introduction to Action-Network-Theory*. Oxford: Oxford University Press.

Latour, B. (1999) *Pandora's Hope: Essays on the Reality of Science Studies*. Cambridge, MA: Harvard University Press.

Lenz Taguchi, H. (2009a) 'Shifting from a linear and one-dimensional to a multidimensional and rhizomatic approach to learning and inclusion', in N. Yelland (ed.) *Contemporary/New Critical Issues in Early Childhood Education*. Philadelphia, PA: Open University Press.

Lenz Taguchi, H. (2009b) 'Writing practices in Swedish teacher education and the inclusion/exclusion of subjectivities', *Critical Studies in Education* 50(2): 145–58.

Lenz Taguchi, H. (2008a) 'The researcher becoming otherwise: the materiality of collaborative research'. Paper presented at *BERA*, London, 6 September 2007 and *AERA*, New York, 26 March 2008.

Lenz Taguchi, H. (2008b) 'Ett intra-aktivt pedagogiskt arbete för inkludering och rättvisa' ['An intra-active pedagogy for inclusion and justice in education'], in R.J. Pettersen (ed.) *Barnehagen som läringsarena* [The preschool as an arena for learning]. SEBU Forlag/Pedagogisk forum/Barnehageforum.no, Norway, pp. 45–69.

Lenz Taguchi, H. (2008c) 'Justice in early childhood education. Justice to whom and to what?' Keynote address at *EECERA* (European Early Childhood Education Research Association) Stavanger, Norway, 5 September.

Lenz Taguchi, H. (2008d) 'An "ethics of resistance" challenges taken-for-granted ideas in early childhood education', *International Journal of Educational Research*, 47(5): 270–82.

Lenz Taguchi, H. (2007) 'Deconstructing and transgressing the theory – practice dichotomy in Swedish early childhood education', *Educational Philosophy and Theory*, 39(3): 275–90.

Lenz Taguchi, H. (2006) 'Reconceptualizing early childhood education: challenging taken-for-granted ideas', in J. Einarsdóttir and J. Wagner (eds) *Nordic Childhoods and Early Education: Philosophy, Research, Policy and Practice in Denmark, Finland, Iceland, Norway and Sweden*. Greenwich, CT: Information Age Publishing, pp. 257–87.

Lenz Taguchi, H. (2005) 'Getting personal: how early childhood teacher education troubles students' and teacher educators' identities regarding subjectivity and feminism', *Contemporary Issues in Early Childhood Education*, 6(3): 244–55.

Lenz Taguchi, H. (2004) *In på bara benet: En introduktion till feministisk Poststructuralism* [Down into bare bone: An introduction to feminist poststructuralism]. Stockholm: HLS Förlag.

Lenz Taguchi, H. (2000) *Emancipation och motstånd. Dokumentation och kooperativa läroprocesser i förskolan* [Emancipation and resistance. Documentation and co-operative learning-processes], PhD dissertation in Swedish, Stockholm: HLS Förlag.

Lenz Taguchi, H. (1997) *Varför pedagogisk dokumentation?* [Why pedagogical documentation?]. Stockholm: HLS Förlag.

Lenz Taguchi, H. (1996) 'The field of early childhood pedagogy in Sweden: a female project of professionalization and emancipation?', *Nordiske Udkast: Journal for Critical Social Science*, 24(1): 41–55.

Lind, U. (2005) 'Identity and power, "meaning", gender and age: children's creative work as a signifying practice', *Contemporary Issues in Early Childhood*, 6(3): 256–68.

Lind, U. (2003) 'Postmodern reconceptualizationof aesthetics for education'. Paper given at *NFPF/NERA Congress* 'Education as a Critical Force: Myth or Reality?' Copenhagen, 6–9 March.

Lloyd, Genevieve (2002) 'Maleness, metaphor, and the "crisis" of reason', in L.M. Antony and C.E. Witt (eds) *A Mind of One's Own: Feminist Essays on Reason and Objectivity*, 2nd edn. Boulder, CO and Oxford: Westview Press, pp. 73–89.

Lorde, A. (1984) 'The master's tools will never dismantle the master's house', in C. Clarke and A. Lorde (eds) *Sisters Outsider*. Fredoom, CA: Crossing Press.

Lu, M.-Z. (1999) 'Redefining the literate self: the politics of critical affirmation', *College Composition and Communication*, 51: 172–9.

Luke, C. and Gore, J. (eds) (1992) *Feminism and Critical Pedagogy*. New York and London: Routledge.

MacLaren, P. (1994) *Critical Pedagogy and Predatory Culture*. London and New York: Routledge.

MacNaughton, G. (2005) *Doing Foucault in Early Childhood Studies: Applying Poststructural Ideas*. London and New York: Routledge.

McQuillan, M. (2000) *Deconstruction: A Reader*. Edinburgh: Edinburgh University Press.

Malins, P. (2007) 'City folds: injecting drug use and urban space', in A. Hickey-Moody and P. Malins (eds) *Deleuzian Encounters: Studies in Contemporary Social Issues*. New York: Palgrave/Macmillan.

Malka Fisher, B. (2001) *No Angel in the Classroom: Teaching through Feminist Discourse*. Boston: Rowman & Littlefield.

Marks, J. (2006a) 'Molecular biology in the work of Deleuze and Guattari', in J. Marks (ed.) *Deleuze and Science: Paragraph: A Journal of Modern Critical Theory*, 29(2, July). Special number on Deleuze and Science.

Marks, J. (ed.) (2006b) *Deleuze and Science: Paragraph: A Journal of Modern Critical Theory*, 29(2, July). Special number on Deleuze and Science.

Marton, F. and Booth, S. (1997). *Learning and Awareness*. Mahwah, NJ: Lawrence Erlbaum Associates.

Marton, F. and Tsui, A.B.M (eds) (2004) *Classroom Discourse and the Space of Learning*. Mahwah, NJ and London: Lawrence Erlbaum Associates.

May, T. (2005) *Gilles Deleuze: An Introduction*. Cambridge: Cambridge University Press.

May, T. and Semetsky, I. (2008) 'Deleuze, Ethical Education, and the Unconscious', in I. Semetsky (ed.) *Nomadic Education: Variations on a Theme by Deleuze and Guattari*. Rotterdam, The Netherlands: Sense Publisher.

Mayberry, M. and Rose, E.C. (eds) (1999) *Innovative Feminist Pedagogies in Action*. New York and London: Routledge.

Mazzei, L. (2008) 'Thinking *with* Deleuze in educational research'. Paper presented at the *BERA Annual Conference*, Edinburgh, Scotland, 3–6 September.

Mazzei, L.A. and Jackson, A.Y. (2009) 'The limit of voice', in A. Jackson and L. Mazzei (eds) *Voice in Qualitative Inquiry: Challenging Conventional, Interpretive, and Critical Conceptions in Qualitative Research*. London and New York: Routledge.

Mendick, H. (2006) *Masculinities in Mathematics*. London: Open University Press.

Miller, D. (2008) *The Comfort of Things*. Cambridge and Malden, MA: Polity Press.

Miller, D. (2005) *Materiality: Positivism and its Epistemological Others*. Durham, NC: Duke University Press.

New, R. (2000) 'Reggio Emilia: catalyst for change and conversation', *Eric Digest*, December. ED447971.

New, R. (1990) 'Excellent early education: a city in Italy has it', *Young Children*, 45(6): 4–10. EJ 415 419.

Nordin-Hultman, E. (2004) *Pedagogiska miljöer och barns subjektsskapande* [Pedagogical environment and the construction of children's subjectivity]. Stockholm: Liber.

Novak, J.D. and Gowin, D.B. (1984) *Learning How to Learn*. Cambridge: Cambridge University Press.

Ohrlander, K. (1992) *I barnens och nationens intresse: Socialliberal reformpolitik, 1903–1930* [In the interest of children and the nation: Social-liberal reform politics 1903–1930]. Studies of psychology and education, nb 30. Stockholm University: Almqvist & Wiksell International.

Olsson, L.M. (2009) *Movement and Experimentation in Young Children's Learning: Deleuze and Guattari in Early Childhood Education*. London and New York: Routledge.

Orner, M. (1992) 'Interrupting the calls for student voice in "liberatory" education: a feminist poststructuralist perspective', in C. Luke and J. Gore (eds) *Feminisms and Critical Pedagogy*. New York and London: Routledge, pp. 74–89.

Osberg, D.C. and Biesta, G.J.J. (2009). 'The end/s of school. Complexity and the conundrum of the inclusive educational curriculum', *International Journal of Inclusive Education*, in press.

Osberg, D.C. and Biesta, G.J.J. (2007) 'Beyond presence: epistemological and pedagogical implications of "strong" emergence', *Interchange* 38(1): 31–51.

Palmer, A. (2009a) 'I'm not a "maths-person"'! Reconstituting mathematical subjectivities in aesthetic teaching practices', *Gender and Education*, 21(4): 387–404.

Palmer, A. (2009b) ' "Let's dance": theorising alternative teaching methods in early childhood teacher education'. Paper presented at the *International Feminist Methodology Conference*, Stockholm, 4–6 February.

Palmer, A. (2007) 'Cold sweat and butterflies in the stomach – teacher-students' attitudes and notions about the subject of mathematics in general teacher-education'. Paper presented at *NPFF/NERA Congress*, Helsinki, 14–17 March.

Patton, P. and Protevi, J. (eds) (2003) *Between Deleuze and Derrida*. London and New York: Continuum.

Peters, M.A. (2004) 'Geophilosophy, education and the pedagogy of the concept', *Educational Philosophy and Theory*, 36(3): 217–26.

Pickering, A. (1995) *The Mangle of Practice: Time, Agency, and Science*. Chicago, IL: University of Chicago Press.

Polanyi, M. (1997) *Science, Economics and Philosophy: Selected Papers of Michael Polanyi*. New Brunswick, NJ: Allen; London: Transaction Publishers.

Popkewitz, T. (1998) *Struggling for the Soul: The Politics of Schooling and the Construction of the Teacher*. New York: Teachers College Press.

Popkewitz, T. and Brennan, A. (eds) (1998) *Foucault's Challenge to the Knowledge, Curriculum and Political Projects of Schooling*. New York: Teachers College Press.

Pramling, I. (1990). *Learning to Learn: A Study of Swedish Preschool Children*. New York: Springer Verlag.

Pramling Samuelsson, I. and Pramling, N. (eds) (2008) *Didaktiska studier från förskola och skola* [Studies in didactics from preschools and schools]. Malmö: Gleerups.

Protevi, J. (2008a) 'Deleuze and cognitive science: one more "next step" '. Paper presented at the *International Deleuze Studies Conference*, Cardiff University, August. www.protevi.com/john/research.html.

Protevi, J. (2008b) 'Lectures on Deleuze and biology'. Paper presented at the *International Deleuze Studies Conference*, Cardiff University, August. www.protevi.com/john/research.html.

Prout, A. (2005) *The Future of Childhood*. London and New York: Routledge Falmer.

Prout, A. and James, A. (eds) (1990) *Constructing and Reconstructing Childhood: Contemporary Issues in the Sociological Study of Childhood*. Basingstoke: Falmer Press.

Readings, B. (1996) *The University in Ruins*. Cambridge, MA: Harvard University Press.

Reggio Children (2008) *Dialogues with Places*. Municipality of Reggio Emilia, Italy: Reggio Children.

Reggio Children (2001) *Making Learning Visible: Children as Individual and Group Learners*. Municipality of Reggio Emilia, Italy: Reggio Children.

Richardson, L. (1997) *Fields of Play: Constructing an Academic Life*. New Brunswick, NJ: Rutgers University Press.

Rinaldi, C. (2006). *In Dialogue with Reggio Emilia: Listening, Researching and Learning*. London and New York: Routledge.

Rorty, R. (1967) *The Linguistic Turn: Methods in Philosophical Method*. Chicago, IL: University of Chicago Press.

Rose, N. (1999) *Powers of Freedom: Reframing Political Thoughts*. Cambridge: Cambridge University Press.

Rose, N. (1996) 'Towards a critical sociology of freedom', *Nordiske Udkast: Journal for Critical Social Science*, 24(1): 3–21.

Rose, N. (1989) *Governing the Soul: The Shaping of the Private Self*. London: Routledge.

Rothstein, E. (2006) *Pattern and Beauty in Mathematics and Music*. Chicago, IL: University of Chicago Press.

Rouse, J. (2002) *How Scientific Practices Matter: Reclaiming Philosophical Naturalism*. Chicago, IL: University of Chicago Press.

Sand, M. (2008) 'Konsten att gunga: experiment som aktiverar mellanrum' [Space in motion: The art of activating space in between]. Doctoral thesis. Stockholm: Axl Books.

Scott, J. (1992) 'Experience', in J. Butler and J.W. Scott (eds) *Feminists Theorize the Political*. New York and London: Routledge, pp. 22–39.

Semetsky, I. (ed.) (2008) *Nomadic Education: Variations on a Theme by Deleuze and Guattari*. Rotterdam/Taipei: Sense Publishers.

Semetsky, I. (2006) *Deleuze, Education and Becoming*. Rotterdam/Taipei: Sense Publishers.

Sinclair, N. (2006). *Mathematics and Beauty: Aesthetics Approaches to Teaching Children*. New York: Teachers College Press.

Sinclair, N., Pimm, D. and Higginson, W. (2006) *Mathematics and the Aesthetics: New Approaches to an Ancient Affinity*. New York: Springer.

Smith, Daniel W. (2003) 'Deleuze and Derrida, immanence and transcendence: two directions in recent French thought', in P. Patton and J. Protevi (eds) *Between Deleuze and Derrida*. London and New York: Continuum.

Steffe, L.P. (ed.) (1995) *Constructivism in Education*. Mahwah, NJ: Lawrence Erlbaum Associates.

Stivale, Charles J. (ed.) (2005) *Gilles Deleuze: Key Concepts*. Chesham: Acumen Publishing.

St. Pierre, E.A. (2009) 'Afterword: decentering voice in qualitative inquiry', in A.Y. Jackson and L.A. Mazzei (eds) *Voice in Qualitative Inquiry: Challenging Conventional, Interpretive, and Critical Conceptions in Qualitative Research*. London and New York: Routledge.

St. Pierre, E.A. (2004) 'Deleuzian concepts for education: the subject undone', *Educational Philosophy and Theory*, 36(3): 283–96.

St. Pierre, E.A. (2000) 'Poststructural feminism in education: an overview', *Qualitative Studies in Education*, 14(1): 71–84.

St. Pierre E.A. and Pillow, W.S. (eds) (2000) *Working the Ruins: Feminist Poststructural Theory and Methods in Education*. New York and London: Routledge.

Tilley, C., Keane, W., Kücker, S., Rolands, M. and Spyer, P. (eds) (2006)

Handbook of Material Culture. London, Thousand Oaks, CA, New Delhi and Singapore: Sage.

Ulin, C. (ed.) (1946) *Från spädbarn till skolbarn: Utvecklingspsykologiska studier i barnens egen miljö* [From infant to school-child: Developmental psychological studies in children's environment]. Stockholm: Natur och Kultur.

Vocate, D.R. (1994) *Intrapersonal Communication: Different Voices, Different Minds.* Mahwah, NJ: Lawrence Erlbaum Associates.

Walkerdine, V. (1998) *Counting Girls Out: Girls and Mathematics.* London: Falmer.

Walkerdine, V. (1988) *The Mastery of Reason: Cognitive Development and the Production of Rationality.* London: Routledge.

Walkerdine, V. (1984) 'Developmental psychology and the child-centred pedagogy', in J. Henriques, W. Holloway, C. Urwin *et al., Changing the Subject.* London: Methuen, pp. 153–202.

West-Eberhard, M.J. (2003) *Developmental Plasticity and Evolution.* Oxford and New York: Oxford University Press.

Williams, J. (2008) *Gilles Deleuze's Logic of Sense: A Critical Introduction and Guide.* Edinburgh: Edinburgh University Press.

Williams, J. (2007) *Poststructuralism, Theory, Practice: Reflections on Creativity.* Dundee: Duncan of Jordanstone College.

Williams, J. (2005) *Understanding Poststructuralism.* Stockfield: Acumen.

Wilson, E.A. (2004) *Psychosomatic. Feminism and the Neurological Body.* Durham, NC: Duke University Press.

Wilson, E.A. (1998) *Neural Geographies: Feminism and the Microstructure of Cognition.* New York: Routledge.

Wood, D. (1992) *The Power of Maps.* New York: The Guilford Press.

Yates, L. (1993) 'Feminism and education: writing in the 90s', in L. Yates (ed.) *Feminism and Education.* Melbourne Studies in Education, Bandora: La Trobe Universty Press.

Yelland, N. (ed.) (2005) *Critical Issues in Early Childhood Education.* Milton Keynes: Open University Press.

Index